Toward a Political
Philosophy of Race

SUNY series, Philosophy and Race

Robert Bernasconi and T. Denean Sharpley-Whiting, editors

Toward a Political Philosophy of Race

Falguni A. Sheth

Published by State University of New York Press, Albany

For information, contact State University of New York Press, Albany, NY
www.sunypress.edu

Production by Diane Ganeles
Marketing by Anne M. Valentine

Library of Congress Cataloging-in-Publication Data

Sheth, Falguni A., 1968–
    Toward a political philosophy of race / Falguni A. Sheth.
        p. cm. — (SUNY series, philosophy and race)
    Includes bibliographical references and index.
    ISBN 978-0-7914-9397-7 (hardcover : alk. paper) — ISBN 978-0-7914-9398-4
(pbk. : alk. paper) 1. Race discrimination—United States.   2. Race discrimination—
United States—Philosophy.   3. Racism—United States.   4. United States—Race
relations.   I. Title.
    E184.A1S5744 2009
    305.800973—dc22

                                                                        2008018838

10 9 8 7 6 5 4 3 2 1

For Bubba

Whose daily outrage reminds me that
we must always care for the world even when
the world doesn't always care for us.

CONTENTS

ACKNOWLEDGMENTS

Writing, despite the stretches of solitude in which it is done, is a complicated social act. There are so many vicissitudes, factors, figures—some long gone—who figure into the making of a manuscript. Perhaps here, I can offer my gratitude to some part of this circle.

The fledgling paper that marked the beginning of this book germinated around the time I finished my dissertation. In December 2002, Vicki Spelman offered to coordinate a forum to present an early version of that paper at Smith College. She followed up in spring 2003, and alas she and members of the Smith College Philosophy Department graciously listened as I publicly aired my confused ideas on this topic for the first time. I don't think I can find more supportive colleagues than the women scholars of the Five College Area. Joan Cocks, Sangeeta Kamat, and Barbara Yngvesson were integral in helping me move past self-doubt to envisioning the completion of this book. Joan and Barbara nourished me intellectually as they read multiple drafts of several of the chapters, and pushed me to be more subtle and nuanced and yet more clear and forceful in my arguments. Barbara went well beyond the call of duty as a senior colleague and friend, as she (and Sigfrid) plied me with excellent wine and food, and listened to me rehearse multiple conference papers; moreover, she was a steadfast intellectual companion and cheerleader during many stages of this project. In the final stage, she generously found the missing pages of a rare text in a library on her end of the country and faxed them to me at the other end, where I was finishing this book! I thank her for her cheerful and warm generosity.

I have been especially lucky to find myself at Hampshire College as I finished the dissertation and wrote much of the initial draft for this book. Hampshire, with its unwavering commitment to intellectual and pedagogical freedom, its institutional self-confidence to support seemingly strange projects, the steady presence of shockingly reflective students, the cheerful and humorous collegiality freely given by colleagues across the schools, and the unprecedented support of the administrators—most notably former President Greg Prince Jr.—were crucial to being able to envision a project that seemed bizarre upon its inception. I thank my colleagues in Social Science, who voted in favor of my regular employment in their school; their collegiality enhances my everyday intellectual and pedagogical life. Vivek Bhandari, Margaret Cerullo, Marlene Fried, Stephanie Levin, Jutta Sperling, Berna Turam, Wilson Valentin-Escobar, Monique Roelofs have been generous and critical interlocutors for a number of sections in this book. I want to acknowledge especially Mary Bombardier, Wilson Valentin-Escobar, Frank Holmquist, Joanna Morris, Laura Sizer, Kristen Luschen, Monique Roelofs, Steve Weisler, and Mario D'Amato for intellectual company and friendship. Chyrell George and Emily Gallivan have made my daily working life much less burdensome with their cheerful accommodation of my ad hoc requests at the office. Deans Barbara Yngvesson and Aaron Berman approved my request for an extended sabbatical in order to complete this book. My students at Hampshire never cease to delight, amaze, and challenge me with their keen insights, willingness to suspend disbelief long enough to listen, their political fearlessness, and generous critical engagement. Among them, I wish to acknowledge especially Katie Bryson, Rachel Leeper, RJ Leland, Nasser Mufti, Patience Okpotor, Ryvka Bar Zohar, and Seth Wessler for enthusiastically engaging and reminding me of important things about the world of ideas, gender, race, and politics. I thank Kim McGuire for her excellent research assistance during the initial stages of this project.

Colleagues, friends, and family from across the country have listened, read, and constructively engaged me in attempts to steer my ideas in a more coherent and sensible direction. They include Marcellus Andrews, Alia Al-Saji, Ellen Feder, Namita Goswami, Jacob Hale, Gordon Hull, Fouad Kalouche, David Kim, Eduardo Mendieta, Charles Mills, Darrell Moore, Mary Beth Mader, Kyoo Lee, Mariana Ortega, Enoch Paige, Jeffrey Paris, Mickaella Perina, Rodney Roberts, Matt Silliman, Ronald R. Sundstrom, Antonio Vasquez y Arroyo, Gregory Velazco y Trianosky, and Naomi Zack. Namita and Darrell especially are responsible for the (relatively more) humble title of the book. Charles has behaved as postgraduate adviser, pushing and prodding me to do more, write more (than one book while on such a long sabbatical!), and work harder. Marcellus, Charles, Mickaella, Ellen, Darrell, Namita, Greg, and my husband Robert, have read and commented on most of what I have sent them for the last five years, and supported me with critical interlocution, delightful (and often wicked!) humor, good will, and pleasurable friendship as I worked to clarify the arguments in this book.

I want to offer a grateful thanks to the Woodrow Wilson Fellowship Foundation. Through its generous support, I have had a luxury that I could never have imagined receiving: an extended sabbatical to read, ponder, and research at leisure and complete a book manuscript without the (albeit pleasurable) distractions of teaching. David T. Goldberg, whose work is a fundamental springboard for my methodological approach, and whose intellectual footprints can be seen all over this book (or so I hope) kindly agreed to "mentor" me during the course of this fellowship. I have appreciated David's hands-off interlocutory style as I have finished the book. His timely responses, excellent advice, warm support, and our political and intellectual conversations enhanced this year immeasurably.

I also thank the audiences and participants for their constructive feedback at the following fora where I presented parts of this book: American Philosophical Association, California Roundtable for Philosophy and Race, Caribbean Philosophical Association, North American Society for Social Philosophy, Foucault Circle, Northeastern Political Theory Association, Society for Phenomenological and Existential Philosophy, Society for Social and Political Philosophy. Thanks also to the audiences at the seminar and lectures series at the University of California Berkeley Ethnic Studies Department, University of Massachusetts Graduate Anthropology Department, University of Maryland American Studies Department, Hampshire College (various departments), Massachusetts College of Liberal Arts, University of Alberta at Edmonton Sub-Altern Speaker Series, California State University Northridge, University of San Francisco Davies Forum, for their constructive feedback. Thanks to them and to the editors of several journals, several presentations finally saw the light of day as articles. An earlier version of Chapter One was originally published in *Radical Philosophy Review* (special volume on Racism and Bio-power. Vol. 7, no. 1: 77–98). Sections of Chapter Four were published as "Unruly Women, 'Muslim Culture,' and Threats to Liberal Culture" in *Peace Review* (special edition on Race, Violence, and Law), Vol. 18, no. 4: 455–463. An earlier version of Chapter Six, "Border-Populations: Boundary, Memory, Conscience," was published in *International Studies in Philosophy*, fall 2005. Vol. 37, no. 2: 131–157.

Special thanks go to the Philosophy department at the University of San Francisco and the Ethnic Studies department at the University of California at Berkeley. They generously provided research facilities and an affiliation as I completed the book while on leave in San Francisco. In particular, I wish to thank Nelson Maldonado-Torres, Thomas Biolsi, and the members of the UC Berkeley Ethnic Studies "Governmentality" Graduate Seminar for their collegiality and generous interlocution during my stint as visiting scholar. Rekha Patel, Tanda Neundorf, Jason Chang, Will Steele, and Kaytan Shah have provided excellent company during the year in which I wrote this manuscript—intellectually stimulating, humorous, and emotionally undemanding. Rekha so generously provided her unique and unrelenting common sense and her beautiful house on the Russian River whenever I needed either. Pilar Schiavo reminded but never pushed me to remember the "real world," even as I was trying to escape it; I appreciate her friendship, support, and encouragement as I grappled with certain forms of political engagement. I discovered the impassioned and loving company of Banafsheh Akhlaghi and Elica Vafaie while in San Francisco. They supported and pushed me to engage in various nonacademic endeavors, for which I will always blame them. Working with Banafsheh at NLSCA has been a treat and a long-term commitment—and I'm grateful on both counts.

San Francisco is one of the most remarkable places in the United States—politically, socially, climatalogically, historically, and certainly intellectually. It has been my psychic home for more than twenty years, and it was a miraculous decadence to be able to return here to gather my thoughts after twelve years of teaching. Here I rediscovered the urgency of progressive and creative politics, alongside deeply thoughtful civic leaders and political activists who represent the marginalized, disfranchised, and others who need much more than hope. The proximity to the beautiful ocean, fantastic bookstores, excellent cuisine, wine country, and of course the best assortment of cafés in which to work have made this city an existential paradise for me. In particular, I wish to acknowledge the sadly defunct Canvas Café, the Beanery on 9th and Irving, Café du Soleil on Steiner and Fillmore streets, Jumpin' Java on Noe Street, the Icafe on Irving and 22nd Avenue, and the Kaleo Café, for their good coffee and laid-back environments—crucial for the writing of books, and the life of the mind. Chateau St. Jean and B.R. Cohn wineries in Sonoma have also provided tasty relief from intense work sessions.

Robert Bernasconi and Jane Bunker have been the kind of editors that a young professor dreams about. Robert solicited this project in its earliest of stages, with the kind of confidence and support that helped erase my doubts about the validity of this project. Jane has been responsive, punctual, prompt, and accommodating as I have had to wrench out various sections under important deadlines.

Then there are the friends and family whose presence is crucial intellectual and emotional nourishment—even through the long stretches without communication—without whom I cannot imagine this journey being even half as joyous, wicked, passionate, and lively. Asim Ali, Amar Bhat, Shirish Balachandra, April Ricotta, Uma Narayan, Laurence Lollier, and Bess Purcell, all long-standing friends, have refreshed and rejuvenated me with their acerbic wit, excellent aesthetic sense, all-round good taste, and important political commentaries. Mickaella Perina has become a sister by a different parent, who scolds, listens, understands, comforts, and is a near-daily interlocutor and unrelenting source of common-sense and reality. The Sheths, Garbers, Prasches, Bhats, and Balachandras have provided crucial humor, and financial, culinary, and other resources during times of need. My nieces Alison, Sophie, and Tara never cease to make me appreciate how delightful it is to be in the presence of strong, young, smart women. My nephews, Krishna, Vikram, and Shankar always manage to make me laugh and rejoice with their unique blends of sweetness, cheekiness, kindness, and love of life. All of them induce me to wake up every morning dreaming of utopian futures.

This list is very long, and yet not nearly complete. I apologize for all accidental omissions, and take responsibility for all mistakes, despite the efforts of my dear interlocutors to save me from error.

Finally, I wish to thank Anita Balachandra and Robert E. Prasch. One is my sister and the other my life-partner. Anita—what to say? How to thank? Impossible to measure, ineffable, the importance of your presence. And to my darling Bob, I owe an unrepayable debt. With you, I have been able to follow my dreams and existential commitments without limitations or regret. I can only ask: whither would I be, if not for you?

Introduction

If You Don't Do Theory,
Theory Will Do You

In graduate school, I took or audited courses that covered class, culture, exploitation, philosophy of history, oppression, time, hermeneutics, conditions of revolution, topics in psychoanalytic and feminist theories, to name a few themes. The range of continental philosophy that I read included numerous conceptual anchors for reconsidering philosophy in the vein of progressive politics. In these readings, with the exception of Hannah Arendt's writings, I did not encounter the topic of race.[1] Indeed in seminar discussions and even in the hallway, the question of race was usually roundly ignored. When it was (infrequently) raised, it was only to be laughed off as contingent, superficial, and ineligible for the status of deep theory. And indeed, it was laughable to think about how Heidegger would handle race, or why race should be a necessary consideration in the framework of the Frankfurt School; after all, Max Horkheimer, Theodor Adorno, and Walter Benjamin had already undergone severe tribulations as a result of racial attitudes under the policies of the National Socialist German Workers' Party; yet they had not thought it an important enough category to consider in conjunction with class or cultural analyses. At the New School where, happily, interdisciplinary study was strongly encouraged, I took classes in political science and sociology, and sat in on seminars in anthropology. The latter two fields were light years ahead, it seemed, when it came to incorporating questions and theoretical considerations of gender and race. But still . . . I wondered, in light of the political backdrop against which we were studying—the beating of Rodney King and the ensuing Los Angeles riots of 1991, the first invasion of Iraq, the random beatings of Asians and South Asians in the late 1980s, the murder of Yusuf Hawkins in Bensonhurst, NY, NAFTA, welfare reform, the Bosnian and Rwandan genocides—why didn't continental philosophy appear to be relevant to those events?

I decided that the problem was not philosophy, but myself . . . continental philosophy *was* relevant, but my knowledge was not yet sophisticated enough to apply the intricacies of Hegel, Heidegger, and Horkheimer to (then) contemporary racial politics. I continued to struggle with the "greats," while the direction of my interests turned further toward the history of modern political philosophy. Reading a range of feminist theorists and legal philosophers in addition to the works of Hobbes, Locke, Hegel, Kant, Rousseau, Marx, and Arendt over and over, I found fruitful sources as I sought out theories and frameworks that seemed more relevant to the pressing issues of the day. There still appeared to be a deep divide between "philosophy" per se and theories that were "relevant" to contemporary politics. In interdisciplinary reading groups, my colleagues in anthropology, political science, and sociology pointed out not unkindly that philosophy was the bastion of dead White men, and a few live White men, all dealing with archaic issues with antiquated solutions. And I defended philosophy—sometimes half-heartedly. My colleagues were right to some extent, but what I found in other fields seemed to be lacking in the theoretical depth and complexity that I both loved and hated about continental philosophy. And yet, much philosophy written in a contemporary American context did not seem to grapple with power as an intrinsic category of political frameworks, nor again with race, which seemed crudely absurd.[2] How could American political philosophy acknowledge slavery and refuse to think about its implications or influence on American juridical or political institutions? I turned to Constitutional law and critical legal studies for answers; while more fecund than many areas of philosophy, there were still few answers there.

In between defending my dissertation and sending out countless job applications, I decided I wanted nothing more to do with philosophy. I turned once more to other fields—critical (legal) race theory, African-American studies, South Asian literature, postcolonial studies—and read the *New York Times* with increasing outrage and anxiety. Arabs, South Asians, Sikhs, Muslims, and Hindus were going to school and work in fear for their lives, while police authorities were conspicuously indifferent, doing little or nothing to protect them. The PATRIOT Act, passed under the auspices of the Bush Administration, handed to then Attorney General John Ashcroft the power to initiate a widespread round-up and "voluntary" interrogation of hundreds of Muslim men, in an ostentatious effort to "prevent terrorism." I turned to Arendt once more for wisdom, insight, and solace and sought out the works of scholars in the tradition of legal critical race theory in an effort to understand how these politics could happen, and the first draft of chapters 5 and 6—the beginning of this book—took shape.

I was still frustrated with philosophy, American political theory, and the academic discipline of philosophy at large. Why did the concept of race have to be dealt with as a stand-alone concept or as an add-on feature to another "core" field? Why wasn't race considered an intrinsic feature of law? Of political institutions? Of political frameworks? For example, in much of the literature on race across the natural and cognitive sciences, the social sciences, and the humanities, the "reality" of race is still being discussed in terms of biology, empirical trends, government policies, philosophical arguments, or cultural discourse. Each of these is crucial to debating the reality of race, as well as racism and its pervasiveness. But what about the underlying framework makes the concepts of "race" and "racializing" possible? What about the discourse on race, as it has been conducted in the United States over the last 200 years, determines and reproduces certain anchors by which race is understood? Correlatively, how does this discourse obscure new, possibly more accurate ways by which to consider race, the racializing of various populations, and the way that race-thinking fundamentally infuses the most "race-neutral" of political and legal institutions?

Theoretical frameworks for race are also unsatisfying. We know that the legacy of slavery in the United States has viscerally affected the way that "Americans"[3] think about race. Black–White relations often tend to determine the dynamics and general boundaries of race discourse. Yet, the presence of American Indians, Mexicans and "Californios,"[4] the entrance of indentured servants from China and Japan, as well as continual immigration from other parts of Asia, Eastern Europe, and the Middle East should influence how we understand the dynamic structures and production of race. To the extent that the need for a change in race discourse is acknowledged, scholars admit that the boundaries of Black–White discourse have to be made more expansive, at least enough so that Latinos and Asians are considered necessary additions to the race discourse. But it is simply insufficient to say that race in America is about Blacks and Whites, and include other populations such as "Asians" or "Latinos" as cosmetic additions. The history of race in the United States, as for nearly all other nations, reflects the history of political institutions and social and ethnic conflicts, and the politics of regulating the inflows and outflows of people through its borders. Race reflects the logics and dynamic of legal institutions, foreign policies, diplomatic relations with other nations, attitudes toward perceived "outsiders," and the need by political authorities to respond or placate its constituencies in order to remain in power.

Another way to approach the complexity of race in contemporary politics is to consider the political categories and concepts that underlie apparently binary race relations. We might see beyond the historical specificity of racial humiliations such as slavery, one-drop rules, and anti-miscegenation laws if we were to understand how these antagonisms emerge from certain configurations of power, sovereign authority, and the vulnerability of different subject-populations. The interpretation of such historical events as pertaining primarily to relations between Blacks and Whites in the United States, eclipses the possibility of seeing these as forms of oppression, colonization, and "racialization" that have occurred to other populations both in the United States and in international contexts. In the United States, by looking to the legal vehicles and political institutions that enabled slavery, segregation, and anti-miscegenation, we might better understand how *power constitutes race*, and how race—not as a social description, but as *a tool of political management and social organization*—infuses the very ground of politics and sovereign-subject relations at every moment of a society's history. We could do the same by looking at race in international contexts; the framework in this book will point to certain theoretical approaches that can function in international contexts, but will stop short of offering a full treatment of race in contexts outside the U.S.

In this book I take certain theoretical—political—categories and frameworks that are generally considered *race-neutral* and illustrate how the notion of race fundamentally informs those structures. I understand "race" to be a mode or vehicle of division, separation, hierarchy, exploitation, rather than a descriptive modifier. Even beyond the discourse of social construction, race is fundamentally instantiated through a range of laws and social policies. Legal and political institutions—as representations of state power—produce race, understood as the vehicle by which populations are distinguished, divided, and pitted against each other. Division and antagonism are the intrinsic functions of racial categories—understood in terms of social or cultural identity (African Americans, Asians, South Asians, Latinos), but also in terms of political identity and the hierarchy of membership (citizens, aliens, residents, immigrants); the dynamic of different populations to each other in relation to the state; and of legality/vulnerability/criminality of different populations in relation to each other.

By showing how race is produced and reproduced through categories that are not overtly "raced," I hope that the argument in this book addresses certain lacunae and contributes to the growing literature in philosophy of race, critical race theory, political philosophy, and legal history. I look to what have been considered traditional "race-neutral" avenues, because they offer fundamental insights about race, transcending the shop-worn debate about whether race is scientifically objective or socially constructed. Thinking about the way race infuses political categories and legal frameworks, the possible permutations of race can be shown to apply to any range of populations—populations who are not necessarily objectively coherent (e.g., through ethnicity, racial identity, geographical or historical affiliations) but often subjectively constituted through certain allegiances, moral, religious, or cultural beliefs, political commitments—and even populations who can only be constituted as a group diasporically.

The concepts and ideas that I consider in this book include (1) the relationship between sovereign power and subject-populations as expressed through certain laws and judicial decisions (such as anti-miscegenation laws, one-drop rules, immigration law); (2) the way that sovereign institutions create political coherence, and manage subject-populations, for example, by threading certain "race-neutral" antagonisms into official definitions of good citizenship as well as of "criminal behavior" (through vehicles such as the selective distribution of certain rights, or through the definition of an "enemy alien," "enemy combatant," or "illegal alien"); (3) the "race-neutral" framework of liberalism (in particular how "reason," "dissent," and "cultural difference," are understood and deracialized within liberal theory). By exploring these political concepts and categories for their hidden "racialization" of different subjects, I wish to illustrate how certain political measures and "security" policies—contemporary or classic—from the "one-drop" rule, anti-immigration measures, to the increasingly widespread profiling and incarceration of Muslims since 9-11, are not only forms of ostracization and persecution, but of creating new "races" of people. Moreover, these practices can be traced to much longer standing structural flaws in our approaches to political philosophy, philosophy of race, and immigration law.

The method of approaching race as a mode of political and social division, and as an intrinsic function of political and legal structures, enables us to understand race as producing not only social identities but political or legal identities. The concept of race can be understood in terms of who is "culturally" or "socially" criminal (understood not as murderers or thieves, but as enemy aliens, foreigners, strangers, illegal aliens, or other kinds of legally designated hostile beings). Viewing the production of race through a legal or political prism allows us to see how race is utilized to divide populations in less conspicuous and more insidious ways than through identity or social stigma. It also reveals an intrinsic function of sovereign authority, namely the continual interest in maintaining a unity and coherence within the polity. This goal is facilitated by the management and limiting of potential unruliness or disorderliness of its subjects through legal and political structures that create or enhance an intrinsic or potential vulnerability surrounding them. In turn, this vulnerability is conducive to the state's interest to invite, cajole, or induce different subject populations to police themselves and by extension, other populations, in order to maintain a vigilant guard against excessive unruliness in one's own "community." We see a popular instance of this in Jeremy Bentham's Panopticon, as analyzed by Michel Foucault, as a site where prisoners help to discipline and govern themselves, and "the will of all . . . form the fundamental authority of sovereignty . . ."[5]

This concern of sovereign authority is conjoined by an interest for each population to help criminalize certain individuals/types of individuals/communities (one's own or others) in an effort to protect one's own "legal" or "favored" status before the law and the state. As might be obvious, this dynamic is based on Hannah Arendt's framework of the pariah-parvenu; with a few changes, I utilize her framework to understand political collectivities or groups in relation to a state. The most recent example of this, and the one that I draw on throughout the book, is the way that the pan-ethnic "Muslim" population in the U.S. and much of the Western world is being racialized and ostracized with the help and collaboration of various state powers in conjunction with vulnerable populations. It has been documented by scholars that the status of immigrant and minority groups—before the law and vis-à-vis other groups—tends to rise by helping to marginalize certain populations.[6] What I wish to do is to augment these accounts by offering an argument for how this collaboration occurs within the context, concepts, and framework of political philosophy.

The argument in this book emerges in response to three distinct discourses about race: First, my argument considers how the notion of racial difference is comprehended within contemporary political philosophy, particularly in liberal theory. This area does not explicitly consider how the concept of race enters into these considerations. To the extent that the notion of race is considered, it is often taken as an empirical category, informed by different populations, identities, and the collective interests of distinct racial groups. But this approach often takes what race is as "given" through the slightly dissonant lens of racial identity, rather than asking how race is instantiated through the state, produced through certain kinds of sovereign-subject dynamics, and institutionalized through certain juridico-political categories such as law, rights, and citizenship.

The "givenness" of race is compounded by the now commonplace debate in philosophy between the constructivists and objectivists, that is, whether race is a "social construction," or has biological/scientific grounds. By returning to the issue of objectivism v. constructivism, this debate deflects the question of how race finds itself taken up and reproduced through legal and political structures such as the U.S. Constitution, laws that institutionalize the "one-drop rule," and judicial decisions that reify certain racial designations and identities at one time or another. My second approach to race addresses this elision. Through these vehicles, certain understandings of race pervade, determine, and direct collective social and political conversations about concrete political controversies. I have in mind—although I don't address all of them in this book—issues such as the U.S. Census counts of different racial identities (Hispanic, African American, White, Asian, Mix-race), gay marriage and anti-miscegenation laws, immigration laws, citizenship and naturalization regulations, affirmative action, due process and human rights for noncitizens (immigrants, illegal aliens, and "enemy combatants" and "terrorists"), among other issues.

My third approach to race emerges from the discrete character of race discourse (biology v. social construction) and its marked separation from the literature on postcolonialism and poststructuralism that treats similar issues of discrimination, exploitation, marginalization of different populations under the banner of "Othering." In the philosophy of race literature, race is often still mired in the objectivist/constructivist debate, and for this reason suffers from the lack of grueling interrogation of the causes of hierarchy and divisiveness offered by accounts of colonialism and structural exploitation that are treated in postcolonial and poststructuralist literature.

My response to the discreteness of the postcolonial and philosophy of race discourses is to explore the insights that might emerge from integrating some key concepts of each literature: Othering, racializing, state-induced production of hierarchy, race as a social construction, race as a scientific category, race as a mode of identification of different populations, etc. These terms, when considered through the lens of political philosophy, can be seen not as variations, but as the products of how "race" is deployed as a weapon for political management. In the humanities, the discourse of postcolonialism rarely considers the separation and exploitation of populations an act of "racializing" per se, but rather of "Othering."[7] Since race discourses have traditionally referred to Black–White relations,[8] and postcolonial discourses refer to the history and practice of invading, colonizing, and exploiting peoples in Asia, Africa, Latin America, and the Caribbean, the two literatures are seen as having some content in common, but as exploring fundamentally different frameworks. But in many ways, racializing and Othering refer to the same phenomenon. The controversies about phenotype and science, and on the other hand about how Othering occurs, lead to a kind of circular loop, which becomes difficult, if not impossible, to transcend originary questions in order to arrive at new and insightful answers. In part, this is because these two disciplines do not look to each other for answers, and in part, it is because there is no turn to the metaphysics, the apparatus, by which racializing occurs.

And so, I begin in chapter 1, by drawing on Martin Heidegger and Michel Foucault to argue that we need to understand race as a technology. Through this approach, I hope to bridge the race and postcolonial discourses as described above. I understand race to function as a technology in three ways: as instrumental, naturalizing, and concealment. It is an instrument by which to channel an element that is perceived as threatening to the political order into a set of classifications. These classifications, in turn, constrain us to think about human beings as belonging to races. I name this element—which can refer to a comportment, character trait, or an entire population—the "unruly." I expand upon this concept in ensuing chapters. The second way by which race is technologized is by concealing the first function behind a more "official" one: namely as the transformation of the "unruly" into a set of "naturalized" criteria upon which race is grounded. Viewing race in this way, that is, peripherally and through a new lens of analysis, reveals something about its essence that is concealed from us when we attempt to look at it head on. The third way in which race functions as a technology is by concealing our relationship to law and sovereign power as one of vulnerability and violence, such that racialized populations stand precariously close to being cast outside the gates of the city. In other words, they are refused a dignified recognition or protection by the state. Finally, the implications of the technology of race can be understood by turning to Heidegger's notion of Enframing, Foucault's notion of the racist state, and the Benjamin's articulation of the inherent violence of law.[9]

In chapter 2, I develop my analysis of the third way in which race operates as a technology, namely by considering how politico-juridical frameworks operate not according to the rule of law, but rather through the drive of sovereign authority to further its own interest and manage its subjects by enhancing the vulnerability of certain populations and ultimately, by working in collaboration with certain political factors to racialize them. I take my lead from Jacques Derrida's argument in his essay, "The Force of Law," where he argues that the law is not procedural, but instead "cuts" randomly in favor or against certain populations.[10] I agree with the first part of his position, but I think *how* populations find themselves on one side of the law or another is hardly random. Instead, I argue, they are "preselected" through a range of factors that work in conjunction with sovereign power. In developing this framework, which I call the "Violence of Law" framework, I take issue with certain descriptions of sovereign power as articulated by Derrida, Giorgio Agamben, and Michel

Foucault. I then build upon a revised version of their arguments to analyze how populations become racialized through juridical and political institutions. I should underscore here that I am interested in how "races" of people are produced politically. As such, I distinguish between "racial" markers—skin type, phenotype, physical differences, and signifiers such as "unruly" behaviors. The former, in my argument, are not the ground of race, but the marks ascribed to a group that has already become (or is on the way to becoming) outcasted.

In chapter 3, I develop the concept of the "unruly," which, as I argue in chapters 1 and 2, is the ground of racialization. I do this by exploring a crucial conceptual ladder between the perception of a group as "not one of us" and their ultimate political outcasting. There are several steps to this ladder, which begin with the notion of "strangeness" as the basis of the perception of a group as "unruly." Strangeness and unruliness are elements of a discourse of "madness" or one of its subdiscourses, or "irrationality." The language of madness or irrationality takes the place of explicit racism, although they function similarly. I draw upon Foucault's writings on madness to develop a key subtext of the discourse of liberalism, namely how reason and unreasonableness become codes for the "madness" of cultural difference. The limits of "acceptable" cultural difference often function as vehicles and justifications by which to preempt or exclude dissenting groups from participating in "pluralistic" or "democratic" discourse. The very premises upon which the foundations of "democratic deliberation" are built—individualism, secularism, a certain general "overlapping" consensus about acceptable collective and public values—are often sufficient to prevent populations whose cultural foundations are in radical disagreement from challenging the prevailing notions of "free" and open debate. Moreover, such radical disagreement is preemptively construed as "irrational" or "illiberal," thereby adding insult to the injury of silencing certain populations. This judgment also adds to the increasing hegemony of various instances of past colonialism and contemporary neo-imperialism, which has justified the enslavement, persecution, or ostracization of certain populations because of the asserted absence of sufficient "rationality"—in other words, stupidity, foreignness, or a dangerous criminal psychology. Consequently, rationality—or its absence thereof—becomes a weapon by which to deem a group as insuffiently rational, and hence dangerous, unruly, mad, or even evil. But in any case, these are all versions of legitimizing a certain racialization without resorting to the explicit language of race.

In chapter 4, I draw on recent examples of the persecution of Muslim men and women to illustrate how they are perceived as "unruly," and consequently, how they are tamed—disciplined—by the state. This chapter applies the elements of the theoretical framework that I lay out in the first three chapters. In the case of Muslim women, I take the example of the "hijab" as a starting point to explore why it is perceived as a threat within the context of a liberal society, arguing that ultimately it is not the hijab itself, but what it synecdochically represents, which is a threat to the principles that anchor liberal societies. Drawing on the example of two Muslim high school students in Queens, NY, who were detained as potential "terrorist" threats, I explore the principles that they appeared to have transgressed by wearing the hijab or full purdah— principles such as "individualism," "transparency," a "neutral" divide between the public and the private, the secular and the religious. The hijab, along with other practices such as reading the Qu'ran, listening to sermons by fundamentalist imams, signify a comportment that is read as a dismissal of a superior (liberal) culture. Per my discussion of strangeness in chapter 3, these practices express an unwillingness to conform to the dominant *Weltanschauung* of the secular Western world. This unwillingness, translated as the unruly, indicates the danger presented by Muslim women who wear their principles "publicly" in opposition to a widespread political censure of all things "Islamic."

In chapter 5, I return to theory, and offer a way to understand how race operates as a "mode" of division within American legal policies and structures. I turn to law to illustrate how certain categories, such as citizen, person, or American, appear to facilitate "race-neutral" divisions between populations, but which actually function as vehicles by which to organize, manage and rank different groups within the polity. We have numerous examples to this effect. In eighteenth- and nineteenth-century United States, various states employed the categories of free White men, free Black men, and slaves, but there were also other legal categories to designate other "outsiders," and distinguish them from other "insiders." During times of peace the American government employed the categories of citizens, legal residents, aliens; during times of war or "alleged" war, as in the most recent few years, the terms "enemy aliens" and "enemy combatants" have reemerged as categories of differentiation, but also as ways to distinguish which kinds of political protections will be awarded or withheld from different kinds of populations.

When these terms underlie the concrete practice of "liberal" or "democratic" procedures in a polity, they construct and reify the identity of populations that may have no coherence in and of themselves until they are framed as a collective group externally—through laws, lawyers, politicians, immigration officials, and other authorities. The way that these terms are deployed legally and politically exemplify Carl Schmitt's statement that the meaning of the enemy can only be understood concretely against the backdrop of a given political event; they also implicitly acknowledge the specific power relations that are in place at any given moment.[11] The added force behind the way these terms are deployed is concealed behind the "naturalization" of the exception through the language of procedure and of the "rule of law."

Chapter 6 is the final theoretical anchor of the framework that I lay out in this book. I argue that the state's attempts to racialize a population succeed, not only by exploiting the range of political circumstances that have rendered that group already vulnerable, but also by managing the power disparities between two other subject-populations to its advantage as well. The racializing of a group occurs against the backdrop of a dominant population and another population that has already been targeted or has already existed as a "pariah." It is in this group's interest to escape its status of extreme vulnerability by functioning as a "Border-Population," a group that serves to guard and demarcate the dominant population from the newly emerging pariah population. I borrow Hannah Arendt's categories of pariah and parvenu, but depart from her analysis in several ways in order to account for the racializing and political vulnerability of groups rather than individuals. In developing this account, I want to instantiate the theoretical point that race, or racial divisions, are tripartite and not binary, as they are typically understood in race discourse.

This tendency has reasserted itself most recently in the striking contrast between the treatment of Muslims in the United States and the sudden "welcome" of Black Americans as part of the core American polity.[12] What accounts for such a disparity in the reception and treatment of these two groups? Although the incident that motivates this chapter occurred nearly six years ago, the answer to this question can only be adequately articulated well after the moment of emergency in which the phenomenon first became conspicuous. Once located legally, socially, and culturally outside the periphery of the American polity, a conspicuous subset of Black Americans have now been reconfigured as what I will term a "Border-population." As such, they are located on the periphery itself, the conceptual or physical site that distinguishes insiders from outsiders. Like any border, the political and rhetorical positioning of this population now serves to protect the "internal boundaries" of a nation, as Johann Fichte calls them.[13] This population is crucial in facilitating a recognition of the significant divide between the core populace and those who stand outside the symbolic boundaries that unite the populace. But in this role, Black Americans function as more than merely a wall dividing "insiders" from "outsiders," or "we" from "them." They also serve as the historical memory and institutional moral conscience that facilitates the American state's capacity to create the newest population of outcastes, namely Muslims in post–9-11 political context. By the terms, "serve" and "function," I am not suggesting a voluntary or ontological status on the part of African Americans or any other group that may be understood as a Border-population. Rather, I wish to show how this group is positioned in light of competing dynamics or antagonisms on the part of different institutions and/or populations. As a moral gauge, a Border-population's reaction (or absence of a unified reaction or referendum) is used by the state and/or inner populace to legitimate the outcasting of another group. Such a transformation of the symbolic position and place of Black Americans—from outsiders to "Border-guards" and Moral Gauge—is neither an incidental occurrence nor unique to American politics.

The final chapter reflects the application of the framework that I have laid out to the case of a little-known immigrant group to the United States. The group in question is "Asian Indian," but this population arrived well before the post-1965 immigration reforms that brought so many South Asians to the United States. Punjabi men—mostly Sikh, although some Hindus and Muslims were also part of this immigration—arrived in the United States via Canada, where they had been summarily kicked out in the early 1900s. Though nearly invisible today, their impact, was felt most deeply in California. There, they worked on farms, often undercutting the going wages for other labor and immigrant populations such as the Chinese and Japanese. They began to acquire farmland and, deprived of the opportunity to bring their Indian spouses to the U.S., began new families with Mexican and Mexican-American women as spouses. As British colonial subjects, they felt the sting of abandonment by the British government in their attempts to stay in Canada, and as they began to settle in the United States, a number of them engaged in nonviolent acts of political agitation to unseat the British government in India. Simultaneously, they became the focus of deep enmity from White working-class populations, as well as other immigrant groups. Consequently, during the first two decades of the twentieth century, they too became the focus of laws aimed to disfranchise, persecute, and exclude them from the United States altogether. I argue that the case of Asian Indians is a classic example of the juridico-political racialization of a population.

The conclusion attempts to offer "solutions" to the problem of racializing populations. By insisting that race and outcasting are endemic to liberal societies as well as to most juridico-political structures, I have left myself open to charges of "nihilism." But I would suggest that seeing certain problems as systemic is less nihilistic than assuming that systematicity means there is no course for redress. As such, I borrow from Tina Chanter's work on the abject to suggest that political resistance can occur in the most "hopeless" of situations. However, the forms that resistance takes change constantly as the problem itself manifests itself in new ways.

Throughout the book I have tried to show that throughout American and international history, the *racial identification and corresponding outcasting* of various groups have their roots in the way that the structures of rights, law, and protections have been set up to protect only those populations who are willing to collaborate with juridical and political institutions in the marginalization of certain groups. How then does one avoid the link between the protection of one population at what seems like the inevitable expense of another population?

One solution is to rethink the disparities between the discourses of human rights and national/political rights in order to consider how to avoid the vulnerability that each framework induces for certain marginalized populations. I suggest that neither the notions of national rights nor of international human rights is successful in protecting vulnerable groups against the potential of being rendered rightless and/or stateless. Instead, we must consider eradicating the conceptual and concrete division between immigration and Constitutional law. It is a solution that addresses the way legal institutions have attempted to outcaste, persecute, or otherwise marginalize different populations by racializing and inferiorizing them. We need to rethink the frameworks of human rights and political rights in order to circumvent the apparatus and infrastructure required to enforce human rights in an international/cosmopolitan arena, and to prevent the ability of nation-states to impose certain (often impossible) criteria for the awarding of rights to "outsiders."

One last word: since many of the chapters in this book address "liberalism" or "liberal" societies in addition to sovereign power and juridical institutions, this might be a good place to explain my understanding of liberalism and show the overlaps and distinctions between the liberal political project and the concept of sovereign power in nation-states.[14] My argument is about liberalism, and not nation-states as such. The latter are, according to Walker Connor, a "territorial-political unit [. . .] whose borders coincide or nearly coincide with the territorial distribution of a national group."[15] I understand nation-states to be predicated on ethnic or national homogeneity, whether they actually are, or whether they take this to be an aspiration or goal. By contrast, liberalism, theoretically or as a self-identification of a society, is predicated on the accommodation of ethnic, racial, political, or sorts of diversity or pluralism. This is part of the ideological framework upon which liberalism is founded. Furthermore, the primary tension for nation-states is about ethno-cultural identity, whereas I am discussing the impulse to exclusion of populations of any configuration. Here, my interest is in exploring whether liberal societies are intrinsically accommodating of difference or radical difference, or whether they are intrinsically exclusionary—contrary to their self-understanding.

Liberalism has become a ubiquitous term in the contemporary world; it designates a range of political attitudes, cultural worldviews, certain public policies, and certain forms of government. It can be used as a polemical term and as a description of a certain theoretical tradition in philosophy. These various versions of liberalism might have the following traits in common: Liberalism is a political philosophy that identifies the rational individual as the primary political unit in society. Liberalism is simultaneously concerned with the freedom and capacity of the individual to accumulate private property and govern his affairs and relationships with limited[16] interference by the state. The cornerstone of a liberal society is a market economy involving limited or minimal regulation. Historically, liberalism emerges as a counter-paradigm to the overwhelming political power of monarchs to govern and regulate the public and private affairs of their subjects. In a liberal society, political power is considered to be equally distributed and held by all individuals, but is expressed by proxy through an elected leader. That is to say, liberal societies are governed by leaders and administrations who, at least superficially, govern and take their power by the rule of law, and popular or majority consent. In liberal societies, it is assumed that governmental authority is respected and obeyed because it represents the political will of all members of that society.[17]

By extension, liberalism is thought to mark a stringent divide between the public/political sphere and private sphere, the former of which pertains to governing society, while the latter is thought to contain the family, and at various moments, the economy. By implication, politics and the public sphere are assumed to be secular or neutral with respect to religion and most moral and philosophical worldviews, in an attempt to limit, check, and regulate the political cache or power that any given individual or organization can wield against others.

Over the last decade, an excellent literature analyzing the coextensive development of liberalism and empire has emerged.[18] Made by scholars in a range of fields, the argument—or at least that part of the argument that is relevant to this book—goes something like this: The British and American empires promoted the ideal vision of liberalism at the same time that they were engaged in an extremely destructive and violent expansionism. As such, there is no reason to believe that the secular, neutral vision of justice promoted was antithetical or contradictory to the expansion, colonialism, and forced labor that were anchors of the Empire project. In fact, a great deal of insight can be gained by understanding how the ideal vision of liberalism and empire were working hand-in-hand. As Charles Mills points out, just because we can read a number of philosophies in the liberal tradition as being race-neutral, this does not mean that their authors understood them as such.[19] It is in this vein that I approach the culture and discourse of liberalism.

Beyond this, liberalism varies by form and degree among and between societies. Thus, while France would be considered a society that requires a secular comportment in its public institutions and its denizens, the United States—at least until President George W. Bush's Administration—might have been considered a society whose public institutions are secular, but that ostensibly accommodates a range of religious and philosophical worldviews from its denizens. Liberalism can be seen as a metapolitical form of government, namely, one that emphasizes that political and judicial decisions are made through the rule of law, or it can refer to a particular kind of society, as described variously by philosophers from Thomas Hobbes, John Locke, and Immanuel Kant, and perhaps most famously in the contemporary world—John Rawls. Liberalism, in its meta- and micro- versions, is akin to the use of the term, "democracy." This latter term refers to a more or less "free society," where political representation is said to take place by the consent of its citizens, or it can refer to the classic form of government that informed ancient Athens, where political decisions were made by the majority of eligible citizens.

In this book, my use of the term liberal refers to societies that take their lead from the rule of law. I also use the term to refer to a certain socio-cultural worldview that highlights individual autonomy, consent, and particular view of freedom as one that involves the active making of "decisions" or "choices," as Isaiah Berlin discusses.[20] This view of liberalism involves a corresponding view of law, morality, and moral consequences. In this framework, legal punishments befall mostly "bad people," that is, those who have violated laws that are generally just or have just cause.

I have just listed several features of liberalism that emphasize the regulation and limits of political power: Government by consent and will of the people; proceduralism; strict separation between public and private spheres; the freedom and autonomy of the individual; limited state regulation of private and economic affairs; and the collective societal agreement to abide by the rule of law. The corollary to this description of a liberal society is that atrocities occur under governments in such societies are invariably considered accidental, incidental, or misapplications of liberal tenets or of the rule of law. Thus, for example, in the history of the United States, events such as slavery, Jim Crow laws, the exclusion and denaturalization of Chinese, Japanese, and other immigrants, the internment of citizens of Japanese, German, and Italian descent, and countless other tragedies are thought to have been the consequences of flawed thinking, or a misunderstanding of how liberal tenets should be applied—because supposedly in liberal societies, political power has been systemically checked and thus is not vulnerable to be usurped or abused except under extraordinary circumstances. This framework supposes the objective nature of law and liberalism. It supposes that the political tenets and juridical structure that undergirds this society are at worst, occasionally flawed, and at best, benevolent. It presumes that laws and public policies are mediated by lawmakers and political leaders who are directly representing the views of the rational citizens who inhabit that society.

It is this picture of liberalism with which I take issue in this book. The belief that political power has been evenly distributed such that no one institution or person can usurp or abuse the power and protections that others may have—this belief is perhaps the most dangerous, because it conceals a very different relationship between sovereign power and law toward its members behind a facade of equality. The actual nature of sovereign power is much more forceful, much more potent than the myth of the liberal political project belies. A number of philosophers whose writings I draw on in this book—Michel Foucault, Carl Schmitt, Giorgio Agamben, Hannah Arendt—have argued this point much more articulately, more persuasively than I can here. Their arguments, however, are different from mine in various ways: Hannah Arendt discusses the nature of sovereign power in the modern nation-state; I am interested in liberal societies as such. Carl Schmitt points to liberalism as the ground of the "political" and the basis for the enemy; I am interested in how liberalism conceals the political. Giorgio Agamben argues that we are all vulnerable to be the exception in any politico-juridical structure; I argue that not all of us are vulnerable at the same time—someone is wielding power while others are the sovereign's targets. Foucault argues that sovereign power is wielded less overtly and more diffusely in contemporary society; I agree that power can be distributed and wielded more diffusely; however, I believe power can also be wielded quite directly by sovereign authorities in a liberal society—this force, I suggest, is built into the very juridico-political structure that emerges from liberalism.

As such, the lens by which I view the relationship between sovereign power and law toward its members in liberal societies is distinct from the way one might understand how sovereign power behaves toward its citizens in a modern nation-state. In the latter case, the relation between sovereign authority and the members of a nation-state *might* be governed according to the rule of law, but it need not be the dominant narrative that is used to describe that relation. Thus, we might consider Jordan a modern nation-state that operates according to the rule of law, but neither the denizens of this society nor political scientists would describe it as liberal. On the other hand, regardless of the current state of affairs of the United States, France, or Denmark, their self-understandings are that they are societies that have traditionally operated on the principles of rule of law, individual freedom and equality, and they still insist upon a secular public sphere. The narrative of liberalism, in which these concepts are the hallmarks, still hold a dominant currency in these societies.

In this book, my interest is in rethinking the relationship between sovereign and subject from within the prism of the "liberal political project." The dominant emblems of liberalism—in particular the idea that legal structures within liberalism are inherently fair and neutral toward all of its denizens (best-case version) or accidentally skewed in favor of some (worse-case version), that atrocities such as slavery, internment, or massacres are accidental mishaps—need to be revised in order to account for other phenomena in liberal societies, which cannot be explained under this account: widescale mishaps, that is, "exceptions" to the rule of law, that generally happen to populations whose access to power is extremely limited or the most disenfranchised (at the moments during which those atrocities occur); the gap in the cultural, economic, and political beliefs of those in leadership or lawmaking positions and of certain portions of their constituencies; the ability of those in leadership or lawmaking positions to shape and impose the dominant cultural and political opinions that certain portions of their constituencies will be forced to accept; and by extension, the marked disparity between the legal (and existential) invulnerability of political leaders and lawmakers in comparison to the legal (and existential) vulnerability of certain portions of their constituencies.

My description in the prior paragraph can also be understood through the lens of "race," and indeed I do understand such uneven access to power as "racial." However, as mentioned earlier, I understand the concept of "race" to be a mode of division that is instantiated through political and legal institutions, rather than a term that consistently identifies certain stable and coherent populations; that is to say, only part of my account of race refers to liberalism. As chapters 1 and 2 illustrate, I am also very much concerned with how sovereign power creates and reproduces race while hiding behind the face of neutrality and objectivity toward which the narrative of liberalism is geared. And so, as I proceed, let me offer one more account about how I understand the relationship between liberalism and sovereign power in this book. While I have attempted at points to illustrate that certain features of sovereign power operate in both liberal and "nonliberal" contexts, most of my examples emerge from liberal contexts, such as the United States. My accounts of sovereign power pertain to liberal and nonliberal contexts, but I find it important to illustrate the way race is created is concealed and naturalized especially easily in a liberal context—precisely because the narrative of liberalism is supposed to be identical to the actual operation of sovereign power (i.e., appearance and essence are considered to be the same), and because the mythical hold of liberalism is so strong that it is easy not to see what in other contexts might appear to be so obvious: first, that law (and laws) are neither necessarily objective nor good[21]—so that the "rule of law" is in fact substantively more flimsy than it might otherwise be supposed to be; second, that sovereign power is distinct from subject populations—in liberal or nonliberal societies, such that the creation and application of laws should be interrogated for their intentions and targets. Thus, in my analyses, liberalism and sovereign power operate side by side when it comes to the creation and institutionalization of race, racial divisions, and the vulnerability of certain populations.

Readers will recognize echoes of Walter Benjamin, Michel Foucault, Jacques Derrida, Giorgio Agamben, among others in the prior description of my project. In this book, I take some of my inspiration from their writings. However it is not my intent to engage in a history of philosophy of their scholarship; rather, I am interested in extrapolating crucial insights in order to understand racialization and racial division as a crucial feature of politics and sovereign power, that is, as an alternative part of any framework of the modern state. It will be clear to some that I am trying to reconcile the frameworks and ideas of philosophers such as Arendt, Heidegger, and some of the above mentioned philosophers (among others) with what are considered ordinary, even banal, truisms of modern "western" polities referred to in ethnic and cultural studies literatures. I am also trying to bridge the conversations that are engaged within Critical Race Theory (legal) literature and postcolonial discourses. In these instances, I am trying to reconcile them because I find important insights in "each,"—if these can be reduced to coherent and distinct literatures. But I have also found that each literature has something in common: they ignore the prevailing and hegemonic discourse of liberalism as they make important inroads and critiques of the workings of political institutions, law, politics, and power. Given that the theoretical discourse of liberalism largely ignores the disparity of power between sovereign (political leaders and lawmakers) and subjects, it is surprising that liberalism as a narrative is still such a culturally hegemonic authority in the United States and other "liberal" polities. It is also surprising that, given its hegemony, the literatures I have mentioned above have not taken on the metatheoretical assumptions of liberalism in their critiques.

Why, for example, does not Agamben's evaluation of the "exception" and sovereign power in *Homo Sacer* account for the narrative of the "rule of law," which cloaks sovereign power in liberal theory?[22] Foucault's brilliant account of disciplinary and regulatory power does, at least implicitly, account for the power involved in "rules" exercised by sovereign power. But his discussion, which offers an exacting account of the way power quietly, "neutrally," and ubiquitously underlies the race wars of modern society, appears to neglect the way sovereign authority still operates directly to create racial divisions, on the grounds that in contemporary society sovereign power operates in a more diffuse manner. Why do insightful scholars in the Critical Race Theory tradition, while offering forceful arguments about how minority populations are persecuted repeatedly within history of American law, appear to neglect the arbitrary dimension of the "rule of law" and judicial opinions? I have in mind opinions such as that expressed by the Supreme Court in the *Knauff v. Shaughnessy* case of 1950, which insisted that *any treatment afforded aliens is due process*—regardless of whether it reaches the standards implied for citizens in the 14th Amendment.[23] Similarly, the ethnic and cultural studies literatures have so many astute theoretical insights about the operation of political and social power and the harassment of various disenfranchised and ethnic populations. But it seems that writers in these fields often refrain from challenging the more entrenched mythological dimensions of traditional political philosophy and liberal theory. And finally, postcolonial theory—while remarkably showing how imperialism and colonialism operated on its subjects then and on its descendants in the diaspora today—shirks from addressing the "racial" dimensions of race literature— with which it has so much in common and which its insights on the operations of political and imperial power could complicate.

It is neither my interest nor intent to blend or muddle the concepts, points of reference, or frameworks offered by these distinct literatures. Rather, it is my hope that by drawing upon each of them the resulting analysis might contribute some new insights to a long-standing topic, and enrich in some small way these existing literatures. In the process, I hope to offer a way by which to understand that race is the consequence of a political, legal process that is meant to manage people. Race and its longtime associate, phenotype, are not the grounds of distinct human groups, but rather are used to justify the deeply entrenched divisions caused by long-standing and powerful political structures.

1

The Technology of Race and the Logics of Exclusion

The Unruly, Naturalization, and Violence

The essence of [race] is by no means anything [racial]. Thus we shall never experience our relationship to the essence of [race] so long as we merely conceive and push forward the [racial], put up with it, evade it. Everywhere we remain unfree and chained to [race], whether we passionately affirm or deny it. But we are delivered over to it in the worst possible way when we regard it as something neutral; for this conception of it, to which today we particularly like to do homage, makes us utterly blind to the essence of [race].[1]

Introduction

The last century has found us entangled in an unending debate over the "reality" of race: scientists, academics, and policy makers argue whether race has a biological foundation or whether its reality is contrived, constructed, or otherwise humanly created. Can DNA offer us true answers, ask social scientists, or are geneticists begging the question? Do physical distinctions between persons tell us something noteworthy about their racial genealogy? If race is "socially constructed," as the phrase is now lobbed around tritely, then how do we account for physical differences?

Another question: Why *must* we search for a "satisfactory" description of one's racial identity? Approaches that take seriously the question of whether race is biological or socially constructed appear to be vulnerable to the snare cited by Martin Heidegger in my paraphrase of his quote above: they regard race as something given or neutral, and thus render us

21

blind to its essence. Heidegger's 1950 lectures on technology are notable
for distinguishing between technology and the essence of technology. Our
attempts to find the "essence" of a thing by looking at it directly often lead
to its obfuscation; instead, by looking to the "Gestell," or the enframing of
an epoch, the truth of a particular thing might be more readily revealed to
us. We might have a similar success in finding the essence of race by not
looking for it directly, but rather by using our peripheral vision, as we
might in order to search for something in the dark.

What if, instead of searching for the objective ground of race, we explored the function of race and racial distinctions in society? Political
philosophers have long pointed to the organization of political power
and the fair acquisition of resources as among the biggest problems in
creating a functional society. If we accept this point, then another role
for race emerges: race becomes a way of organizing and managing populations in order to attain certain societal goals, such as political coherence, social unity, and a well-functioning economy.[2] These goals require
the collective awareness of the political status, social role, and the pur-
ported relationship between each member of society. As such, race becomes a way not only by which to distinguish populations, but to use
these distinctions to maintain social and political harmony[3] among
them. Understanding race in this light requires a consideration of how
political and legal institutions such as sovereign authority, law, and the
judiciary collaborate in cohering societies. In this picture, race is no
longer descriptive, but causal: it facilitates and produces certain relationships between individuals, between groups, and between political
subjects and sovereign power. The function of race, then, is similar to the
function of technology: Technology, commonly considered as equip-
ment, facilitates the production of certain "goods." It requires the input
of certain raw material which, mediated through a device, is transformed
into a "new" product. In turn, this product is thought to meet certain
needs that we might have. Similarly, within a juridico-political context,
race becomes an instrument that produces certain political and social
outcomes that are needed to cohere society.

At this point, it might make sense to return to Heidegger and take
our lead from him by understanding race as a technology. I will sketch
this position briefly here and develop it further in this and ensuing chapters. I want to suggest that race functions as a technology in three dimensions: first, it is a vehicle deployed by law to channel certain elements
in order to produce a set of classifications that constrain us to think
about human beings as belonging to races. The elements in question are
perceived as unpredictable, undependable, or threatening to a political
order; I will refer to them as "unruly."[4] The second dimension by which

race can be considered technologically is through the juridical capacity to conceal the first function behind a more "official" or "procedural" one. Once the unruly elements are transformed into new categories, the process of this transformation is buried behind a set of "naturalized" criteria[5] upon which race is "grounded," such that the categories in use appear unshakably solid or ontologically rooted. Viewing race in this way reveals something "lofty and ambiguous" about its essence that is concealed from us when we attempt to view it head on.[6] The third way in which race functions as a technology is that it conceals our relationship to law and sovereign power behind seemingly objective moral and political judgments. And so, in liberal societies,[7] this relationship appears to be grounded securely on the rule of law and principles of fairness, equality, and protection rather than on vulnerability and violence,[8] in other words, as one where populations are susceptible to being thrust outside of the gates of the city, beyond the aura of law's protection, to abandonment by the law.[9]

To return to Heidegger: to understand the *Gestell*, or the enframing, of an epoch—that is, the cultural, legal, political, existential apparatus that characterizes a mode of existence—might "reveal" the implications of race as a technology, especially in its second and third dimensions.[10] Thus, at least part of the apparatus, which "drives-forth" race in its deployment as a technology, emerges from a basic tension between the ethos of sovereignty and the context of liberalism: the fundamental purpose of sovereign power is to maintain order and discipline, and otherwise to manage its populace while promoting the ideology of equal protection and universal freedom. If this is the case, then we might understand how race is deployed effectively in liberal societies, namely as a way to create political order by using such "naturalized" categories as objective grounds by which to identify populations who are immoral, inferior, or evil. The primary function of such characterizations, I maintain, is to identify and justify "outcastes" or "exceptions" to the promise of universal protection so as to retain a focus on the value of liberalism's freedoms and thus to facilitate a collective social interest in managing its populace.[11] The tendencies that exemplify such a social interest—through the use of race as a technology— are what I refer to as the "political metaphysics of race."

While I take my lead from Heidegger's "Technology" essay, my understanding of how race functions technologically—especially in its second and third dimensions—draws on Michel Foucault's understanding of technology as well. As mentioned earlier, I understand technology in an instrumental sense, to be "productive," that is, to produce certain kinds of outcomes (qua racial classifications). In this sense, I draw on Foucault's discussion of technology as he alludes to it in *Discipline and Punish*, that is, as a way of breaking down the body and rearranging it,[12] and as well—"conquering it . . . [and] rendering it more useful and docile."[13] However, in this argument, it is not the body that is rearranged and rendered docile, but human beings as part of collective populations that are to be managed and maintained through sovereign power.[14] In this regard, race as an instrument of production can be linked and understood in connection to its second and third technological dimensions, namely through the naturalization of "racial" or "racialized" classifications,[15] and as the concealment of the expression of the violent and vulnerable relationship that subjects have with sovereign power.[16] The third dimension of technology takes its lead from Foucault's understanding of the "regulatory technology of life"[17] as that expression of "disciplinary coercions that actually guarantees [sic] the cohesion of that social body."[18] However, I depart from Foucault's discussion of race in connection to biopower, by suggesting that the regulatory technology in question is one of the ever-present, ominous, and yet concealed violence that underlies the relationship among subjects, collective populations, and sovereign power. This violence is expressed through the "taming of the unruly,"[19] as it leads to the production of races. Race, then, can be understood as a technology as well as an existential mode of sovereign power, which threatens and coheres simultaneously. Race, as I construe it, is that which lies between the "right of sovereign power and the mechanics of discipline," and is distinct from the exercise of disciplinary and regulatory power.[20] This violence is hidden behind a moral discourse of inferiority, criminality, and evil, and encourages the deployment of racial divisions by different populations in attempts to become less vulnerable to the law.[21]

I offer this argument as a way to bridge what appear to be two fundamentally distinct discourses. One discourse, which I call "Biological Race" (BR), emerges from contemporary American philosophical conversations about race, and *utilizes or challenges* biology, genetics, phenotype, and genealogy to ground its arguments.[22] An important implication of BR is that regardless of the position one takes in this debate, the givenness of race constrains its terms, and thus inhibits the possibility of understanding the meaning of race within a different framework altogether. The second discourse, which I will call "Political Othering" (PO), refers to political structures and worldviews such as colonialism, orientalism, and imperialism to discuss the methods by which certain populations have been construed as "foreign," "Others," "aliens," on grounds such as culture, political structures, status, or territory.[23] The latter discussion appears to be fundamentally distinguished—even excluded—as "not really" about race, *because of the nonbiological grounds* by which "Othering" occurs. One of the more important contemporary implications of this distinction is that discussions of exclusion that pertain to populations such as refugees, political prisoners, immigrants, or the participants/victims of a civil war, are seen as fundamentally "not about race" and instead about their political, cultural, ethnic, national, caste, or religious affiliations. Another implication is that the discussions of BR preclude us from recognizing conflicts among the "same" populations as being about racial identity and division.[24]

These discourses, BR and PO, while based on different criteria, are nevertheless both forms of understanding populations as different or "other" through race, their foundations derive from similar impulses. The similarities between these discourses can be located through a "political metaphysics" of race, or a generalizable systematic analytic by which races are understood and distinguished, and would allow us to understand a range of social divisions and racism as part of the same political phenomenon. Identifying the tendencies and implications of such a metaphysics of race would enable us to understand certain excluded populations as the focus of a racialization that does not conventionally resort to eighteenth- and nineteenth-century European classifications of race.[25] Through an exploration of race as a technology, I want to explore how a population can be divided and produced as a "breed" or "species" extremely or completely dissimilar in fundamental ways from the population against which it is juxtaposed. By extreme dissimilarity, I wish to invoke the idea that "they" could never be part of "us," because "they" don't embody the fundamental traits required to be "human like us."

As I have indicated, I draw on both Heidegger's and Foucault's writings to consider the meaning and implications of race within the context of sovereign power. While the frameworks of these two philosophers are not necessarily consistent, I believe their mutual interlocution through the medium of race creates a productive tension.[26] Read together, their works facilitate an illumination of the metaphysical terrain upon which race—as a mode of existence, a technology, a vehicle of division, and an engine of political power—operates. This chapter does not extensively engage with Foucault's discussion of bio-power.[27] I should note that his prescient lectures on racism and sovereign power, as well as his other writings, have influenced my argument powerfully. His insights about the function of race as a political mechanism of sovereign power, expressed as a metaphysical division, are crucial to the formulation of this argument. Through my disagreements with his arguments in the 1976 lectures, I hope to acknowledge as well as redirect some of his powerful insights on race and sovereignty in order to contribute to the contemporary philosophical literature on race and racism.

First Dimension: Taming the Unruly

The technological deployment of race is exemplified through attempts to understand "what race is"—biological or social. The focus on this question is influenced by, among other things, eighteenth-century writings[28] that turn to race as a way of systematically classifying and justifying the intuited or perceived differences between populations. Even recent discussions in philosophy often focus on the "received view" of race as biological in the attempt to confirm or shed doubt on it.[29] In these debates, race is deployed as a scientific instrument, producing a certain set of results, constraining us to think about race as either biological or socially constructed, and to look for evidence to confirm one position or the other. Even beyond this binary debate, within the context of juridico-political management, the instrument of race is used to seek out uncategorized (raw) material and transform it to produce certain categories of identification. These categories can be biological,[30] political, or legal.

Race locates something that is real, the identification of which is always shifting.[31] Within the dimension of the real, the important character of what is being picked up is what I call the "unruly."[32] This is the element that is intuited as threatening to a political order, to a collectively disciplined society. As this term suggests, this element threatens to disrupt because it signifies some immediate fact of difference that must be harnessed and located or categorized or classified in such a way so as not to challenge the ongoing political order. The "unruly" is marked out within some dimension of the "real" that should not be interpreted merely at the visual level (as in the case of persons who appear White but are recorded as Black, or of some segment of an otherwise "homogenous" population that becomes marked as being "different than us" or of a different "race" or an "Other"). That which is unruly can be evasive enough to be "intuited" or "felt" rather than seen or perceived—because the intuition is one of "danger."[33] It is this intuition—together with an awareness, memory, or collective narrative about a certain history, culture, or politics with which the "unruly" is associated—that facilitates the acceptance of a certain classification. This element, as located in the dimension of the "real," can be "represented" by something as tangible as skin tone or headdress or as intangible as a bodily comportment, a gesture, or an accent. However, it signifies something even more subtle, such as a religious affiliation, an unusual behavior or practice, a hint of another's migratory or ancestral past (having once been chattel) or the social history of another's tribe, caste (having once been "untouchable"), or kin. We could even say that the "unruly" denotes the real *in association* with its perceived degree of threat.

The context of the "real" is what I take to "be responsible" for the occasion of the deployment of race as a technology. For example, did someone's ancestors come to this country in chains or to another locale as conquerors that are now vanquished? This fact may not be expressly recorded on one's body, but in a public, or official narrative, such as a birth certificate, or an oral genealogical history. And it is such a fact, which can be identified as the ground of the real in which the unruly signals as that which is dangerous, and in need of being tamed or regulated. This taming occurs through something like a legal classification of blackness in the U.S. or—until Indian independence—something like the legally sanctioned outcasting of the Shudra caste in India—*because they were understood as polluted and thus considered untouchable*, and consequently, restricted to menial labor, sanitation jobs, and even specific clothing restrictions.[34]

The element that becomes identified as the "unruly" can vary according to the moment in which it is found. In this regard, it is a floating signifier, pointing to something that insinuates a threat to the political order.[35] If we look at the treatment of race in American legal history, then we find the unruly instantiated and then tamed through the constant deployment of certain rules or hermeneutic devices. One common example is the one-drop rule in the United States, which legally distinguished those who were deemed "Black," from those who were not, until the latter part of the twentieth century and is still in informal use today.[36] At one level, the one-drop rule, which did not have a uniform definition across various states until the twentieth century, facilitated a way by which to *circumscribe the essence of blackness, or nonwhiteness*, as denoted by genealogy or blood. Thus, a woman who was blonde and blue-eyed and whose lineage could be traced to an enslaved African-American ancestor—understood in terms of fractions, which decreased as the relation to said ancestor diminished—might be designated as Black or a "Creole of Color" in Louisiana but White in South Carolina at the same moment in the nineteenth century.[37] The paradox of being distinguished as White in one state and Black in another might be correlated to the different degrees of threat that same person presented in each state on any number of issues: miscegenation, ascending social class, aspiring to be legally free, or accumulating capital.[38]

Such a potential threat illustrates the other dimension of the one-drop rule, namely its formal memorialization of one's ancestral history, as this has been recorded: for example, as the evidence/offspring of a forbidden sexual interaction, a sanctioned rape, or the caste-doors or legal and economic avenues through which *some of* one's ancestors entered this country. It is the collective social awareness and judgment of a person's past that is being crystallized through the one-drop rule. At another level, the one-drop rule might mark a specific comportment or mode of behavior that needs to correspond to it, that is, presenting oneself as "Black." A departure from this mandate will also signify an "unruly" comportment, one that defies the political and social place that is to be inhabited.

The "unruly" is the perspicuous element that is picked up on by sovereign power, but it is one of several stages that mark a group's transition from merely "different" to "racialized." I discuss this process in more detail in chapter 3. In chapter 4, I apply the framework to the case of "Muslims" in recent political history.

Second Dimension: Naturalizing the Unruly

The originary ground of a certain racial category—the "unruly" element— is classified and channeled through certain legal and social practices, such that these become the basis of distinguishing one population from another.[39] However, there is a simultaneous move that occurs, which involves the "naturalizing" of this classification. After the initial "processing" of the unruly through the production of certain categories, the process—the political context—of classifying becomes forgotten, concealed, or reified. Thus, it appears as a "natural foundation" for racial categories. So, to return to the example of the "one-drop" rule, the awareness of one's past is transformed into the metonymy of blood, but this transformation is concealed behind its "facticity." Blood is construed *as the factual ground of biological ancestry*, while simultaneously understood as the measure of blackness. *Blood(lines)*—the symbol of neutrality and objectivity—locate a person whose "known" background conforms to this definition—as Black despite all other contrary visible signifiers. Blackness or nonwhiteness—as this is expressed *not* through the fact of biology or blood, but through a *"known" and selectively interpreted genealogical history*—is what is "naturalized" through the one-drop rule. Thus, according to the statute in effect in late nineteenth-century Louisiana, judging a person as Black requires having any traceable "Black ancestry." For example, then, to determine a person as having "one-eighth (1/8) Black blood" requires reading her as having one great-grandparent as "Black," and another great-grandparent, two grandparents, and two parents as "not Black," or at least not traceably so. It goes without saying—although not without consideration—that these are "blood" relatives, that is, related to her by dint of the series of sexual acts that produced her.

The act of singling out one person as "responsible" for her public recognition via state law as "Black," raises the question of which end this identification, and selective, stylized, form of identification serves. Clearly, if her genealogical history had not been known, or surveyed under the state regulation, the question of having a "Black great-grandparent" would have not have been publicly acknowledged, and indeed, short of the one-drop rule, might very well have been irrelevant in terms of her public "racial" identification. Among other reasons, the insistent naming of a person as Black under such specific conditions is designed to relocate or "demote" her status on a legal, social, or political scale. Moreover, if this blonde, blue-eyed, person wishes to be registered as "White," the fact of her great-grandparents' interactions—construed as miscegenation—is explored in legal terms, and raised as a way of disciplining her for desiring to ascend to the more dominant status of "whiteness."[40] A moment of unruliness—a history of miscegenation, a whisper that one is not as one appears—is hypostatized and reified through the means of a rule understood as a "definition" and "demarcation" of race.[41]

Then, the one-drop rule *depends on the concept of blood as a "natural" category—as the ground of race—which blinds us to the essence of race.* But rather than seeing "blood" as the device that it is—a "trope" by which to remember and judge the singular process of one's ancestral, social, and political past, it is reconstituted as a biological—objective, ontological— proof of race, and hence, drives forth the quest to understand the origins of race as "natural."[42] By then taking up the question, as Robin Andreasen does, of whether races could ever be distinguished biologically, one receives the product of such a technology (one-drop rule) as a neutral, *prima facie*, fact about the ground of race (biology qua common ancestry).[43] In so doing, one is blinded by the technology, and thus participates in reifying the unruly, that is, in its concealment and transformation as a "natural" basis of race.[44]

I have explored the first two dimensions of how race can be deployed as a technology by taking up the question of the "one-drop" rule and its manifestation as an "objective" mode of understanding different racial groups. But one need not depend on—what are maintained to be—objective, scientific, or racial criteria in order to deploy the technology of race to create new racial groups. In later chapters I explore other examples by which race can be deployed to "racialize" populations, using more nebulous criteria. These criteria are consistent in being perceived as "unruly" elements that threaten a given political order.

Race as a Tool for Sovereign Power: Dividing Populations

In this section I offer a schematic overview of the third technological aspect of race, namely that which conceals our relationship to sovereign power as one of violence.[45] First, I begin with the premise that race is instantiated through sovereign power. In so saying, I explore several fundamental insights of Michel Foucault who, in the late twentieth century, offers a new narrative of sovereign power in modernity. He claims that the modern state is, at bottom, a racist one, in that it is the agenda of any given sovereign to distinguish and compel one population to live from another population's mandate to death.[46] Foucault links his analysis to bio-power, in other words, that authority of the sovereign to make decisions concerning life and death through certain biological priorities. Then, for Foucault, racism is the tendency or the drive to fragment, divide, or create breaks in the "biological continuum of the human race."[47] The racism of the sovereign lies in the ability to *create races* of subjects, using any number and quality of characteristics within the domain of life—over which it has control[48]—by which to demarcate them, in order to create divisions between the living and the dying. Races, and racism, are predicated on the "biological continuum" of life, and the mandate of sovereign power is to divide that continuum through the various policies, technologies, and circumstances by which the health and life of populations is regulated and managed. This is true, according to Foucault, even for modern and contemporary sovereign authority. As he suggests, the only characteristic that changes is the *telos* of that authority: whereas in the Hobbesian model of the state, the *Leviathan* decided who it would "make die and let live," the contemporary state uses a power of "regularization" or "normalization" to decide who it will "make live and let die."[49] Thus, says Foucault, race wars underlie the peace and order of a society, dividing a single population into two—through the treatment of human beings in their physical dimension as living beings.[50]

For this argument, it is important to emphasize that according to Foucault, bio-power is a "technology of regulation," which is implemented as the *unique and modern expression of the intrinsic racism that lies at the heart of sovereign power*. It is implemented to manage, control, and regulate its population through these distinctions, and this function is "normalized" as an intrinsic practice of sovereign power. In other words, for Foucault, as it was for Hobbes, it is life that is being held as leverage against populations in order to secure the cohesion of a polity.[51]

Foucault's observation that the state is fundamentally racist, and takes as part of its mission the creation of hierarchies and divisions between groups within a population, seems correct—to an extent.[52] I want to delve briefly into the relationship between this mandate of the state and its treatment of race in its agenda; I will develop the contrasts between Foucault's account of sovereign power and my revisions of it more extensively in chapter 2. It seems correct to say, along with [Hobbes and] Foucault, that at least one, if not the, primary purpose of sovereign power is to enable a certain control and management of its population. For Foucault, this purpose is coextensive with the deployment of biopolitics. And yet it is hard to subscribe to Foucault's position that the racism of the state is expressed through the sheer, and mere, expression of divisions between populations, as exemplified through biopolitics. It is also somewhat difficult to reconcile Foucault's insistence on the inherent racist character of the state with his explicit acknowledgment that, "It is . . . *between these two limits* [namely, a right of sovereignty and a mechanics of discipline] *that power is exercised.*[53] It would seem that the essence of race lies somewhere *between* Foucault's position and one side of the discourse of BR,[54] namely that it is fundamentally grounded on something physical, phenotypical, or biological.

It is possible to consider the mission of the sovereign power as that of cohering its populace through the control and management of its populace. It is also one method of management—conquest—to divide its populace through any number and combination of criteria. These criteria could include the physical or biological, or they could be expressed in the division in the biological continuum of human life, as Foucault argues, as manifested through health policies, pension plans, etc.[55] Yet, it seems to be insufficient to point to the biological, to life, to man-as-species,[56] as the ground of division, and thus as the essence of the "new racism" of modern sovereign power. Two questions still remain: first, what determines the criteria by which populations are divided? The expression of racism—as manifested through biopolitics, still seems to require some prior element that drives any particular regulation of biological processes. Second, is it not possible that the biological—as this represents the domain of life—is not the only mode of division? Foucault's analysis does not appear to account for other, fundamentally existential (or ontological), vehicles by which race is expressed. These vehicles may draw on bio-power,[57] or they may not, but they can still account for divisions and breaks in the population.

We could, as Carl Schmitt does in his incisive critique of the liberal state, understand the same mission to divide as the expression of the secularized divine omnipotence of the state. "The juridic formulas of the omnipotence of the state are, in fact, only superficial secularizations of theological formulas of the omnipotence of God.[58] In this secular role then, the state is driven to maintain its power and its coherence by making and shaping its men, that is, its populace, by rendering itself forcefully "political." In other words, the coherence and strength of the state requires a prior element, namely something that *already* renders it unified politically. For Schmitt, writing in the wake of World War II, this mission was satisfied through the identification of an external enemy, which would enable a people to understand itself as allied, coherent, and wholly united. This external enemy could not simply be identified as an economic competitor or private antagonist, but rather as one who was fundamentally opposed to the state in a "concrete and existential" sense.[59] And so, how is an enemy identified? Schmitt's response: ". . . the context of a concrete antagonism is still expressed in everyday language, even where the awareness of the extreme case has been entirely lost . . ."[60] He explains that seemingly mundane terms can be polemicized only when they are articulated in close connection to a concrete situation and a specific conflict. "Words such as state, republic, society, class . . . are incomprehensible when one does not know exactly *who is to be affected, combated, refuted, or negated by such a term.*"[61] In other words, the polity must already know or have an idea of who the enemy is.

I would augment Schmitt's description of how an enemy is identified: not only in terms of a concrete situation, but one that is based on a threat. That threat is perceived *even as it is something barely perceptible.* At the beginning of this article, I identified the target of race, namely the taming of that which I call the "unruly." The unruly is the element— often intangible, but possibly represented as physical or biological— which constitutes a threat to the coherence of a polity, and needs to be domesticated or at least managed in order for the state to maintain control of its population. It is the "unruly" that is picked up as the ground of classifying, distinguishing, separating, dividing. To return to Foucault's formulation of the state as fundamentally racist, where race is the biopolitical expression of division, I would modify his understanding of race as follows: The state is fundamentally racist, where bio-power is *one* expression of that division; there can be other expressions of racial division. But in any case of racial division, biopolitical or otherwise, there must be some element that "drives" the *character* and the *criteria*, and the *lines* by which the division is instantiated.

As such, I would again like to suggest that race is the transformation of the "unruly" into a set of categories by which to divide populations against themselves—biopolitically, culturally, socially, etc. It is one method by which sovereign power can fulfill its mandate to control and manage its populace, maintain its hold over them. Then to return to Foucault, it seems that the state's mission to divide is not dictated by random biological or material characteristics, but rather by locating that which is potentially pernicious to sovereign power and managing it through the technology of race: the production of a classification in which the unruly is embedded; its subsequent naturalization or reification as an objective category; and finally, its concealment as the expres-

The Technology of Race and the Logics of Exclusion   33

sion of the relationship between sovereign power and its populace as one of potential violence.[62] Any or all of these technological dimensions may be augmented or informed through biopolitics; however, there must be an "unruly" threat that drives the Foucauldian manifestation of race.

To return to an earlier example, here is a definition of race from 1923 that acknowledges and challenges the definition of race as exemplified in the one-drop rule that was cemented in 1896. Compare the weight of ancestry as it supposedly demarcates race in the one-drop rule upheld in the earlier *Plessy v. Ferguson* (1896) to the weight of ancestry in *U.S. v. Bhagat Singh Thind* (1923):

> They imply, as we have said, a racial test; but the term "race" is one which, for the practical purposes of the statute, must be applied to a group of living persons now possessing in common the requisite characteristics, not to groups of persons who are supposed to be or really are descended from some remote, common ancestor, but who, whether they both resemble him to a greater or less extent, have, at any rate, ceased altogether to resemble one another. *It may be true that the blond Scandinavian and the brown Hindu have a common ancestor in the dim reaches of antiquity, but the average man knows perfectly well that there are unmistakable and profound differences between them today; and it is not impossible, if that common ancestor could be materialized in the flesh, we should discover that he was himself sufficiently differentiated from both of his descendants to preclude his racial classification with either. The question for determination is* not, therefore, whether by the speculative processes of ethnological reasoning we may present a probability to the scientific mind that they have the same origin, but *whether we can satisfy the common understanding that they are now the same or sufficiently the same to justify the interpreters of a statute—written in the words of common speech, for common understanding, by unscientific men—in classifying them together in the statutory category as White persons.* In 1790 the Adamite theory of creation—which gave a common ancestor to all mankind—was generally accepted, and it is not at all probable that it was intended by the legislators of that day to submit the question of the application of the words "White persons" to the mere test of an indefinitely remote common ancestry, without regard to the extent of the subsequent divergence of the various branches from such common ancestry or from one another.[63]

The Supreme Court's opinion states that it cannot acknowledge the brown Hindu and the blond Scandinavian as both being "Caucasian," and thus as White. Here, the same burden of evidence—blood and genealogical history—which is used to distinguish those passing for White from "real White persons," (in *Plessy*) is discarded in favor of using visible phenotypic differences to distinguish ethnic Indians from free White persons for the purpose of barring them from becoming naturalized citizens.

In *Plessy*, common ancestry qua blood is reconstituted to deny one's past. In *Thind*, one's past is reconstituted in order to deny common ancestry. The unruly becomes a floating signifier for any particular element that leads to the unexpected, unpredictable behavior of a population, which threatens to overthrow an existing power relatinship—a regime—in some way. The status of being "Caucasian" is now threatened by an Indian national who, by most acknowledgments of the day, could claim an originary title to this status, just as the status of "being White" was threatened by the deceptive appearance of Homer Plessy. The court utilizes the unruliness— in this case, translated as the demand to be recognized as White, to be equal—as the ground by which to classify, relocate, and transform an individual or population who appears to threaten the state's ability to order and manage. If we see both cases through the lens of race as a technology, then the unruly in each case is real, but not necessarily physical.

Further, by institutionalizing the classification, the source of the "unruly" becomes hypostatized as a "natural" entity—one that demonstrates the proof of the existence of a certain race, or the absence of eligibility to be located in a superior race. By locating the classification of "Aryanness" or "Caucasian" under the guise of a neutral definition that acknowledges the history of a term, but narrows its scope, the second dimension of race as a technology occurs. That is, by purporting to resort to the "rule of law" to make its objective ruling that Indians cannot possibly be entitled to the same political status as Whites, the court "naturalizes" the exception, and not only reinforces a certain political status for Indians, but links this status to a certain re-racialization of the same group.[64]

To illustrate this point, let me offer a parallel to the one-drop rule: it is that of the caste-system in India. The ground of the caste-system is that status into which one is born. It depends neither on phenotype nor on physical features, but it does enforce distinctions between populations on an ontological ground, namely whether one is Brahmin, Kshatriya, Vaishya, or Shudra, and ties these ontologies to vocation, occupation, marriage, and pollution. It is not a system of classification endorsed by the modern secular Indian state, but its initial instantiation remains as a powerful force that divides populations even in the face of aggressive attempts by the state to undermine those divisions in favor of other attempts *to reclassify, redivide, and manage its populations.*[65] And so while legally the modern Indian state has attempted to challenge pervasive cultural caste-based discrimination through affirmative action for Shudras, Dalits, and Adivasis, there is no such protection for Muslims. Moreover, there have been other statutes, akin to and following from the American PATRIOT Act, which allow for the indefinite detention, interrogation, and incarceration of Muslims without writs of habeas corpus—on the grounds that as Muslims, they are *potential terrorists*. This phenomenon has had the unlikely effect of unifying Hindus across caste against Muslims—although it has not altered their status with regard to each other.[66]

Such traits—cultural, religious, or otherwise complex and intangible become the grounds for classification, but as signifiers they also shift in importance to accord with shifts in perceived threat, which then divides populations against each other in relation to such perception. And so, contra Foucault, the mandate to divide populations against each other, neither deploys race, solely understood as bio-power, nor does this mandate lead to a merely bi-racial war. It is certainly the case that the contrast between two populations nearly always emerges through the assertion of some characteristic or set of characteristics deemed to be present in the first group or population, and their dialectical opposition, stark absence or negation as manifested in the second group. But as what becomes denoted as the "unruly" shifts in relation to the perceived threat by sovereign power and other populations, so do these divisions shift as the perceived threat or interests of other populations *induces coalitions and coalescences.*

I think the important element of division, though, is not the fact of division, but something else. This is what I take to be the identification of something unruly, which is at once the essence of race, but also something that reveals itself to be apprehended in precisely the way that it is thrust forth by the context, the apparatus in which it is located. In other words, race is predicated on something that is always-already-threatening. That which already is the ground of race is that which is taken up, categorized, managed, and treated so as to identify a population as a whole unto itself.

Enframing Race: Vulnerability and Violence

To return once more to Heidegger, "so long as we represent [race] as an instrument, we remain transfixed in the will to master it." In that spirit, I want to move to Heidegger's notion of enframing in relation to technology in order to see how race is similarly enframed: it seems that enframing refers to the cultural, political, social, moral, methodological apparatus that both shrouds and infuses our current quest for the meaning of race. Heidegger suggests that enframing conceals, drives, challenges forth a particular understanding of the role and function of technology. He points out that the parts of the technology in question seem familiar to us, and yet while the activity of assembling these parts "always merely responds to the challenge of enframing, it never comprises enframing itself or brings it about."[67] For him modern physics becomes the "herald of enframing [modern technology], a herald whose origin is still unknown."[68] We might have a similar success if we understand the relationship between race as a technology and its enframing analogically. Is it possible to think of the current debates on race as challenged forth by the set of parts that have been assembled together in the unique way that leads us to look to DNA or genetics to understand its essence? It appears that the way race is enframed— as a term that reflects the genus, the species, the (biological) genealogy, and more recently, the cultural and sociological and demographic uniqueness of populations that have been taken as distinct from each other— perhaps induces us to take the outcome of the instrument of race at *face value*, rather than looking past the specific configurations of racial identity—towards the *eidos* of race. By the specific configurations of racial identity, I mean, for example, those now manifested as multiple racial classifications as induced by the U.S. census[69] or those "politicized identities," which attempt to resist what has been intuitively understood as attempts to distinguish and divide human beings in a given polity by taking on and reconfiguring those identities instead of interrogating the fact of classification.[70] Instead, by considering instead the *eidos* of race, described as (1) that which in everything and in each particular thing endures as "present," and also (2) that which "precisely is not and never will be perceivable with physical eyes," we might be able to discern its essence, and if not, then perhaps its meaning.[71]

The enframing of race exemplifies not merely division, but a method of using the unruly in connection with a certain mode of political existence, namely one in which our relationship to society must be understood as one of *vulnerability and violence*. If so, what would facilitate the conceptual link between the discourses of BR and PO—as about race and not merely about random division—is the thesis that it is also in the interest of sovereign power to cultivate a vulnerability or the threat of potential violence among its populace. Walter Benjamin suggests that

> "lawmaking pursues as its end, with violence as the means, *what* is to be established by law, but at the very moment of instatement, does not dismiss violence. Rather, at this very moment of lawmaking, it establishes as law not an end unalloyed by violence, but one necessarily and intimately tied to it, under the title of power. Lawmaking is power making, and to that end, an immediate manifestation of violence."[72]

I would now like to think about Benjamin's comment in relation to things that I've discussed thus far in this chapter: to the function of race as a technology and in connection to sovereign power. When race is deployed through law to demarcate distinctions between populations, violence per se is not immediately manifested through these categories. But more accurately, and this is what I think Benjamin is suggesting, the sheer capacity to instantiate such distinctions gains its power of enforcement through the potential violence that is inherent in it. Thus, when the U.S. Supreme Court insists, as it does in the case of *Bhagat Singh Thind* that while it may be the case that a long ago common ancestry may indeed find a Hindu Indian National and an American White man to both loosely be understood as Aryan and hence, Caucasian, this inconvenience could not possibly stand as a way to classify two individuals in the same box. The reason is that such a classification threatens to unleash the "unruly"—that which had already been provisionally tamed through the classification and subsequent enfranchisement of Caucasians in contradistinction to non-Caucasians. Such a move would be anticipated to wreak havoc on the political and social order of that moment in society. How so? This question leads us back to the enframing of race in relation to sovereign power: Were there an agreement that an Indian National were indeed Caucasian, and therefore eligible for naturalization— contrary to its prior statutes, the sudden upheaval of the established hierarchy of the moment—the implied potential havoc—would undermine the capacity of sovereign power to retain its hold on its populace. This is because it would have thrown the established norms of that moment into question. But the relationship of this understanding is what gives this judgment its weight: By ruling against the possibility that a Hindu Indian, understood to be the initial bearer of the status of Aryan/Caucasian, could be naturalized as a "free White man," the judgment implies an inherent potential *violence*. Specifically, the Indian national is neither guaranteed nor eligible for the potential protection of American law granted to its citizens. The abandonment of the law's protection implied by this ruling is not merely the specter of violence that looms over the horizon, but also the expression of sovereign power to decide whom it will grant or rescind its protection. In this vein, the success of opposing two populations depends upon a sense of vulnerability of being thrust outside "the gates of the city."[73]

But there is another step that is missing here: it is that of the fundamental tension of liberal society that facilitates the success of opposing two populations in relation to a third, dominant, group. I will return to this point in chapter 6. The potential violence implied in the judgment of the law can only make its weight fully felt when it strains at the fundamental tension, which infuses the relationship that a populace has toward sovereign power. The promise of the universal protection of the law can only maintain its value when it is prevented from truly being extended to everyone. But the *sheer value* of the liberal promise is that it cannot shirk its obligation to all who fall within its purview. The only method by which to circumvent this fundamental tension, then, is to create categories of those to whom universal protection of the law will apply—selectively, that is, *in such a way as to justify the exclusion of some while reiterating the importance of the law's protection for "everyone,"—that is, for everyone who counts.*[74]

In order to be part of the "everyone" who counts, then, certain key distinctions must be drawn—based on abstract categories such as individuals, persons, humans, citizens, categories that become infused with meaning—as Carl Schmitt reminds us—only in connection to a concrete situation, *but also through the deployment of race in conjunction with its implied threat of violence.*[75] At each and every given moment then, the deployment of such categories will also insinuate who is *evil, immoral, inferior,* a *terrorist,* and therefore not a *person,* a *human,* a *citizen.*

And so, as we see through any number of legal judgments, race is never merely about "race." It is in the drawing of lines between "evil beings" and "moral beings," between persons and nonpersons, human beings qua citizens and those who cannot be citizens because they are "not human like us," where we find the salience of race. Understood as a vehicle by which to draw and redraw the boundaries by which select populations are assured the protection of the law, race becomes deployed as a technology. It is when we understand it as a technology that we begin to understand how race locates and domesticates the "unruly," and in so doing, "reveals" the apparatus by which the normative ground of racial classifications was once naturalized and concealed.

In its function of concealment, the technology of race also becomes the expression of a certain mode of existence, which links certain key classifications with violence in order to enact discipline and order, and to effect a continual sense of vulnerability. It is only in the search for the concrete meaning of abstract terms like "citizen," "person," "American," that the technology of race reveals the violence and vulnerability that inheres in the relations between sovereign power and its populace, a vulnerability that perhaps can only be unconcealed at dusk.

I think it is this sense of vulnerability that facilitates the continual reenactment of race. It is manifested in the tendency of one population to help cement the ostracization of another group. Giorgio Agamben and, in effect, Carl Schmitt both argue that the key to managing populations requires that populations must always find themselves in danger of being "abandoned" by the law, at the same time that they find themselves subject to it. This fear of abandonment lies at the heart of the effectiveness of race as a technology, in that it draws on the fundamental tension of liberalism by engendering a sense of the "scarcity" of rights (as a kind of resource), and thus helping to induce a fear that facilitates a sense of order and a willingness/complicity to help thrust another population outside the bounds of the law's protection—on the grounds that already exist: the "unruly" becomes the basis by which to identify enemies, evil others, and those who are "fundamentally not one of us."

These are what I take to be some of the key moments that constitute the technology and metaphysics of race. Historically, race has to do with how populations are not just distinguished from each other, but divided, separated, and hypostatized into self-cohering wholes who are to be despised, vilified, and if not cast outside the gates of the city, then at least subordinated and exploited, if not physically or psychically managed. Yet these divisions are still predicated upon an impulse to tame the unruly. It is possible to offer a much weaker claim about what race is, but at least methodologically, many of these attempts to identify race appears to be anachronistic reifications, new concepts that are imposed upon some prior vision of the world that never existed, except in imagination. On this weaker reading—to invoke Heidegger once more—we stand in the essential realm of enframing,[76] and so we still run the risk of blinding ourselves, of obeying the call of this particular technology, rather than listening to what it reveals to us about [race].[77]

2

The Violence of Law

Sovereign Power, Vulnerable Populations, and Race

We have just ended a century of violence, one possibly more violent than any other in recorded history: world wars and colonial conquests; civil wars, revolutions and counterrevolutions . . . The modern sensibility is not horrified by pervasive violence . . . What horrifies our modern sensibility is violence that appears senseless, that cannot be justified by progress.

. . . [T]he history of the modern state can also be read as the history of race . . .[1]

Introduction

In this chapter I develop the third dimension of how race works as a technology, namely by considering the relationship between sovereign power and subjects in a new light. I reject one of the dominant narratives of modern political philosophy, namely the story of liberalism, which tells us that the fundamental *function* of law is to ensure justice for all individuals, and that the basic purpose of law is to protect all who fall within its purview.[2] In order for that narrative to hold, the story of modernity as an epoch of violence, brutality, and dehumanization must be construed as a series of never-ending aberrations, mistakes, and misapplications of justice. On this view, events such as the enslavement of African Americans, the internment of Japanese-Americans, and the current harassment and torture of Muslim or Arab men would be accidental deviations from the framework of liberalism. There are too many such events for this reading

41

to be accurate. As I will argue in ensuing chapters, there is an inherent subtext to liberalism that systematically engenders "exceptions" to the ideal framework of equal rights and protections.[3]

I want to suggest a different framework by which to think about modernity, one that is more consistent with the story of modernity as one of violence. This framework, which I will call the "Violence of Law," holds that the purpose of the state (in its various formations) is to preserve itself, and in that interest, to manage its populations.[4] The state protects those segments of its populations whose interests are thought to conserve its own existence, and abandons those populations that are considered a threat to the existing order. I understand this framework to underlie the structure of liberalism, and other forms of politics. This is the fundamental structure of sovereign-subject relations in the modern era. In this framework, racialization and racial division are crucial features of politics and sovereign power.

Law, Violence, and Undecidability

In contrast to the premise that the purpose of the state and law is to ensure justice, the Violence of Law framework is informed by a distinct view of law from the one we hear in the story of liberalism and deliberative democracy, but it resonates more fully for a range of populations that have been disenfranchised, outcasted, or abandoned in various ways.[5] If we view the series of brutalities of the eighteenth, nineteenth, and twentieth centuries through the prism of the second framework, then they are illuminated as manifestations of the crucial form that justice takes when we understand that justice is not about fairness, but about something else—power, division, and violence. This violence exists alongside the vivid, almost ordinary, brutality and destruction that we have become accustomed to considering of late, but it has existed well before. It is a violence imposed, enacted, administered, and managed by state power; it permeates our legal structure and, as I will argue, it is a fundamental source of racialization and racial division.

There are two dimensions of violence in this framework. The first dimension refers to what Jacques Derrida calls the "mystical" foundation of law's authority.[6] Derrida points to violence and obedience as the sources for this authority: violence constitutes the legitimacy of the law, its ground, and its very beginning. At the original moment of law, there can be nothing else that grounds law—nothing *a priori*, nothing higher, and no transcendental principle but force itself. As such, there is nothing normatively just or unjust about the law, because there is no prior foundation that grounds it.[7]

Since the origin of authority, the foundation or ground, the position of the law can't by definition rest on anything but themselves (*sic*), they are themselves a violence without ground. Which is not to say that they are in themselves unjust, in the sense of "illegal." They are neither legal nor illegal in their founding moment . . . (943)

The original formulation of this position is found in Benjamin's essay, "Critique of Violence."[8] In Benjamin's framework, the end of law is to preserve itself, to maintain itself. Benjamin says, "the law's interest in a monopoly of violence vis-à-vis individuals is not explained by the intention of preserving legal ends but rather by that of preserving the law itself; that violence, when not in the hands of the law, threatens it not by the ends that it may pursue but by its mere existence outside the law."[9] Derrida shares this position when he notes that "European law tends to prohibit individual violence and to condemn it . . . because it threatens the juridical order" or the strategic ability of the legal system to *maintain order by retaining sole control over violence* (985). The law's interest, continues Derrida, is to conserve itself "or in representing the interest that [justement,] it represents" (985). This is an important point to which I will return shortly.

The other side of the law's authority comes from the absolute compunction to obey it, or as Montaigne, quoted by Derrida, says: "And so laws keep up their good standing, not because they are just, but because they are law: that is the mystical foundation of their authority, they have no other . . . Anyone who obeys them because they are just is not obeying them way he ought to" (939).[10]

In this framework, contra the justice of liberalism, justice is neither about fairness, procedure, nor is it formulaic. Rather, "justice is an experience of the impossible," because arriving at a just decision in a juridical structure is ultimately incalculable (947). It is not possible to arrive at a fundamental procedure by which to figure a fair decision, because a decision that can be computed is not a just decision—it can only be a calculation.

There is apparently no moment in which a decision can be called presently and fully just: either it has not yet been made according to a rule, and nothing allows us to call it just, or it has already followed a rule—whether received, confirmed, conserved or reinvented—which in its turn is not absolutely guaranteed by anything; and moreover, if it were guaranteed, the decision would be reduced to calculation and we wouldn't call it just. (963)

Every decision must undergo a moment of radical undecidability before arriving at a judgment (963). This is to say: it is not grounded in procedure, it is literally ungrounded—completely free. There may be immediate concerns that are taken into account, but ultimately, they have little bearing on the decision.

> The undecidable is not merely the oscillation or the tension between two decisions, it is the experience of that which, though heterogeneous, foreign to the order of the calculable and the rule, is still obliged . . . to give itself up to the impossible decision, while taking account of law and rules. (963)

Each decision, at its very instantiation is infused by a kind of madness—an instant of unreason, reflecting the impossibility of taking into account the infinity of knowledge, rules, and conditions that might apply to the decision (967). Ultimately, it is this madness that not only defines justice, but that leads to the "cutting" power of any decision of law. "Justice, as law, is never exercised without a decision that cuts, that divides," and does so with authority (963). This capacity—to cut, to divide—expresses the "irruptive violence," which is the very heart of the force of law (969). As mentioned at the outset, this violence is expressed in the originary authority of law.

> Its very moment of foundation or institution (which in any case is never a moment inscribed in the homogeneous tissue of a history, since it is ripped apart with one decision) the operation that consists of founding, inaugurating, justifying law (*droit*) making law, would consist of a coup de force, of a performative and therefore interpretative violence that in itself is neither just nor unjust and that no justice and no previous law with its founding anterior moment could guarantee or contradict or invalidate. (941, 943)

This founding violence is also beholden to no prior or outside ideology to which "it would have to accommodate or bend to when useful." This statement suggests that there is no preordained target of the law's violence (942). Derrida's position also constitutes a radical break with structuralist positions that argue that politico-legal regimes are already embedded in a system (capitalism, patriarchy, White supremacy), which predetermines the population most susceptible to exploitation according to some material category such as class, gender, race.[11]

Finally, let me point to the second dimension of violence in this framework, which I locate in Giorgio Agamben's *Homo Sacer*: This form of violence finds its final expression in terms of the relationship between sov-

ereign power and its subject, specifically, in the ever-present potential
abandonment of a population. This is a population that is required to
obey sovereign power's dictates without being guaranteed the penumbra
of protection that would deflect the violation of their rights and freedoms.[12] This potential abandonment is the intrinsic relationship between
populations and sovereign authority. In this framework, sovereign power
is neither the beneficent magistrate of the Lockean polity who adjudicates
disputes impartially, nor is it the collective expression of Rousseau's general will, which gives itself the law it must also obey. Rather, sovereign
power is understood as standing simultaneously inside and outside the
juridical order, constituting its boundaries while also declaring the
exception to this order, to its protection.[13]

> If the exception is the structure of sovereignty, then sovereignty
> is not an exclusively political concept, an exclusively juridical cat-
> egory, a power external to law . . . , or the supreme rule of the ju-
> ridical order . . . : *it is the originary structure in which law refers to life
> and includes it in itself by suspending it.*[14]

For Agamben, the basic expression of sovereignty simultaneously circumscribes the polity, those who will be acknowledged and subject to the
law, as well as those who will be forced outside those parameters. The
latter does not "incidentally" become the exception, but rather is intrinsic to the instantiation of the group who will be included or protected.[15]
In other words, the aura of sovereign power is meant to circumscribe
who will be subject to its law and its protections, while delineating the
limits of its protections and the exclusion of certain populations from
those protections (while still remaining subject to its law). But the important dimension of this abandonment is that the sovereign renders a
subject or a population ready to be marginalized or eradicated without
necessarily being seen as being sacrificed: "The relation of exception is a
relation of ban. He who has been banned is not, in fact, simply set outside the law and made indifferent to it but rather *abandoned* by it, that is,
exposed and threatened on the threshold in which life and law, outside
and inside, become indistinguishable."[16] This population is not seen as
being sacrificed, because it has no value; its abandonment becomes a
matter of routine.

There are several features, or absence of features, in Derrida's and
Agamben's (collective) framework that I want to note: (1) The madness
embedded in the cutting power of law for Derrida, as well as the vulnerability of being abandoned in Agamben's understanding of sovereignty is
not predetermined to single out any particular population. That is, the

decision is random; (2) neither framework acknowledges a temporal or historical dimension with regard to the legal decision or the population in question; (3) there is no acknowledgement of a power differential between *different subject populations* in relation to each other or to the sovereign, that is, the unit of analysis is an individual subject; and each subject is thought to have the same relationship, and same vulnerability in the face of the sovereign; (4) the decision and the abandonment of the population are seen as exceptions to the ordinary juridical relationship between sovereign and subject, that is, as out of the ordinary.[17]

Such a metaphysics of sovereign power is useful in its abstractness. An important consequence of this framework is that it successfully challenges the overdetermination of certain historically specific theories of exploitation, such as the materialist perspective that class and ideology primarily determine the differential of power between sovereign and subject (or capitalist and worker). However, the position that the law is either random in its decision of whom to cut against (Derrida), or alternately, that *all* populations are equally vulnerable to being pushed outside the gates of the city (Agamben), rings too consistently with the lesson of liberalism, that is, that atrocities are accidental deviations. Moreover, the atemporal character of each framework is also consistent with that of liberalism; and this too is a detrimental consequence: liberalism's emphasis on procedure, calculation, and abiding by the "rule of law"—starting anew each time, except when a precedent is invoked[18]—distracts us from the ability to see patterns that deviate from this emphasis, instead deceptively enabling us to think of aberrations as unique and accidental.

All of this points to a larger concern: in between the utter madness of the irruptive violence of law and the ubiquitous vulnerability of abandonment, I am arguing that there is a third facet of law, which *does find itself consistently favoring one kind of population while targeting another.* There are certain premonitions, forewarnings, certain symbols that help weigh the "undecidability" of any decision to abandon one party over another. In what follows I will suggest that the "madness" that defines the instant of decision is neither as ungrounded or random as Derrida suggests, nor ubiquitously addressed to all subject-populations, as Agamben suggests. Rather, the decision of law as to whom to cut against is guided by two elements: the population to be abandoned by law or sovereign power is *already* a(n unruly) threat and *already* vulnerable. In the final section I will augment this analysis by arguing that a continued perception of threat and vulnerability of a population, along with the creation of certain juridico-political categories, leads to its racialization. That section addresses the atemporality of the Derridean and Agambian violence of law frameworks.

Sovereign Power

First I should clarify the role of sovereign power in this framework. The Violence of Law framework holds three perspectives on the role of sovereignty, which are modifications of Michel Foucault's discussion of sovereign power. Foucault argues that we should understand the central function of the government as that of maintaining a social order by managing and regulating its populations. His argument applies to modern societies, and he distinguishes this, the art of government, from the "self-referring circularity" of sovereignty, which is to exercise itself. His argument about sovereignty is applicable to early modern societies—namely to those where sovereign power is understood as the authority of the king in relation to his subjects. In the "Governmentality" essay, Michel Foucault offers a distinction between the art of government and the "reason of state," in order to illustrate an important transitional understanding between the sixteenth and eighteenth centuries. He suggests that the function of government is to "manage things" in order to preserve a certain order in society. The end of the sovereignty, on the other hand, is itself—to maintain itself, to keep itself in power, and to ensure that the sovereign can keep its holdings and subjects.[19] Because the notion of sovereignty—as the internal rationality of the state—remained the primary paradigm throughout the seventeenth century, it served as the primary obstacle to the development of the art of government.[20] But as the framework of an economy became central foundation for the "science of government,"[21] the art of government as that of management replaced the paradigm of sovereignty beginning in the eighteenth century. This is not to say the problem of sovereignty disappears, as Foucault points out, but rather it remains as acute as ever.[22] And so, Foucault locates it in a triadic form of modern society, in a relationship with discipline and government, all of which are concerned with the management of populations.[23] Thus the aim of sovereignty is refocused on the "choices of government."[24]

This position is consistent with Foucault's discussion in "Society Must Be Defended" lectures, where he suggests that sovereignty has become diffused and refocused as biopolitics.[25] As he argues, his project is to illustrate how "relations or operators of domination" rather than "the basic elements of sovereignty" are the ground of power.[26] There, he also argues that where once upon a time the state was instrumentalized in this way to create a racial division—a race war, this framework was transformed into an understanding of all struggle as about class struggle. A race war still underlies the contemporary world; however, today this war takes the shape of biopolitics, namely as about regulating men-as-species through the control and regulation of populations in their biological, scientific dimensions. As such, Foucault argues, there is no centralized sovereign state; rather this regulatory power appears from any range of institutions and sources within society. Furthermore, the modern state no longer is an instrument used by one race to dominate another. Instead, the State must be the protector of the "integrity, the superiority, and the purity of the race. The idea of racial purity, with all its monistic, Statist, and biological implications: that is what replaces the idea of race struggle."[27]

Foucault's argument is a deeply insightful contribution to our understanding of how the modern state manages its populations. It is true, as Foucault argues, that racial management has been decentralized and naturalized under the rubric of science and scientific understanding of "race" and biology. He opens up a new prism by which to analyze the micro-sites of power and the biological/scientific façade of modern race politics. Still, his analysis is troubling on a number of counts. First, Foucault's notion of biopolitics, because it is decentralized and ubiquitous, cannot account for the distinct disparity between those who are the personification of the state and those populations who are subject to its authority and caprices. Not all aspects of the populations are subject to regulatory power in the same way, nor are they equally vulnerable to the dictates of the state. Ultimately, someone (or some few) still control the trajectory of power—disciplinary and regulatory. Similarly, Foucault's discussion of the Panopticon, which insists on the ubiquity of power, does not attend to the institution of this form of surveillance—made by a prison warden or legislators or other representatives of state power. This disparity suggests that sovereign power does not disappear altogether in contemporary polities, even in the midst of regulatory and disciplinary power. Moreover, racial division takes multiple forms, even in an era infused by biopolitics. The new millennium has ushered in an enormous terror-management industry, which certainly includes among its weapons-disciplinary and regulatory power, for example, torture, incarceration, rendition, and racial profiling. But it also depends on that dimension of power that Foucault suggests disappeared at the end of the seventeenth century and was transformed into bio power, namely direct sovereign power. It is this power that I am interested in here as another integral mode not just of creating racial divisions, but as sovereign authority's way of managing populations. The rest of this section is inspired by Foucault's profound analysis, although I shift Foucault's framework on several counts.

First, sovereign power is that form of authority that has, not only as its function, but as *its end*, its own self-preservation.[28] Second, the notion of a centralized state or sovereign authority is not obsolete; such an authority, as we have seen vividly not just over the last few years but for decades, can and does act in a direct fashion. This power is directly felt, despite the fact that it can be expressed through a range of institutions, such as judiciaries, state legislatures, and various federal and state bureaucratic offices; moreover the power of the sovereign can be felt through "informal" or "unofficial" actions, such as mobs and political groups. Finally, biopolitics and scientific management are two dimensions of how race operate in modern society, but they do not exhaust the modes by which sovereign power instantiates racial division. Sovereign institutions utilize numerous methods by which to instantiate and naturalize racial divisions.[29]

Unruly and Vulnerable Populations

With regard to the population that will be cut against, it will be one that sovereign power considers a threat to its own conservation and to the prevailing regime. The nature of the threat that is so posed to sovereign power can be rather ambiguous or broad. It need not *in fact* be a clear or inevitable challenge to an existing regime; it need only be perceived as such. The features that constitute this threat then, can be as ambiguous and ever-shifting, although there are some consistent elements that can be ascribed to the threatening subject (or population).

The perceived unruliness of a population is one element that guides the moment of decision.[30] As I mentioned in chapter 1, the "unruly" threat is a transgression of the prevailing order; it signifies something intangible, such as a contrasting ideological framework, like Islam, or the memory of a dangerous or troubling history or discourse surrounding that population, for example, slavery, colonialism, Nazism, the Cold War, and the "Clash of Civilizations." *But the danger can be represented or manifested by something else that may or may not be tangible,* such as outward garb, physical comportment, phenotype, accent, skin color, or something even more subtle.[31] I want to note that within the context of the eighteenth to the twentieth centuries, such physical signs are understood as the ground of racial classifications. By the end of my argument, it should become clear that these physical signifiers are not the basis, but the final representation, of the process of racialization that was historically prior.[32]

In addition, the subject-population is seen as unruly because it threatens to unseat those who perceive themselves to be—*not necessarily in power—but on the verge of losing power.* This loss can be in the realm of the political, economic, social, or that of a prevailing dominant worldview. This perception of loss occurs against a larger *political backdrop/ explosion* through which this population first becomes conspicuous. There must be some event that is the focal point, the occasion, by which the threat is perceived, such as a riot or a bombing. There can also be serial political explosions or ripple effects that induce a sustained focus on the (perceived) threat posed by a population, which continually appears to indicate a loss of power for a dominant group, such as conflicts over claims to certain rights.[33] There is also a crucial feature that provides the basis for the vulnerability of a population: the unregulated existence of this group is believed to engender potentially detrimental consequences for the larger population.

The second element that guides the moment of decision is that of an already entrenched *vulnerability* of the group that is considered threatening. This vulnerability has its seeds sown in the structure of that framework years, even decades before, perhaps even longer. The vulnerable population is characterized by being able to trace a set of events that have it as the focus, even if that focus is implicit. These may include extralegal acts of harassment, violation, or murder. The other element of vulnerability is a lack of protection: allowing violative acts to go unpunished; withholding opportunities in the name of procedure or rule of law; or formally, in legislation passed that is directed towards them, even if not in name.[34] We can see this in any number of instances of groups who have been cut against by law of sovereign power: Whether in the case of the Japanese internment in the United States 1942–1945; the massacre of Tutsis by Hutus in Rwanda in 1994, or in the forced conversion/massacre of Jews (in 1492) and Moors (in 1497) under Catholic Spain. In each instance, the group in question was given the decision of law—not purely randomly, but because they met both of the elements that I have described above: unruliness and vulnerable to abandonment by the law. I will explore several of these examples later on.

There is a third element that guides the decision of the law: It requires another population or even two, who are crucial to the sculpting of the unruliness and vulnerability of the population. It requires at the least a dominant group whose interests are perceived to correspond, or even be identical, to those of sovereign power. This is true for all vulnerable and unruly populations. There is typically another "good population" or "more worthy" population against which the threatening group is contrasted. This contrast has the function of heightening the disadvantages posed by that population, and the advantages that the other population(s) provide, and thereby crystallizing the racial, unworthy quality of the group under vilification.[35]

These features, the perceived "unruliness" and the vulnerability of a subject population, along with a clear view of another dominant population, often preselects a population that will be at the mercy of, subject to, the violent judgments of sovereign power.

The Racialization of a Population

Beyond these two features, I want to explore another dimension that, if augmented to these features, leads to the juridico-political, or institutional, racialization of a population. By racialization, I don't mean pregiven racial identities; rather, the perceived threat and vulnerability that characterize a certain subject-population becomes part of the ground of its outcasting as a species unto itself. How does racialization occur? We know that racialization has numerous dimensions. Here, I want to discuss the political and juridical processes by which racialization occurs, and *how these are embedded in the set of regulations designed to govern an existing population.*

There are several primary features that contribute to the racialization of a population some of which are built upon those features characterizing an unruly and vulnerable population. First, there must be a description of the group, which can but need not necessarily be phenotypical; it might be a nationality, ethnicity, tribal description. This description is not a racial designation of a group in the sense in which I am arguing. It is a description marker. This description has the function of delineating a group against the background of a different population.

I want to reiterate the distinction I am making between racialization and racial identity. Racialization is the process of delineating a population in contrast to a dominant (or powerful) population and a corresponding political tension; this population can be highlighted according to any range of characteristics—none of which have to be "racial" qua phenotype or blood or physical characteristics; they might be religious, economic, social, etc. But in the course of a series of events that highlight the conflicts between this group and a dominant population, it becomes racialized, that is, as a separate species. The weight of an identity as "racial" (in contrast to a descriptive identity) is the remnant of such racialization; it is akin to picking up a sand dollar on the beach. What we see is the tent, or shell, of a creature, which becomes a stand-in for the creature itself. Similarly, a racial identity—the transformation of an identity from a descriptive marker to a racial designation—is the consequence of the process by which a group has become racialized—singled out as a race or an outcasted group. The process of racialization is what I am attempting to lay out in this chapter.

Second, there is a normative description of set of behaviors and/or features that are identified with this population. The threatening features in question are taken in isolation, severed from historical, political, sexual, social, cultural context, and reified as features that are intrinsically representative of those populations,[36] with allowable exceptions. These reified features are then targeted as violating the beliefs, principles, or trajectory of a prevailing regime. This normative description is equated with an inferior moral, ontological, physical, social status, or outright criminality (terrorists, heathens, non-Christians, Muslims, anarchists, insurgents). Third, the unchecked (unregulated) existence of this group is shown to engender potentially detrimental consequences on the larger population.[37]

These features are augmented to the description of an unruly and vulnerable population as I described the process in the prior section. I want to reiterate that these features emerge through a series of events or political explosions, and are continuously embedded in legislation, political actions, and cultural discourses that are antagonistic to the sub-population. Those events locate the unruly population within a historical memory or temporal framework that is embedded politically, culturally, juridico-politically.

What are the additional steps that render a group racial? Since I am addressing the metaphysical structure of law and sovereign power, I will turn to the legal features of a model of the modern state. In any given polity, even (and especially) in liberal societies, which claim to extend protections to all who live within their purview, there is always an escape valve by which to render someone on the threshold between being protected and being abandoned—an *a priori* legal loophole. There are two crucial characteristics of this loophole: First, there must be a legal instantiation of the fundamental way in which the group in question cannot possibly be—or be recognized as—a part of the larger population. This is the "exception" feature. This feature takes on salience in relation to a set of boundaries that govern the limits of membership of a polity. Members of a polity will be designated using one set of terms; by extension those categories will imply the terms that can be used to show how some subset of the population can neither be included, accommodated, nor have a legitimate claim to be legally—positively—recognized. This is a dialectical relationship of recognition but it is unlike the intersubjective relationship found in Hegel's framework of recognition. In Hegel's analysis, recognition is accorded and received mutually as long as both subjects are in a relationship of equality and reciprocity. The absence of mutual recognition results in the unequal relationship between the master and slave, whereby the master is recognized by the slave, but refuses to return the acknowledgment. He appropriates the slave's labor for his own purposes, and thus objectifies him in the act.

By contrast, in the Violence of Law structure, the withholding of recognition is implied through the dialectical opposition to the category that institutes the terms of membership within law itself. As such, articulating certain categories of membership simultaneously implies the categories of exclusion also. The withholding of recognition can be engaged in explicitly—through active misrecognition of people, again articulated as intrinsic legal/political categories. Examples of terms that create the parameters of membership include, in the context of the United States, "natural-born citizen," "White men," or "Caucasian."[38] "Naturalized citizen," "legal or permanent resident," might appear on the continuum as well, although these are generous modifications of intrinsic or "authentic" claims to membership. What one notices about these terms is that they engender a character of membership whose opposites have to do with inauthentic, indirect, or "unnatural" claims to membership. These can include categories such as aliens, immigrants, and illegal aliens. The latter terms define one's legal status, or varying degrees of illegitimacy grounded on the terms of one's entry—or one's parents' status and their entry—into the polity.

Thus, on an immediate level, the terms of membership are grounded on the legitimacy of claims to territory. But half of these claims also expresses claims to legitimate, authentic, necessary sovereign protection, while their oppositional categories express no legitimate claims to protection—except as granted by fiat, contingency, political generosity or indulgence. "We are granting you protections out of the goodness of our hearts—you have no claims and we have no obligations to protect you." As I mentioned above, the latter categories are introduced into the political discussion as "built-in" exceptions to the obligation of universal protections of all within the purview of a sovereign authority. Further, as exceptions, this loophole must be able to appeal to a "rule," or "principle" of law.[39] Because of this apparent ground of the appeal, as well as its repeated, endless instantiation, the category becomes naturalized as a part of the fundamental legal structure.[40]

The second dimension of this loophole must have the effect (or potential) of rendering the population in question *inhuman, dehumanized,* in other words, explicitly and fundamentally unworthy of the protection of the law.[41] This feature is an extension of the prior loophole. Limiting protection to "legitimate" members of a polity initiates the practice of the lack of protection for the "exception" populations.[42] Repeated lack of protection has the effect of dehumanizing that same group. The dehumanization of a population does not necessarily have to take an explicit form or label, although there may be plenty of examples that exemplify this practice. Rather, the dehumanization feature is the consequence of the repeated lack of protection for a population. This feature is especially vivid within the context of a human rights framework, which endorses the position that human beings are worthy of protection by law; the consequence of dehumanization is found in the contrast of treatment of a range of groups who are repeatedly and openly abandoned by the law.

This phenomenon is one that is tangentially referred to by Schmitt, who points to the creation of enemies—often explicitly unnamed, but which are understood within context to connote specific populations. The dehumanization feature that I describe here is an attempt to augment Schmitt's analysis by pointing more specifically to the way this phenomenon functions within the law: by creating a limit category: citizens, and (morally upstanding) resident aliens. These categories indicate those who are human *and* worthy of protection. These two descriptors are intrinsically linked in the recognition of those who fit this category by sovereign power or law. The limit categories are juxtaposed against terms such as terrorists, enemy combatants, enemy aliens, which indicate those who are *not* worthy of protection, and by extension in a human rights framework—not human. This phenomenon is an exemplification of Giorgio Agamben's description of that which is "bare life." It is the repeated absence of protection accorded to a group that renders it not only an outcast population that is vulnerable, but inhuman as well. We have seen this feature repeatedly. In the history of the United States, we see the explicit refusal to apply Constitutional protections to African Americans—both during slavery and after Emancipation,[43] as well as to Japanese Americans during the internment, for gays and lesbians and transgendered individuals,[44] and of course immigrants generally.

These last two features are the *key* to the (juridical) racialization of a population, in distinction to a population that is distinguished (and potentially vulnerable) culturally, sexually, economically, or politically. The "unruly" and the "vulnerable" dimensions of a group enable the law to move through and past the moment of radical undecidability to a decision—to cut in favor of one group and against another in relation to an existing regime.[45] The force of law, the irruptive violence, which instantiates its force, is expressed by meeting the threat of the group in question, which is a threat to law itself and transforming it (989)—with a view toward conserving itself and its own juridical order (985). The kind of population that might be consistently cut against would be circumscribed against the backdrop of something that/who would be always-already threatening, and thus would need to be tamed, domesticated, managed by law—or sovereign power. Derrida says "That which threatens law already belongs to it, to the right to law, to the origin of law," but "[o]nly the yet-to-come (*avenir*) will produce intelligibility or interpretability of this law . . . ," which suggests that the effect of the law will only make sense after the decision (Derrida, 989, 993), and that the founding power of law constitutes the order that renders it comprehensible, legible, well after the moment.

As this law to come will in return legitimate, retrospectively, the violence that may offend the sense of justice, its future anterior already justifies it. The foundation of all states occurs in a situation that we can thus call revolutionary. It inaugurates a new law, it always does so in violence. Always, which is to say even when there haven't been those spectacular genocides, expulsions, or deportations that so often accompany the foundation of states, great or small, old or new, right near us or far away. (991)

Derrida refers to this as the founding or revolutionary moment of law, which "interrupts the established [law] to found another" (991). I think his words here confirm another dimension of violence, which is also involved in the cutting power of law: In the moment of founding, the law has already constituted who it will protect and who it will abandon, and in the process, continually reshapes the current onto-juridical regime, the current cultural worldview, and—consequently, a new racial order whereby some population is casted out of the law's protection.

As Agamben says about the value of the population who is to be abandoned: Sacrifice is the mark of giving something up of precious value. If there is no sacrifice, then at least in this regard human life in question either has no value or value beyond comprehension. In naming life both "bare" and "sacred," Agamben appears to highlight the double meaning of human life, which is abandoned to vagaries of sovereign power; as he says, "The life caught in the sovereign ban is the life that is originarily sacred—that is, that may be killed but not sacrificed—and in this sense, the production of bare life is the originary activity of sovereignty."[46] When applied to subjects, the concept of exception—understood as a "routine exclusion"—enables us to understand how it is that human life, once considered a sacrifice to end, is now rendered "bare" or "naked" life, that is, life that can be marginalized or eradicated as a matter of fact or procedure. This marginalization or abandonment is the other violence found in the law; it is the violence manifested in the knowledge that there is no sovereign power to appeal to for help, that one exists in the world left to the horrors of a Hobbesian state of nature—for certain populations, but not all.

But unlike Agamben, I think that this does not render all subjects in a state of exception all the time. At least, it is not such a stark situation. For Agamben, the state of exception is constituted by the sovereign, so that we—all subjects—are in this state all the time. But this suggests that the moment of abandonment—and the population to be abandoned—is random, and due fundamentally to the undecideablity of law (Derrida) or the sovereign's indecision.[47] And as I've suggested above, neither the

group to be abandoned, nor the moment of abandonment is random; nor
by extension, is the state of exception quite so constant, ubiquitous, or
baldly authoritarian. The mode of creating "exception" populations is
more subtle—it utilizes the rule of law to appear as a natural, necessary
phenomenon. This again, is the purpose behind the creation of limit categories in law—the juridical function naturalizes the exception within law.

The Unruly and the Vulnerable Manifested as Categories of Law: Immigrants, Aliens, Enemies

In what follows, I'd like to offer two brief examples that illustrate how the
framework of Violence of Law works. In chapter 7, I discuss a third example in more detail, namely the racialization of Asian Indians in California during the early twentieth century. Here I will review a case of
racialization that occured to Japanese Americans in California during
the first half of the twentieth century. The other case is the Rwandan
genocide of 1994.

For many observers, the mass and systematic murder of close to
1 million Tutsis by Hutus across Rwanda in the period of one month in
April 1994 seems to defy explanation. And indeed in many ways, that is
certainly an accurate assessment. But at least in terms of the legal and political apparatus that created the conditions of possibility of the genocide, there are a few things that can be said. There is a correspondence
here between the earlier, more abstract discussion of the relationship between sovereign power and subject, and how this relationship finds its
vivid manifestation in the genocide of 1994, whose foundations were laid
over several hundred years, and through a myriad of events. The vulnerability of Tutsis—the decision to render them and Hutus in racial terms
did not happen overnight. Still, it is possible to locate specific moments
when certain moments of racialization are embedded in laws, identity
cards, and other evidence of the legal and political institutionalization of
key categories pertaining to political membership, sovereign protection
and abandonment, and the ever-degraded status of Tutsis as "bare life,"
in the words of Agamben.

The division between the Tutsis and Hutus, while stemming back
many centuries, appears to have been politically formalized during the
period of Belgian colonialism of Rwanda, specifically during the Belgian
reform of the colonial state, between the middle 1920s and 1930s.[48] At that
time, Tutsis were identified as distinct from Hutus in a variety of ways:

the Tutsis were understood to have emigrated there from neighboring areas, and generally had possession of larger amounts of land than Hutus, as well as cattle. There is an internal discourse that distinguished the two groups phenotypically,[49] although many Hutus and Tutsis acknowledged that it is often difficult to identify who is Tutsi or Hutu correctly. Belgians institutionalized the common lore by employing Tutsis as their colonial administrators and go-betweens, creating a hierarchy between Tutsis and Hutus. Members of each group were also given identity papers identifying the groups to which they were said to belong.

The prevailing lore of the time considered the Tutsis to be a "Hamitic race." From the Biblical story of Noah, Shem, Japheth, and Hamm, the normative implications of this story were Tutsis were the more shameful, "darker" Caucasian race, and consequently, they were not indigenous— not Bantu as the Hutus were thought to be.[50]

There are several important factors here: First, Tutsis were in the hierarchical upper echelons under Belgian colonization. During the transition from their status as a colony to an independent nation, the Rwandan Nationalists argued that as "outsiders," Tutsis should not have any political authority to rule in Rwanda. Ultimately, the Belgians were convinced of this argument, and handed political authority to the Hutus, on the grounds that Tutsis were not indigenous. Second, the status of Tutsis changed from being outsiders to insiders in correspondence with their classification changing from being a race to an "ethnicity." Third, their "racialization" was primarily a state-induced phenomenon as was that of Hutus: from identity cards, to legally instantiated, and shifting categories of insider/outsider, race/ethnicity, and correlated political status: Hutus and Tutsis, depending on who was in power, were both at alternating moments of political power, thwarted out of colleges, jobs, and land. Tutsis had undergone another massacre, 1959–1963, though on a comparatively smaller scale than the events of 1994.

The racialization of Tutsis is entrenched in the history of Belgian colonization, namely the creation of economic, political, and social hierarchies by the Belgian colonial administrators, as well as the institutionalization of the distinction between Hutus and Tutsi through national identity cards and the restriction of civil service jobs for Tutsis under colonialism. The history of the antagonisms between Tutsis and Hutus was furthered along via the institutionalized nationalism instituted by the Belgians as they prepared to turn over Rwanda to its "indigenous" population, the Hutus. In the process, they reified the lore that the Tutsis were "from away," and augmented the creation of a racial identity for the Tutsis—one that distinguishes them as a species that is distinct from the Hutus. The irony of this distinction is that—"[Non-Rwandans] can't tell us apart . . . [Rwandans/Hutus/Tutsis] can't tell us apart," as many Hutus offered testimony after the 1994 genocide.[51] The singularity of the racial identity for the Tutsis is heightened, when compared to the reconstitution of Tutsi identity as an "ethnicity," under President Habyarimana's government.[52] The Tutsis' racial identity, in my framework, is part of the "racialization" that is enabled under sovereign power.

The period during which Tutsis are marked as an ethnic group is one of relative calm, although the series of events that outcasted Tutsis is still seared in the collective Rwandan memory. And this series of events is marked by a shift of sovereign power, from the Belgians to the Rwandan Nationalists (Hutus) unsympathetic to Tutsis, and again back and forth between them and a political party that was somewhat sympathetic to the Tutsis. Note here that the subject-population is distinguished and sculpted through the existence of both sovereign power and the Hutus.[53]

Through the period between the turnover of power to the Hutus by the Belgians and the events of April 1994, there is also a consistent dehumanizing discourse surrounding the Tutsis—one noted most vividly by the constant references to them as "cockroaches," and the almost ordinary daily cultural discourse—promulgated through radio, neighbors' conversations, and throughout different strata of society—that referred to the need to kill them. This discourse is in existence prior to the 1959–1963 massacre of Tutsis, and well entrenched after this massacre.

As importantly, the racialization of the Tutsis is augmented by two other influences: the first is the enabling of this racial identity through the creation of escape categories such as: indigenous, foreign, citizens, aliens, which instantiate the juridico-political parameters of the polity: In other words, the creation of nationalist categories of membership are intrinsic to the racialization of the Tutsis. I want to note again one of Derrida's earlier quotes:

> As this law to come will in return legitimate, retrospectively, the violence that may offend the sense of justice, its future anterior already justifies it. The foundation of all states occurs in a situation that we can thus call revolutionary. It inaugurates a new law, it always does so in violence. Always, which is to say even when there haven't been those spectacular genocides, expulsions, or deportations that so often accompany the foundation of states, great or small, old or new, right near us or far away. (991)

And as I said earlier, Derrida refers to this as the founding or revolutionary moment of law, which "interrupts the established [law] to found another" (991). The case of the Hutus and Tutsis reinforces the dimension of violence involved in the cutting power of law. The Tutsis became the population cast outside the law's protection in the shaping of the new racial order, a move prefigured centuries before when the Belgian colonial administration made the decision to embrace one side of the division between the Tutsis and Hutus. Thus, at the moment of founding, the law has already constituted who it will protect and who it will abandon, and in the process, has reshaped the current onto-juridical regime, and cultural worldview.

Let me now turn to an example that occurs in the United States: the case of the Japanese-Americans 1942–1945. Through an executive order issued by President Franklin D. Roosevelt in the aftermath of the bombing of Pearl Harbor, Japanese-Americans were ordered to report to assembly centers throughout the (western) United States, from where they were later sent to "internment camps" for the duration of World War II. This population had resided in the United States for as many as 60 years, bringing forth second- and third-generation Americans of Japanese descent. Many of them of were American citizens. Despite these facts, this group was summarily ordered to turn themselves in for the safety and security of the United States. However, this event can be grounded in a series of moments occurring decades before, which foreshadow the depiction of Japanese as unruly and vulnerable to outcasting by the time President Roosevelt's executive order is issued in 1942.

The Japanese immigrate to the United States shortly after Chinese immigrants are barred from entering the U.S. in 1882. As racial animosity against Chinese laborers in the United States increases, Japanese immigrants arrive on the mainland in 1891, serving as substitute labor for the Chinese. Their major initial presence is in Hawaii, where they emigrated to work on sugarcane fields, until the 1907 Gentleman's Agreement with Japan, whereby the Emperor of Japan agreed to refuse visas to Japanese laborers, effectively prohibiting them from immigrating to the United States.

The mainland's welcome of the Japanese as inexpensive labor to substitute for the increasingly marginalized and persecuted Chinese labor beings to wane with the 1907 Gentleman's Agreement. Beginning in 1910, followed in 1913, and again in 1920, a series of Alien Land Laws was passed with the intention of disfranchising settled Japanese immigrants from the lands, business, and other properties that they had purchased in the United States.[54] The increasing hostility that they faced through the law is accompanied by a larger cultural hostility, which serves to exacerbate and reinforce the predisposition of the law to weigh in against them: concerns (expressed in 1919) about "the high birthrate of Japanese immigrants," which "would eventually create overpopulation in the state" and the "pronounced antagonism" of the Japanese toward integration an assimilation; there were concerns (expressed in 1921) that Japan had "evil designs on the United States and that the early facilitators of its intentions were the immigrants."[55]

These hostilities in turn are expressed, as with other Asian immigrants, through anti-miscegenation laws (passed in 1930), barriers to naturalization (in 1922) as they are categorized as "aliens "ineligible for citizenship," and the 1924 Immigration Act, which prohibited Japanese immigration entirely.[56]

In turn, these laws refocus the hostility on the "strangeness" of the "inscrutable Japanese," with inexorable and disastrous consequences. As Tetsuden Kashima argues, the internment of Japanese immigrants and Americans of Japanese descent was precipitated by concerns and planning to persecute this population well before the internments camps following the 1941 events at Pearl Harbor. Through ample documentation, Katsuden shows that the Japanese had become the targets of wariness by federal organizations with regard to "internal security," beginning in the 1920s.[57] In the aftermath of the 1931 invasion of Manchuria by the Japanese, the United States worried throughout the 1930s that "'[w]hen war breaks out, the entire Japanese population will rise and commit sabotage. They will endeavor by every means to neutralize the West Coast and render it defenseless.'"[58] This U.S. State Department memo was augmented by concerns on the part of then President Franklin D. Roosevelt anxieties about the potential betrayal by persons of Japanese origin or background, leading to his suggestion that every Japanese citizen or noncitizen who met with Japanese ships arriving in Hawaii should be "secretly but definitely identified and his or her name placed on a special list of those who would be the first to be placed in a concentration camp in the event of trouble."[59]

The potential "unruliness" of the Japanese, represented through their physical identities and ethnicities, could be located in international relations between the U.S. and the Japanese, as well as comparisons with other temporarily "good" or possibly "better" immigrants who were arriving in the U.S., such as Asian Indians, Koreans, Filipinos, and Europeans. Natsu Taylor Saito shows that at various points the Japanese population was contrasted with their Chinese counterparts. As early as 1894, a court in Massachusetts ruled that the Japanese were also part of the "Mongolian" race that included the Chinese, and therefore both populations were ineligible for naturalization.[60] At other times, such as in 1941, they were identified as "enemies" of the United States in deliberate contrasts with Chinese immigrants, who were portrayed in a positive light as "friends."[61] But it is hard to imagine that the "unruliness," whatever the myriad sources, was "incidental" to the "rule of law" that created and enforced the subsequent internment of Japanese immigrants and American citizens. By the time President Roosevelt's Proclamation 2525[62] and infamous Executive Order 9066[63] were put into effect, 120,000 persons of Japanese ancestry were arrested and interned, the various rights, protections, and the recognition of the humanity and rightful legal status of the Japanese had been gradually stripped for nearly three decades. The law was cutting—continually, nonrandomly, and with a deliberate vengeance, and had been doing so for quite some time.

Conclusion

Both Derrida's and Agamben's understanding of violence is not beholden to a prior ideology or another outside authority; law is its own authority. Let me suggest a different formulation of the position shared both by Benjamin and Derrida: The law's interest in a monopoly on [protection] of individuals is not explained by the intention of preserving legal ends but rather of preserving the law itself; that [the protective function] when not in the hands of the law, threatens it not by the ends that it may pursue, but by its mere possibility outside the law and thus by its challenge to the preservation of law.

This description might help us understand better the relation of law qua sovereign power to its subjects. *The instability of law emerges when it is threatened by another lawgiver—understood as that which is capable of protecting against other sources of violence.* This monopoly on protection can be pursued by the corresponding function of law, namely to be able to regulate violence—by outsourcing violence to private parties, by looking the other way when private parties use violence, handing out contracts to kill, and selectively enforcing order through violence on certain populations, and correlatively, by abandoning populations of its protection—and thus inviting others to commit violence on those abandoned populations.

Something of Derrida's understanding of the founding violence of law changes through this reformulation: suddenly we see the law not as moving through the moment of "undecidability" to a nondescript decision that has cutting power—that cuts and divides randomly. Instead, we see the cutting power of law as in fact quite selective: it cuts in favor of that population that will help to preserve itself, and against another which it understands as threatening to its own existence. It is that which is anchored by the "unruly" and thereby poses a challenge to an existing onto-juridico-political regime. This "protective" function of law kicks in when it understands its obligation to those populations who support, reinforce, or whose interests are consistent with that of the prevailing regime.

Why do I refer to this phenomenon as a form of violence, and not merely as the abrogation of responsibility by sovereign power? In part, the nature of violence—physical violence let's say—is one of discipline, coercion, and management of the subject. As Foucault has famously noted, violence (in the form of regulatory and disciplinary power) is a form of molding persons to conform to a certain vision of subjectivity— whether soldiers, citizens, or prisoners. Presumably the pressure to mold someone into a certain subjective shape can be understood as coercion, but does not necessarily have to be understood as violence. Why then, do I refer to the abandonment of populations as a form of violence? In part because, in the world of nation-states, the inevitable consequence of abandonment of subjects by national power is a return to a Hobbesian state of nature, where human beings are forced to use their own re- sources, strength, and skills to defend themselves from the exigencies of others' whims. Even more to the point, violent actions are those that will inevitably lead to a violent end result as its consequence.

Walter Benjamin begins a description of the second kind of violence when he points to it as existing in the basic nature of law. Lawmaking, he says, is power-making, and to that extent, an immediate manifestation of violence (Benjamin 1978, p. 295). The intrinsic effect of the authority of law is its ability to enact a certain end. Benjamin suggests that the violence of law can reside either in its ends or in the means required to achieve cer- tain ends. Thus, the violence expresses itself in the capacity of the law to make itself felt. Moreover, the purpose of mythical lawmaking is power, whereas the purpose of divine lawmaking, or sovereign power, is justice.

Benjamin concedes that not all agreements are bound to conclude in violence. He points to examples of contracts between private persons, or other relationships, whether the means and ends are fundamentally agreed upon by all parties. As he says, "[n]onviolent agreement is possi- ble wherever a civilized outlook allows the use of unalloyed means of agreement."[64] But in the case of a polity, there is a fundamental disparity of power between state authorities and subjects/residents in the polity. This must be the case even in a practicing democracy. Despite the claims that democratic political participation is ideally a case of procedures enabling equal access to a public forum for the purposes of debating and agreeing upon policies, the fact remains that not everyone has equal access to public space qua the effective ability to be heard, nor to power, understood as the capacity to make law.

What I'd like to suggest here is that the purpose of lawmaking, the kind exhibited through the state, is a case of power rather than justice. In any kind of polity, more than just the disparity of power, it is the intrinsic understanding of the state that it is fundamentally at odds with some part of the population that resides within the confines of its jurisdiction: These antagonisms have been especially evident in U.S. history. We can point to the history of slavery, to the labor strikes of the late nineteenth and early twentieth century, the continuing antagonisms between corporate capital and labor—domestic and international—as manifested through NAFTA, FTAA, GATT, and most recently, CAFTA. We can point to the internment of Japanese-Americans, to the atrocious Tuskegee experiment of the mid-twentieth century, and so many others. There are many ways of understanding these disparities: they may be antagonisms of class interests; the antagonisms between racial populations; or the overlap between race and class in the antagonisms between different groups. What each of these conflicts has in common is the following: besides the class and race antagonisms expressed in each of them, the state has always taken a side, if not driven the antagonisms, created the sides, and expressed itself through the side that has imposed, exploited, and oppressed another.

But what these antagonisms also point to is the "cutting" power of the law as working against—systematically—the interests of a certain population, those who are deemed threatening—both to another population's ability to remain on the good side of the law, and to the law's ability to maintain power, and a certain kind of hierarchy. There is something that is intuited about the unruly, something that renders that population conspicuous, incapable of blending in, or fitting into the larger population without attracting notice or fear.[65]

This is not to say that the state is always oppressive—one could argue that the state has also found itself on the side of oppressed groups in ending slavery, ending apartheid, in integrating schools, in the promotion or defense of gay rights in certain states. Regardless of whether one agrees with the interpretation that the state has often had a hand in meting out justice, it still holds, I would suggest, that the state has played a strong role in creating, administering, managing conflicts between populations. And the larger purpose behind this role is in creating unity and managing a certain coherence within the polity.

And so, the violence of which I speak emerges from the fear of being put outside the gates of the city, so to speak, or at least put outside the jurisdiction of the law's protection. This is the fear, I contend, that drives the collaboration of different populations with state authorities in creating outcastes. The most recent example of this is the outcasting of Muslims from the Western world. It is certainly the case that the acts of Muslim terrorists over the last few years have both alerted and helped to entrench the idea that Muslims are to be feared, that the presence of certain Muslims signals a threat to our existence. And yet, the war on terror, or what I call a war on Muslims, is driven not only by the Bush Administration, as certain simplistic narratives would explain. Rather the war on Muslims, I would suggest, emerges from a deeper impulse, the impulse to manage and cohere the unity of a populace by drawing on their fears of this violence.

As I have tried to argue, there is already a preexisting vulnerability, which enables the state to weigh the undecidable moment of law to abandon one such population over another. It already speaks to the violence of the law, that moment of originary founding violence that is waiting . . . not to cut randomly, but to cut decisively, in a way consistent with not protecting that already intuited as being threatening. In any case, I would suggest that the framework that I have laid out above is a more accurate gauge for law to decide who will be abandoned . . . who will become the subject of violence. But this abandonment, as conspicuous as I have hoped to render it, is rarely so conspicuous—that is the beauty of the technological. Technologies—especially technologies of law—help to produce certain outcomes while concealing the factors of production behind the veil of naturalization.

3

The Unruly

Strangeness, Madness, and Race

We have yet to write the history of that other form of madness, by which men, in an act of sovereign reason, confine their neighbors, and communicate and recognize each other through the merciless language of non-madness; to define the moment of this conspiracy before it was permanently established in the realm of truth, before it was revived by the lyricism of protest . . . We must describe, from the start of its trajectory, that "other form" which relegates Reason and Madness to one side or the other of its action as things henceforth external, deaf to all exchange, and as though dead to one another.[1]

Introduction

The last two chapters described the racialization of populations as engaged in by juridical institutions. In chapter 1, I discussed the ways in which race is used as a technology to channel certain elements into the production of racial divisions that appear to be grounded objectively. In chapter 2, I argued against Derrida's argument that the judgments of law cut randomly in favor of or against certain groups, calling this a part of the mythology of liberalism—that individuals are automatically protected by law except under certain—unusual or contingent—circumstances. Rather, I argued that a subject population is often preconstituted to attract the disciplinary wrath of the state, and in turn, that this disposition is the ground of the racialization of a population. Here, I want to discuss the dialectical counterpart of institutional racialization, namely how and why certain groups attract the hostile attention of the state. The two primary features that circumscribe such a group, "unruliness," and "vulnerability," highlight the broad parameters by which a group is isolated as ripe for racialization. But there are two other stages that must be augmented to those prior features, strangeness and madness. These features are related to the normative behaviors that are ascribed to a group—those that deem a population unruly.

Madness has been leveled as a social diagnosis, and utilized as one of the currencies of political and social outcasting for hundreds of years. In the twentieth century, the charge of madness has been leveled against colonized and anticolonial populations, ethnic minorities, immigrant groups, homosexuals, transgendered populations, or others who deviate from "mainstream" class and cultural comportments. As Foucault points out, madness becomes the weapon by which one part of humanity confines another, relegating it to confinement, forcing it to hide, rereading its logic as one of animality. One of the fears that men "of reason" have of insanity, of the mad, is the nearly flawless capacity to imitate the logic, the discourse of reason.

> The marvelous logic of the mad which seems to mock that of the logicians because it resembles it so exactly, or rather because it is exactly the same, and because at the secret heart of madness, at the core of so many errors, so many absurdities, so many words and gestures without consequence, we discover, finally, the hidden perfections of a language.[2]

If the mad resemble those endowed with reason, if they appear to speak the language of reason but with very different imaginations and desires, then not only are the mad dangerous, but they can also hide among us, undetected, and infiltrate and transform the logic of civilization before there is a chance to stop them. The danger of the mad is as follows: Madness, irrationality, unreason are affiliated with those who can not use "right reason" to see and acknowledge that way of looking at the world that appears to be obvious to "everyone else."

I want to step away for a moment and distance myself from the descriptive employment of the discourse of madness; I want, instead, to think about the subtle ground of madness. Embedded in the charge of madness is a set of subterraneous norms and fears that lead to the creation of unruly populations. In the prior chapters, I indicated that the "unruly" is the lightning rod by which a population becomes singled out for outcasting. The behaviors associated with the unruly and their physical representations such as skin color, phenotype, language, accent, comportment, outward garb[3]—are part of the scaffolding by which madness is understood. Madness itself is a refined discursive apparatus by which some other uneasiness is indicated, one that often seems too murky to excavate. I think uneasiness is one ground by which the process of racializing or outcasting begins for some groups in the contemporary age. In order to escape the baggage of other words that have often been used to connote a similar kind of phenomenon, I will simply refer to it here as "strangeness." The sophisticated vocabularies of strangeness can become one initial impetus by which groups are eventually deprived of their status as legitimate rights-bearing members of national or international political communities. There are plenty of examples in the history of the world, where cultural or social strangeness has been read as a form of unruliness, and ultimately indicted as madness. This diagnosis has been used to confine the "guilty" as if they were defiant transgressors of established widespread norms.

In what follows, I will develop the notion of "strangeness," as the ground of the eventual perception of a group as "unruly." Then, after developing the concept of the unruly in further detail, I explore these terms as they might apply to more recent history. Of late, the indictment of madness has reappeared to justify the political and legal vulnerability of yet another group, and consequently, the state's hostile attention and its racialization of this group, namely Muslims or Arabs (loosely perceived as such) in liberal polities.

Strangeness

In using this term, I want to evoke the connotation of the unfamiliar, perceived as unfriendly, hostile, and ultimately, diffident. The *Oxford English Dictionary* (OED) records the usage of the root "strange," as first appearing in 1290, to evoke the description of someone who belongs to a place or locality "other than one's own."[4] A second definition evokes a character for a person, language, or custom that is foreign, alien, or from another land or country. Yet a third definition identifies the "strange" as alien, different, or diverse. Another meaning ascribed to the strange is that which is unfamiliar, unknown, not met with, or experienced before, and again as unfamiliar, abnormal, or "exceptional to a degree that excited wonder or astonishment." And finally, a fifth usage, pertaining to persons—and one that most immediately describes "strangeness" in similar terms—signifies that the strange is that which is unfriendly, cold, distant, not affable, not familiar, or encouraging, cold, aloof—moreover, an action is ascribed to the "strange person": one who is uncomplying, unwilling to accede to a request or desire.

My point in turning to the OED is to initiate a discussion of strangeness, but my point in this exercise is to illuminate the links between the unfamiliarity of a phenomenon—or group—and the way that unfamiliarity is apprehended, rationalized, internalized by a dominant group or institution in power, and then transformed into a strategy of political management. Embedded in this relationship is another crucial impulse: the transformation of the unfamiliar into a sense of wrongdoing on the part of the "strange" group itself—in modern parlance, a "blaming of the victim," so to speak.

Since race as an explicit category for those peoples who "appear" unfamiliar does not explicitly develop until the eighteenth century,[5] "strangeness" might be the most apt term to describe a phenomenon that can be found in writings as early as those of Pliny the Elder's (23–79 CE) *Natural History*, which discusses a range of Monstrous Races. He offers descriptions of the Panotioi,[6] Cynocephali,[7] (dog-headed people), and hermaphrodites,[8] among other unfamiliar peoples. Depictions of Monstrous races can be found in medieval maps dating back to 600 CE, which locate Jersusalem in the center of the world.[9] The depiction of Jerusalem in the center also points, perhaps too obviously, to the codevelopment of the languages of monstrosity and rationality within the context of Christianity. The races in question stood out because of their abnormality of appearance, because they were gruesome or otherwise conspicuously marked as different. Thus, the need to explain the unfamiliar emerges and is transformed into a narrative about another's inferiority, savageness, not quite human-ness. The category of race, which has become such a familiar one today, might be successfully explained as operating on a similar principle. The writings of Buffon, LeClerc, Herder, Kant, Hegel, and others[10] in the eighteenth and nineteenth centuries focus on the development of races of peoples in other parts of the world. These theories take their lead from the observations and reports of anthropologists and explorers, who are traveling to the Americas and Africa and the South Pacific, happening upon strange peoples—peoples whose customs, languages, features, cultures are not only unfamiliar, but perhaps translated as "cold," "distant," "uncompliant," "unfriendly," or any one of the other terms that are offered as definitions of that which is "strange." And thus the great question: how does a political institution manage that/those who are "strange"—intellectually, culturally, politically, and in relation to those who are its own (and familiar)? The projects of colonialism and imperial expansion are but two answers to this question.

Strangeness is not identical to foreignness, although there is clearly much overlap between the two. Foreignness is often the language by which populations are alienated and recognized as alien to a society. In Europe and North America in the early twenty-first century, foreignness is almost exclusively devoted to the "immigrant question," similar to the way that the term pertained to the "Jewish question" in Europe, or the "Japanese" question in North America during the beginning of the twentieth century. In each of these instances, the term foreignness is used to identify, focus on, and expose to suspicion the trait that a group is from outside the national context. This is one facet of the hostility that was visited upon these groups. The term falsely closes the door to other traits—and other more nebulous factors—that raise fear and suspicion within a "domestic" context.

In this sense, strangeness is more apt when used as a term to consider the grounds by which a group begins its process of being racialized within a larger society—at "home." The notion of strangeness implies a certain primordial fear, which for centuries has appeared to required that certain "housecleaning" strategies must be employed to eliminate or manage the strangeness. The actions, the rationale of a stranger or a strange group cannot be predicted. The appearance of a stranger in one's midst often disrupts the everyday harmony of a society. The unfamiliar practices of a new group appear to threaten the order of an already ongoing set of customs and culture. Moreover, the strange group cannot automatically be counted on: are its commitments, scruples, sense of loyalty the same as ours? Will this group turn on us in a time of crisis? The strangeness of another group is often immediately linked to a potential danger that it poses to another group.

Let me review an excerpt of the definition of the unruly that I offer in chapter 1. There, I describe the "unruly" as

> the element that is intuited as threatening to a political order, to a collectively disciplined society . . . The "unruly" is marked out within some dimension of the "real" that should not be interpreted merely at the visual level (as in the case of . . . some segment of an otherwise "homogenous" population which becomes marked as being "different than us" or of a different "race" or an "Other"). That which is unruly can be evasive enough to be "intuited" or "felt" rather than seen or perceived—because the intuition is one of "danger." . . . It is this intuition—together with an awareness, memory, or collective narrative about a certain history, culture, or politics with which the "unruly" is associated—that facilitates the acceptance of a certain classification . . . [T]he "unruly" denotes the real *in association* with its perceived degree of threat.[11]

At which point does the strangeness of a group become perceived as unruly? Contra the OED's definition, I suggest that it is not the "unfamiliar"

or the strangeness of the group that is perceived as unfriendly or dangerous; rather, it is the perceived "unwillingness" to "adapt," pay deference,
consciously or explicitly self-deprecate, or assimilate to the norms of the
larger population. Often, what makes a group strange is often too nebulous
or too fecund to pinpoint, and certain practices become the stand-in for the
more general "strangeness" of that group. These become fetishized as
the core representation of that group's singularity, and their continual
practice—read as the absence of conformity, adaptation or assimilation of a
group's practices within a larger society—is what is viewed as unruly. Bonnie
Honig offers a similar observation when she says,

> Foreignness is a symbolic marker that the nation attaches to the
> people we want to disavow, deport, or detain because we experi-
> ence them as a threat. The distinction between who is part of the
> nation and who is an outsider is not exhausted nor even finally
> defined by working papers, skin color, ethnicity, or citizenship.
> Indeed, it is not an empirical line at all; it is a symbolic one, used
> for political purposes.[12]

The absence of conformity or adaptation appears to imply an "unwillingness" to conform or a refusal to see "right reason," in other words,
that the practices of the dominant group are better or correct, or at the
very least, the definitive status quo toward which a new group has an
obligation to assimilate. This "perceived" unwillingness, or some other
striking feature of a group—a feature that cannot be obscured, becomes
the source of the perception that an unruly threat is being posed to the
larger society. And so the unruly signifies the threatening aspect of the
strange; it is threatening because it will not melt away into some com-
fortable, familiar, configuration but continues to be conspicuous, like a
protruding excrescence.

There are numerous ways that we might see the emergence of an
"unruly" feature in a certain context. To return to the example from
chapter 1, the scenario of "appearing" White, even behaving as White,
while being registered as "Black,"[13] gives rise to a sense of danger that a
person is not conforming to the convention norms or scruples of a political regime. In the contemporary era, another way that the unruly is noted
is through the discourse of cultural difference, as I will discuss below.

The perception of an unruly threat might be one way to explain Carl
Schmitt's 1932 statement that the "political," and not the state, will constitute who the enemy is perceived to be.[14] To say that there is always an
enemy doesn't answer the question why there must always be one. Contrary to Schmitt's position, the threat of the foreigner or of heterogeneity

is not a natural one. And yet, such a danger might very well be a political necessity for the preservation of sovereign power. In earlier eras, the category of race, or monstrosity, or the abnormal, or ultimately, madness, enabled the possibility of confining, conquering, colonizing, and civilizing the unruly.[15]

But since the mid-twentieth century, refined Western—liberal—society has learned to manage its fear of the strange by controlling the degree and quality of cultural difference that will be tolerated and accommodated or refused outright. Liberalism, as a political project, prides itself on the ability to tolerate a range of political perspectives, personal viewpoints, varieties of culture.[16] And yet, "nonconformity," understood as a strange practice or marked "cultural" difference that will not fade, strikes a disruptive blow even within this framework. It suggests something askew, a distance or separation even beyond the standard "unique" perspective. Nonconformity indicates a (self)conscious distance from the group, one that suggests an affront—even if neither self-conscious decisions nor deliberate affronts are necessarily in evidence. But nonconformity is another way of articulating an avowed stance of difference, which is itself not offensive in a (global, capitalist, liberal) world where differences—as long as they are generally the same—will be tolerated, accommodated, and perhaps even accepted.[17]

In a world that, since the end of World War II, has espoused a tolerance of multiculturalism, *banal cultural differences* such as "exotic" holidays, traditions, or food are insufficient to marginalize a population, since they can be construed as—or transformed into—simple consumer or aesthetic preferences and, in a world marked by global capitalism, welcomed as marks of cosmopolitanism. By contrast, *significant cultural differences* are understood as profound and defiant practices that extend far beyond capitalism, searing the very heart of an apparent primordial political and cultural homogeneity. In the complicated contemporary Western political and legal landscape, significant cultural difference has become another way to understand a population as dangerous, and as belonging to a different logic—or an altogether illogic. And illogical, incomprehensible populations are nearly always perceived as threatening. One of the urgent concerns of the post-Reformation secularized Christian (liberal) world is the perceived danger of a cultural heterogeneity that departs radically or challenges a prevailing political-cultural order. This turmoil is characterized by the idea that culture is an expression of rationality, as Richard Rorty has suggested.[18] This view of culture presupposes a common set of practices that function as the reassurance of a shared cultural comportment, namely that you and I are sufficiently similar. When widely shared, this cultural perspective appears as the dominant norm—or a universality. The uncritical equation of a set of norms with rationality establishes such norms as universal and renders them beyond dispute. Except in those cases where differences are understood as mere preferences (rather than deep-seated beliefs or cultural ontology), this view of culture renders the dissenter—she who does not share the dominant norm—an outsider and a threat to the singularity of that culture.

The mark of strangeness precipitates the question of loyalties, commitments, allegiances. This is why assimilation becomes such an important imperative. We tend to believe that those who accept and internalize "our" norms are more likely to share our allegiances. As a result, they are less likely to betray "us." But radical heterogeneity is more than merely difference or strangeness—it is an unruly threat to a shared culture. Radical heterogeneity represents a challenge to the values of a liberal-secular political order, and to "reasonable" and law-abiding members of the polity. Those who are affiliated with such heterogeneous practices are, by extension, understood as unruly creatures; they are considered irrational and thought to share few characteristics with "rational" human beings, who by definition ascribe to the prevailing cultural regime. Their public perception as a threat, even a potential insurgence to a current regime, prompts a political or sovereign response that would suppress the potential threat. Judith Butler has already pointed to this phenomenon. Referring to the 1991 invasion of Iraq by the United States, she says, ". . . the Arab 'other' is understood to be radically outside the structures of democracy and reason, and hence calls to be brought forcibly within."[19]

The fear of betrayal to "outside force" prompts the concern that radical heterogeneity is threatening. As such, the perceived danger of radical cultural heterogeneity is treated with a fundamental hostility from sovereign institutions;[20] this hostility is directed toward individuals whose comportment seems to threaten the fundamental political-cultural order on which the state is based. That treatment is often naturalized as the proper response of a state toward a threat to its people. As William Galston states, "Liberal public institutions may restrict the activities of individuals and groups for four kinds of reasons: first to reduce coordination problems and conflict among diverse legitimate activities and to adjudicate such conflict when it cannot be avoided; second, to prevent and when necessary punish transgressions individuals may commit against one another; *third, to guard the boundary separating legitimate from illegitimate variations among ways of life;* and finally, to secure the conditions—including cultural and civic conditions—needed to sustain public institutions over time."[21] By preempting the possibility of challenging a prevailing set of norms, the question of reasonableness is already instantiated by those who understand themselves as "full members of the polity." And so, a dominant population can create the conditions by which to reproduce itself and its norms while defending itself as extending full and equal rights to all "members," of the polity—in other words, others like themselves. And thus the practice of distinguishing "legitimate from illegitimate variations among ways of life," enables the state to justify why certain populations—especially if the members of that population are seen to be culturally homogenous—are not entitled to its promise of "universal protections." As Galston says, "Value pluralism is not relativism. The distinction between good and bad, and between good and evil, is objective and rationally defensible."[22]

I want to explore the distinction that Galston raises, between legitimate and illegitimate, good and evil, ways of life. Galston, like many who write in the tradition of liberalism, reserves the capacity to make judgments about who is sufficiently acceptable for membership in a polity. This reservation is often quite explicitly stated and catalogued without a conceptual or logical explanation of the grounds of inclusion or exclusion; here, though, I want to explore the conceptual grounds. Galston, like many who are sympathetic to liberalism and the values of pluralism, reserves this distinction because he implicitly accepts that in a modern culture of liberal toleration,[23] cultural difference alone is not a sufficient reason to deprive a group of rights. It is significant cultural difference—seen as a *threat* to other reasonable and hence law-abiding members of the polity—which is understood as holding the potential for criminality. In the case of Muslims, for example, the actions of the group of 19 on 9-11, have become a synechdoche for the "nature" and unique cultural practices of all members of that ethnic and cultural group. And thus, this synechdoche reinforces the perception of the entire group as engaging in a set of culturally heterogeneous practices that emerge through the affinity for another tradition or "another" God, and thus, another authority than the culture that binds us as a community. Hence, these practices are seen as profane or criminal practices, i.e. as transgressing or departing from the *common culture that members of a group should share.* If we can ascribe this interpretation to a given group, then we might better understand the logic behind the pre-emptive hunt for "potential terrorists," qua enemies: the idea of "innocent until proven guilty" does not apply to those who are "not-like-us" or "not-human-like-us."

Radical differences cannot be comprehended as familiar or possibly acceptable. And yet, lack of familiarity or acceptability does not necessarily mean that they are unreasonable—except through the lens of the dominant framework through which they are exclusively evaluated. Often, what is being judged is the strange logic of the difference of practice, a logic that is being couched as "making sense" or even "rational" within another worldview. Matthew Abraham refers to the concept of the "reasonable person," a key category of American legal jurisprudence, "as a normative concept in that it isolates a particular subjective position as ideal, deploying this position as rational, reliable, and most important as possessing the capacity to make a legitimate material inscription within legal discourse."[24] In other words, the pronouncements of a "reasonable person" make a "meaningful, discursively recognized utterance that carries the force of law with it. In other words, it's that 'which counts.'"[25] This concept carries a cultural weight that extends beyond the judicial system, even though that is where we see the crystallized impact. It becomes the implicit standard by which reasonable and unreasonable practices, comportments, and behaviors are measured. It is easy to see then, how the charge of irrationality, rendered by a person of authority, can discredit the claims of someone from a strange background.[26] And it is this strangeness that is being equated with irrationality, and consequently with "illegitimacy."

Huntington and Rawls: Islam, Madness, and the Menace to Liberalism

Consider the threat of radical cultural difference as it has been articulated by Samuel Huntington and John Rawls. In his now infamous article, "The Clash of Civilizations," Huntington, a well-known liberal nationalist, suggests that there might be a number of "civilizations" that have the potential to be antagonistically positioned against the "West." He most consistently devotes his attention to the example of Islam and Arab countries. There are several features by which a civilization is distinguished from another, the most important of which is religion. The contours of a particular civilization rest on the views of "the relation between God and man, the citizen and the state . . . as well as differing views of the relative importance of rights and responsibilities, liberty and authority, equality and hierarchy."[27] In this framework, Huntington considers the relationship between religion and politics to be the primary axis by which a civilization is defined. In his argument, he points out that "economic modernization and social change" is often a destroyer of a group's (national/regional/local) identity. The vacuum left in the wake of these identities' destruction is most often reshaped by religion. As Huntington builds his argument, what is most striking is the way he catalogs a range of civilizations on the basis of culture (such as the "Asianization" in Japan or the "'Russianization' in Boris Yeltsin's country"), but always locates one particular civilization on the basis of religion: "Islamic" civilization; and the 're-Islamization of the Middle

East."[28] Indeed, by the end of his article, religion—most prominently understood as Islam—features as the key source of antagonism between the West and East. Not surprisingly, this interpretation is consistent with his view of what distinguishes the West from the East, namely the ability (or inability, in the latter case) to abstract out religion from the political and economic framework of a civilization.

A similar equation is manifested in John Rawls' *Law of Peoples*.[29] He offers the imaginary example of a decent, hierarchical Muslim people called "Kazanistan."[30] Elsewhere he calls Kazanistan "Islamic."[31] Rawls's use of this example is notable for its ascribed assumptions and features. The people of Kazanistan are hierarchical because they do not allow non-Muslims to stand for office, although they may be in the armed forces and higher ranks of command; they are nonliberal because they do not accept the separation of religion from the state, and they are "decent" because they are not aggressive toward others. They observe the Law of Peoples, and accept and respect human rights; they are also decent because they do not arbitrarily discriminate against non-Muslims, nor do they treat them as inferior in social or political relations, and because "[u]nlike most Muslim rulers, [they] have not sought empire and territory. This is because their theologians understand *jihad* in a moral and spiritual sense, and not in military terms."[32] These statements offer a narrow view, even patronizing of Muslims, who are portrayed as either sympathetic to (and thus "decent") or in tension with liberal tenets (and thus hierarchical and "nonliberal"). More hopefully, Rawls insists that this hypothetical people might be able to accommodate the needs of a range of groups, in the spirit of cooperation, and to respect the religious minorities within Kazanistan. Moreover, the members of government who disagree with government policies must be able express dissent. This dissent must be respected through responses that explain "how the government thinks it can both reasonably interpret its policies in line with its common good idea of justice and impose duties and obligations on all members of society."[33] Meeting these goals would establish this Muslim people as not only decent but also "reasonable," in part because they might instigate changes in the direction of liberal reforms. But, suggests a resigned Rawls, while this will not render Kazanistan a just society, it can nevertheless be decent; and this is truly the best that we can hope for from a nonliberal people. For Rawls, Muslims are nonliberal, because they are unreasonable: that is to say, they do not accept the premises of liberal public reason, namely that public reason should be formal and not substantive. And the unreasonable is that which is strange, even bizarrely unfamiliar, and thus unacceptable.

But here is how the logic is couched instead. Rawls insists that public reason applies only to politics and not other features of one's life; by extension public reason employs a political conception of justice, which is procedural and not substantive.[34] In other words, comprehensive doctrines, that is, those that have at their core certain moral or religious beliefs, cannot be the foundation of public reason nor of an ideal liberal democracy. The reason behind the exclusion of comprehensive doctrines from the space of politics is that deep-seated moral, religious, or philosophical beliefs ultimately can offer neither authoritative guidance nor rational superiority in debates about the distribution of goods, because they are ultimately personal, individual, beliefs. Were we to argue about religious or moral beliefs, the argument continues, we would get into an infinite battle that ultimately can never be concluded except perhaps through violence or force (and hence is itself an unreasonable avenue to resolve this debate), and which is ultimately not relevant to questions of political (procedural, democratic) conceptions of justice.

As should be obvious at this point in history, Islam is considered, by prominent Western intellectuals, to be a fundamentally distinct form of religion in contrast to mainstream Judaism, Catholicism, or other variations of Christianity, in that it integrates religious and political principles, an integration that appears fundamentally antithetical to a Western liberal regime. The ideal of shared or public reason prohibits the infusion of political life with religious principles—since the latter would promote a substantive—rather than a procedural—form of justice. This aspect of Islam is thought to be not only a fundamental violation of liberalism, but an inferior cultural-political regime, insofar as it is understood to ground political justice upon religion.[35]

There are several other remarkable factors in Huntington's and Rawls's descriptions. The first is the insistence that a liberal-secular political regime cannot consider a people or a civilization fully cooperative and eligible to interact in Western-style political governance until they share the premise that religion and the state must be separate and that all individuals must have the equal capacity to run for office and participate in government. Thus, still thinking of the "Islamic" peoples of Kazanistan, Rawls cautions us,

> "Of course, fundamentalist religious doctrines and autocratic and dictatorial rulers will reject the ideas of public reason and deliberative democracy. They will say that democracy leads to a culture contrary to their religion, or denies the value that only autocratic or dictatorial rule can secure.[36] They assert that the religiously true, or the philosophically true, overrides the politi-

cally reasonable. We simply say that such a doctrine is politically unreasonable. Within political liberalism, nothing more need be said."[37]

This conception of justice draws substantial distinctions between that which is properly political and that which should fall outside the realm of politics. Simultaneously, it raises the stakes for potential dissenters by equating this division to the line between the *reasonable* and the *unreasonable*. Rawls insists that religion and morality have no place within a liberal framework, and that *objections to this exclusion are not open to debate, and furthermore, are "unreasonable."* This move preemptively excludes dissenters from the set of people who are sufficiently "rational" to have an open debate about the concerns and questions of justice. But as Chantal Mouffe points out, "appeals to rationality,"—a typical authority in liberalism—often "disguises the necessary frontiers and forms of exclusion behind pretenses of 'neutrality.'"[38] And thus, "rationality becomes the key to solving the 'paradox of liberalism': how to eliminate its adversaries while remaining neutral."[39] Mouffe argues that "the very distinction between 'reasonable' and 'unreasonable' is already the drawing of a frontier; it has a political character and is always the expression of a given hegemony."[40]

Political reason, as Rawls describes it, locates disagreement in a narrow space. It implies a certain common set of logics, shared procedures, a certain cultural singularity—or at least commonality, which appears to manifest itself as a "universal consensus." Thus, if we accept that culture is an expression of rationality, and that rationality is an expression of humanity, then the implication is that *a group who does not accept the basic premises of a liberal society is somehow fundamentally, ontologically, cognitively, and culturally, different*[41] *from one which does*. In concrete terms, then, an Islamic society is incompatible with a liberal society. It is not only different, it is strange, unfamiliar, and its persistent existence is testament to the unfriendliness of those who insist on subscribing to it.

We should note that much of the West subscribes to a version of the same hierarchies, although it substitutes nationality for religion. Thus, it would seem that this is more than a descriptive distinction. Huntington and Rawls subscribe to the moral and political superiority of "secular" polities—those who can separate their religious identity from their political self-understanding—over those whose "ethnic and religious" identity intrinsically informs their self-understanding.[42] Even more to the point, in both Huntington's and Rawls's writings, the inferior group is most often substantiated by the population called "Muslims," whose questionable ascription to religion as the ground of their political worldviews renders them a suspect group, and ultimately, a potential threat to the Western world.

The decision to exclude certain practices, views, or peoples under the guise of the "free exercise of reason," does more than conceal the non-neutrality of the liberal state. It also hides the antagonisms and violence that the liberal frameworks of Locke, Rawls, Huntington, and other liberal theorists profess to have managed through the procedural rules of democratic participation.[43] And so, I would suggest that rationality, and its free exercise thereof—manifested as a universal or common consensus of what constitutes a legitimate, reasonable, acceptable, tolerable, way of life, is the expression of a *certain cloth of cultural singularity.*

The acceptance of the law—as the immediate ontological expression of political reason—is the basis of that commonality. But what is the implicit and underlying structure of political "reason?" I think there are two dimensions. The first is that within the context of polities and sovereign authority, the capacity of political reason is the post-facto interpretation of Law, and of laws. It is the tranformation of a prescription into the description of the state of the world. What becomes concealed in this transformation is that a certain vision of the world has been imposed and reconstituted as a "fact." We see this within the characteristics of citizenship in classical liberalism: masculinity, heterosexuality, family, patriarchy.[44] In contemporary liberalism, these shared characteristics take on a more sophisticated form: the capacity to deliberate, communicability, shared interests, a commitment to—or at least a respect for—proceduralism in decision-making, a desire to reconcile one's culture and a shared political framework—that is, between particularity and universality.[45]

Difference, Madness, and Race

But the cloth of cultural singularity appears to hypostatize the fear of difference, of strangeness, to the level of threat or danger that will overturn one's world(view), or much of what a particular society values. In other words, the fear of strangeness leads easily to the fear of an enemy. Is an internal enemy truly required? As I suggested at the beginning of this chapter, the threat of the foreigner or of heterogeneity is not a natural one, although it is endemic to the framework of a shared cultural or political ontology.[46] There are practices in every culture that catch our attention, regardless of whether they are widespread; they become representative of the strange, "foreignness" of a *different* culture. The focus on the practice, in combination with what it is thought to (mis)represent and other practices with which it is (mis)associated, raises its status to the level of extreme threat. In the language of liberal political thought then, those who emerge from cultures that are "radically heterogeneous" are the irrational. Like the "strangeness" that sets them apart, they become part of the "unruly" that threatens the state.

In ensuing chapters, I will argue that "Muslims," "Arabs" are subject to such racializing, because—at least superficially—cultural heterogeneity of the forms, for example, represented by Islam and Muslims/Arabs are perceived to be an offense to "Western" culture/liberalism. But I don't think that this is the fundamental problem, at least not directly. I think this is the language of the current moment of racialization, but the practice of racial dividing can be engaged in under numerous guises. The practice of racializing Muslims is the consequence of a recent phenomenon.

There has been a dialectical unfolding of two new discourses that have led to the current renewal of the discourse of "acceptable" and "unacceptable" cultural differences, which can be seen as a euphemism for the paradigm of madness. First, since the end of the twentieth century, the use of "race" to outcast people has generally been forbidden in the Western world. Since the concept of race, understood as a mode of distinguishing a hierarchy of different groups, has been discredited by scientists and politicians alike, the concept of race as a ground by which to marginalize people can no longer proceed in the same vein or at the same pace as it did in the eighteenth, nineteenth, and part of the twentieth centuries. And so it seems that the attempt to distinguish people— enemies, as Carl Schmitt says, requires a new logic, a new mode by which to make similar distinctions.

Second, since the end of World War II, and official adoption of the Declaration of Human Rights, it has become more difficult to deprive persons of rights, although the attempts to do so by various institutions continue. There is a certain set of rights that are thought to be extended to all individuals, regardless of race, caste, sex, political or religious creed. In the language and logic of the UNDHR, rights are extended to all human beings, as an attempt to seal the loopholes that enabled the incarceration, torture, and death of certain categories of human beings. All persons, after 1948, were thought to at least have the guarantee of protection through their membership in the category of Human being, since in the rhetoric of human rights talk, the category of human being has been catapulted into a political category denoting a certain aura of protections.[47]

In chapters 1 and 2, I have argued that it is in the interest of sovereign power to conserve itself. The project of conserving itself is predicated on a fundamental distinction between the interests of those in charge and their constituency. The prospect of remaining in charge requires attention to two further interests. Sovereign power has to appeal to that constituency that is conscious of and supports these two developments—in other words, the prospect of universal human rights as a solution to any potential outcasting, and the discrediting of race as a political or scientific category—and that understands itself as part of the liberal project of tolerance and accommodation. As such, the notion of "cultural difference as a proxy for madness takes the place of race and enables a new loophole to the framework of universal human rights.

How so? In the milieu of science and medicine in Western worlds, the category of madness, with its attendant language of irrationality, unreasonableness, etc., creates a fissure in the tight fabric of political equality and cultural difference. This fissure, as I've tried to argue in this chapter, enables the possibility of locating an "objective" ground by which to single out a group for extreme political suspicion and hostility, if not ultimately for political outcasting. In the world of universal human rights, legal protections cannot be withdrawn from any human subject, on the assumption that they are "human," and worthy of protections. Such an assumption cannot be easily ruptured—this is the point of the human rights framework as represented by the Universal Declaration of Human Rights. But the loophole that allows the violation of this bulletproof protection is the possibility that someone is not human—or at least not recognizably so with the culturally predetermined framework of a post–World War II world. Madness has the potential for such a violation, since it denotes someone who is not fully rational, and therefore possibly not capable of utilizing their rights appropriately. Race—qua madness—can become the new objective grounds for political inferiority.

Madness is particularly conducive to the creation of new outcast groups. At least for the past few centuries, the diagnosis of madness has always belonged to science: it takes on an objective aura as one that requires that a group be singled out and "treated" so as to be returned to a "normalcy," so it can return to join the rest of the population. Foucault argues madness is a new form of racism, borne by psychiatry in order to single out the abnormal, to isolate "individuals who, as carriers of a condition, a stigmata, or any defect whatsoever, may more or less randomly transmit to their heirs the unpredictable consequences of the evil, or rather of the non-normal, that they carry within them."[48]

Foucault distinguishes madness as a medical racism that is distinct from "ethnic racism," although, he adds, it was augmented by the Nazis onto the ethnic racism that was particular to that era.[49] His point is certainly true of Europe, where nation-states are predicated on ethnic and kinship affiliations, but less so in the context of the United States. Instead, I would suggest, madness as a "scientific" racism prevails as the new form of "ethnic racism" in the U.S. The apparatus of madness as a discourse of racism is especially useful in a nation whose popular self-image—as a "nation of immigrants"—is in tension with a competing (ideal) image of a coherent nation whose ties run long and deep, as ethnic ties might. The discourse of madness enables the construction of an internal enemy against which sovereign power and the "political"— "citizens," "Americans," can be allied. Madness as a form of scientific racism can alleviate the struggle of sustaining a coherent political unit(y) in the absence of those ethnic and blood-ties. And so new allegories and images metaphorically take on the role of "family ties" can help form the bond of the "We."

Then, in the case of certain kinds of populations that may not automatically consider themselves to be a group, but who nevertheless are part of the project of ostracization by a state, the diagnosis of madness enables them to be removed from the realm of members who are extended due protections and rights. The discourse of strangeness, madness, and its moral extension, "evil" can help to create a new enemy, sudden danger, while simultaneously circumventing the issue of human rights, avoiding charges of (literal) racism. Moreover the "scientific"—or political "scientistic" context in which the charge of madness is leveled, lends the entire phenomenon an aura of an "objective," if not a medical, condition.

Liberal Hegemony and Heterogeneous Populations

As we saw above, the charge of madness, like racism—*as a form of racism*— can be played out using a sophisticated vocabulary—one where some person or group can be diagnosed as "mad," or "inferior" without ever using the explicit term.[50] The insidious genius of such a vocabulary is that it can be deployed using an "objective" procedural apparatus, which can then be used to persecute, outcaste, and/or confine someone for alleged crimes, which in fact are crimes of transgressing a prevailing discourse rather than actual harms. The language of difference becomes an apparatus by which to distinguish banal differences from those that are perceived as avowed stances of nonconformity (what I have been referring to as the unruly). The former—as long as they are generally the same—will be tolerated, accommodated, and perhaps even accepted,[51] whereas the latter becomes the target of the state's wrath.

And so, which differences are acceptable and which will be rejected? The dialectical counterpart of madness is the notion of rationality, whose application is informed by a hegemonic consensus. The concept of hegemony[52] often presupposes a certain ideology that envelopes us, swooping us into its midst. It presumes that there is a space of discontent, disagreement that is being repressed, concealed, or ignored in the quest for a certain consensus. Instead, I would suggest that in the project of liberalism, the conception of rationality, or the exercise of rational procedures with a view toward consensus, insists upon a certain singularity, where disagreements are generally minor, relatively trivial, and the cost of disagreement—within the group itself—are inconvenient, but neither tragic nor calamitous.

The drawing of frontiers, as Mouffe says, signifies that others who disagree are still in a sense on the same terrain as ourselves, but their presence is merely on the other side of that frontier. Rationality is predicated on a certain cultural commonality that is presumptuous enough to be the norm. In this form, the trope of rationality serves a powerful function. By appearing as something that emanates from each member of a society, while also reflected within the law itself, it appears to be the intrinsic ontological trait of human beings. As Judith Butler says, "To establish a set of norms that are beyond power or *force is itself a powerful and forceful conceptual practice that sublimates, disguises and extends its own power play through recourse to tropes of normative universality.*"[53] In this form, the trope of rationality serves a powerful function. By appearing as something that emanates from each member of a society, while also reflected within the law itself, rationality appears to be an intrinsic trait of human beings. And hence, rationality is more than a shared set of understandings, procedures, framework. It is the ontological cloth by which one can be recognized as human, not only by others but also by sovereign authority and by law. And so, if rationality is understood in this way, then it would, it seems, also make sense that unless one accepted the "rational" premises that undergird a particular community, and shared the traits that belong to the members of that community, then one is precluded from not only from mere membership but from the acknowledgment or recognition that one is human as well.

From the perspective of a world that is governed by nation-states, the preclusion of such recognition reveals most vividly the expression of an intrinsic sovereign authority—a sovereign expression of *violence and coercion*—which is crucial to the successful maintenance and reproduction of a liberal state. So, one could ask at this point, what is the meaning of the violence and coercion that are the intrinsic expressions of sovereign authority? Laclau and Mouffe respond that these are attempts to limit and manage the undecidability of heterogeneity, in order "to make way for actions and decisions that are as *coherent* as possible," even as they also point out that such a management can never be complete or successful.[54] I certainly agree that coherence is an aim of a sovereign agenda that is motivated by the impulse to preempt the chaos of a potentially unmanageable population. And so, while "coherence" may be read, on the one hand, as "an ordered intelligibility," that is, an explicit political agenda that constitutes what is reasonable (rationality as an explicit condition of a free society), what the majority wants (hegemony), the outcome of procedures of negotiation and accommodation (pluralism and toleration). But what they term "undecidability," is not the messiness that lies at the boundaries of the political. Rather, "undecidability" is really the intrinsic fear embodied by liberal sovereignty. It is fear of the unruly, which threatens to wreak havoc on the order, the established laws and norms of a polity, which not only support but *guarantee* the force of sovereign power.

The implied solution is to coerce others "to prove" they are one of us rather than accepting them under the stated conditions by which people are allowed to enter the polity—criteria such as deliberative rationality, cooperation, a commitment to equality and rights. And so, here might be another way by which to understand the rationality that secures and undergirds the liberal framework: rationality—expressed as abiding by the rule of law—is the stance of coercion, which is designed to cohere (not just render intelligible, but to bring together) a population, while simultaneously excluding others. Rationality then might be understood as a moment of self-identification and recognition. Certainly, this is the way it has been understood in any number of discourses, from Kant and Hegel on to contemporary discourses of political justice, multiculturalism, to name a few.[55] But what I am interested in emphasizing here is the moment of rejection, aversion, and exclusion that appears to be intrinsic to recognition and self-identification.

Vilem Flusser calls this the "criminal aspect of self-determination." "The act of self-identification constantly throws one into crisis, because self-identification requires one to differentiate oneself from others, to discriminate against others . . . Identity is thus the consequence of a crisis, a criticism—a 'crime' in the the precise meaning of the word. 'Who am I?' is a criminal question."[56]

The question, "who are we?" has similar implications of criminality— depending upon who is asking the question. By this question, I am referring not merely to the self-naming of one population among many—since this is a response to a slightly difference question, namely "what are we?"—or a question of what we have in common.[57] Rather the question of "who we are," at the moment of asking, serves to establish the ever-impending frontier that Mouffe describes as being implicit in the aspiration toward a rational consensus. It doesn't just demarcate the line between the us and them, but it insists that there necessarily must be such a demarcation.

There might be a number of ways to reply: One of them is that such a demarcation is not necessary, if some common ground, or shared understanding can be found. This is one answer—and in part it is the understanding offered by Rawls and even Galston. But this response seems to locate the *not-We*—to some degree—back in the original group—because the set of disagreements, differences, is not extreme enough to threaten the coherence of the "We," and thus, by extension, does not threaten the sovereign power whose function it is to manage the "We." Moreover, I think this is the response to a different question—not of the "who," but of the "what" we are.

I think the correct—the only—response to this question has been offered by Carl Schmitt in his discussion of the political. The political, as Mouffe as pointed out, is nothing other than power—contra the facade of the liberal state—that power exists and that it is power that is primarily responsible for how the question of "who We are," is to be answered.[58] But the capacity to identify the enemy presupposes the confidence to ask the question of the "We," and the authority, and legitimacy of being able to answer the question preemptively and to enforce the answer. And so, it's not merely any population—ethnic, sexual, racial group—that can ask and answer. Rather, this power of the political emerges from *law*— law as the expression of sovereign authority, and hence, as holding the power of enforcement. As Walter Benjamin suggests in his discussion of lawmaking,[59] the sheer capacity to instantiate such distinctions gains its power of enforcement through the potential violence in which it is inherent. This is an excellent description of how certain legal categories function technologically: when concepts such as citizen, person, human being are read in certain selective ways and are enforced selectively, that is, to demarcate distinctions between populations, they serve to criminalize—or at least to scapegoat or caste-out the populations who are excluded from the category. And so while violence per se is not immediately manifested through such categories, by implication, the enforcement of these categories—as seen through the privation of legal protections or rights—serves to remind populations on which side of the law one needs to be—and by extension, which side of "rationality" one needs to take up and internalize.

As such, this reminder and its uptake instantiates the sovereign authority of that population that does ask the question. By extension, "Who are We" implies an identity, or at the very least, the presumption that there is a set of common threads that link a group of individuals together. And so, the question of "who we are" implies a certain cultural fabric. But does this act of collective self-identification necessarily imply the criminality, or at the least, the antagonism, the exclusion, of those who are not part of the "We"? The issue here is whether the existence of the enemy is intrinsic to the recognition of the "We," or if it emerges, as Rene Girard argues, only during times of crisis. Girard's general point is that moments of emergency eradicate all differences between different populations—which by extension eliminates all identities as well. Therefore, in order to reestablish certain hierarchies and norms, a scapegoat needs to be found as a "guilty" party so that the "innocent" can be reinstituted, renormalized.[60] Such scapegoats can be found throughout history, even when there are no overwhelming crises to capture a national imagination: slaves, the poor, immigrants, women, the insane have all played this role. This might suggest then, that an excluded other is necessary to the very constitution of the "We," rather than one that emerges in response to certain conspicuous political moments.

4

The Newest Unruly Threat

Muslim Men and Women

"[A]lthough we may . . . sometimes persecute people because they are foreign, the deeper truth is that we almost always make foreign those whom we persecute."[1]

Introduction

In chapters 1 and 2, I argued that the concept of race can be deployed as a technological device by which to distinguish and divide populations for certain societal purposes, such as political coherence and social unity. In this chapter, I present a concrete example of the racializing and outcasting of a population that had neither been a coherent group nor a race prior to becoming the focus of the state. This example will build on the first dimension of race as a technology: the singling out and taming of "unruly" features, which deem a population to be threatening and in need of discipline/taming. In chapter 5, I will continue to develop the example I begin here, by exploring some of the specifics behind the second and third dimensions of the technology of race, that is, how such taming happens through "procedural" or "official" avenues, and the role of sovereign power in racializing a new group.

I have given a preliminary explanation of how I understand "liberalism" in the "Introduction"; however, in light of chapter 3, it might be useful to revisit my deployment of that and related terms, such as "Western" or "secular" liberalism. In this chapter and elsewhere, I employ "liberalism" in the following manner: it refers to that dominant political-cultural worldview that has encompassed nations and cultures as wide-ranging in priorities and values as France, Denmark, Holland, Germany,

England, the United States, Italy, Sweden, Turkey, Canada,[2] and others. In the context of the argument that follows, these "North Atlantic" countries have in common a national/collective self-understanding that pledges a commitment to procedure, rule of law, and the tolerance of a range of populations that hold distinctly different cultural/ethnic/linguistic/religious values, that is, a commitment to pluralism. This pluralism is rooted in a specific interpretation of the public-private distinction. Plural values are tolerated in the private realm, but the private realm is delimited by those norms that are valorized in the public realm. My contention here is not only that this pluralism is more limited than most North Atlantic cultures will acknowledge.[3] In addition, these societies have directly excluded Muslims and "Muslim culture" on the grounds that they are "unreasonable" and a danger to the harmony of "liberal culture." This exclusion stems back decades before 9-11, possibly further. We see it in the range of policies cataloged above—from the prohibition of the hijab, the integration of religion and politics, the coerced (and stylized) assimilation of Muslim immigrants to "be Western/modern," that is, to be "not Muslim," or at least not recognizably so.

And so, symbols of the Muslim faith, but also other "Muslim" practices such as certain kinds of religious/political speech or beliefs, disproportionately attract the hostile attention of the state because of their "unruly" character. Let me revisit also what I mean by the "unruly." An "unruly" symbol is one that appears to present a threat within the specific political or cultural context in which it appears. Its presence is perceived as a challenge to certain prevailing norms. While this symbol may itself appear as mildly or hardly transgressive, its existence in fact indicates a larger (perceived) danger. That danger is in fact the perceived transgression of a prevailing juridical/political order.[4] An "unruly" symbol might be tangible, and thus intuited, such as a physical comportment, phenotype, accent, skin color, or one's name. Or it might be something intangible, such as the memory of a crime committed long ago, or a moment of exploitation, a hidden history of miscegenation (all in reference to a population perceived as "dangerous").[5]

The Racializing and Outcasting of Muslims[6] in the United States

In December 2002 hundreds of mostly male Muslim immigrants in the United States—under the aegis of the newly created category of "potential" terrorist—were rounded up, questioned, and detained for the purposes of "intercepting and obstructing terrorism." This agenda was carried out without extending the benefit of Constitutional protections routinely offered to non-Muslim American citizens (and often indulgently granted to noncitizens during times of relative peace and security) such as writs of *habeas corpus*, and various Fourteenth Amendment rights such as the right to an attorney, due process, and equal protection of law.[7] The aegis for this action came from the USA PATRIOT Act, an acronym for a bill whose formal name is "Uniting and Strengthening America by Providing Appropriate Tools Required to Intercept and Obstruct Terrorism."[8] As is well-known today, this is a several hundred page document that takes as its premise that terrorism can be duly understood and eradicated through preventive and preemptive measures. The PATRIOT Act authorized a striking increase in the scope of police powers afforded to the Attorney General's office, the recently created Department of Homeland Security [DHS] (the new overseer of the Bureau of Citizenship and Immigration Services [BCIS]).[9] Until 2003 the forced registration and detention of Muslim men was covered sparingly in the national media, but it has withstood several judicial challenges.[10]

Since then, Muslim men—and women—have been subjected to remarkably cruel treatment in the name of stopping or preventing terrorist activity.[11] Which transgressions have engendered such treatment? Liberals and conservatives alike have argued that the Bush Administration's "war on terror" is a legitimate war, with its objective the elimination and prevention of threats to the (physical) safety of American citizens.[12] They suggest that preemptive policing strategies must take precedence in a world threatened by terrorists. The goal of preventing terrorism is important and defensible; however, their views do not account for the hostile attention that has been visited upon Muslims in a range of arenas unrelated to terrorism, and spanning back decades before the "war on terrorism" began.[13] Preemptive strategies fail to account for the abrogation of protections thought to be afforded all persons under a human rights framework, such as writs of habeas corpus, a right to judicial review, nor what is implicit, and the most important freedom: the right to be considered innocent until proven guilty. Racial profiling, targeting, and harassment since September 11 has not been successful,[14] nor are these new strategies in the treatment of Muslims.

I think a more compelling case can be made that Muslims or Arabs or Middle-Easterners have become the focus of the state's attention as an undependable, unpredictable, unruly, population whose existence poses a threat—not to society at large, as the Bush Presidential Administration has insisted in defense of its extreme treatment of Muslim men[15]—but to the secure existence of the current juridico-political regime. As I described in chapter 3, a similar anti-Muslim hostility can be traced to a worldview best exemplified in the proliferation of books and articles that locate the threat of terrorism in the content of Islam. Samuel Huntington's writings, for example, caution against the hegemony of anti-secular, anti-liberal ideals in the political foundation of Islamic states; John Rawls's final book employs the casual use and acceptance of examples of "illiberal" and "unreasonable" peoples as being Muslim. Others locate the threat of terror in the "culture of Islam."[16] Feminist and nonfeminists alike have criticized a monolithic Islam as the source of Muslim women's oppression.[17]

As I began to argue in chapter 3, Western society's more urgent concern is the danger of radical cultural heterogeneity or the *threat to a fundamental cultural homogeneity.* The treatment to which Muslims have been subjected manifests a *fundamental hostility that sovereign institutions*[18] *direct toward individuals whose comportment seems to threaten the fundamental political-cultural order on which the state is based.* This hostility is a response to "unruly" signs or practices that conspicuously challenge or violate a dominant "neutral" cultural or political norm, such as public secularism. On another level, these signs serve as proxies for other more elusive threats to an onto-political[19] regime, in this case, liberalism. An "unruly" sign might appear as mildly or barely transgressive, while it actually displaces the larger threat.[20] The larger threat is the violation of the metaphysical underpinnings of any juridico-political regime.[21]

There are several traits that have been ascribed to Muslims since 9-11—traits that, when combined, represent a powerful indictment of Muslims as an "unruly" threat to the "Western" world, most notably in this context, the United States, but also to much of Western Europe. These traits take on a singular potency when understood as part of an effort to create a new outcaste population. Through these traits, Muslims have begun to be depicted as a new race—an evil and less rational race. In turn, this transformation has been parlayed into their depiction as a new pariah group, and has legitimated the withholding from them, as a group, the "universal" protection of human rights and Constitutional law.

Most of the following criteria apply to any "newly" noticed population in any society. In the United States, the histories of Chinese, Japanese, Mexican, Filipino, Puerto Rican, and other immigrants follow similar patterns of being received as outsiders and racialized eventually, if not immediately, through a range of similar criteria.[22] We find similar examples outside of the United States as well.[23]

Perhaps the most important criterion regarding "Muslims" or "Arabs" is their status as immigrants, along with their "strange" habits or appearances. Their identification as immigrants facilitates the indictment of Muslims as outsiders, and as another race altogether. There are several aspects to a group's status as immigrants: one is the association of immigrants with outsiders or the "not quite one of us," through physical markers—skin color, outward garb, etc., and cultural differences.[24] In the case of Muslims, they are generally neither legally nor "culturally" Americans already, and instead perceived as holding onto a distinct ethnic, national, or regional description: Arabs, Yemeni, Middle Eastern, etc. Second, they appear visibly different—for reasons of skin color, facial aesthetics, dress.[25] Their practices are culturally different, they speak another language, eat different foods, engage in distinct cultural practices (holidays, prayer, mosques), etc., and thus threaten the general nebulous quality of "American culture," with such "conspicuous" and distinct practices. Third, a group's economic status, combined often with educated or skilled backgrounds, and perhaps an intragroup willingness to combine economic resources, can render it a threat not only to unskilled labor, but also to more privileged groups in the domestic labor force. We see examples of this across different industries and regions.[26]

Finally, following patterns similar to those of other immigrant groups,[27] Muslims have become delineated and outlined through an obsessive focus on Muslims as the targets of the War on Terror by local, national, and international media. The media are both following the lead of the equally obsessed United States government on the identification of terror investigations and "potential" terror suspects with men and women of Muslim background. The media and various prominent cultural and religious leaders have not only followed the lead of the state, but contributed to the amplification of the fearful identification between Muslims and terrorism.

The singularity of the perceived threat of Islam and Muslims can be heard from numerous sources. A myriad of newspapers and magazines, including *Newsweek* and the *Atlantic Monthly*, asked the question of what about Islam led to 9-11, suggesting that the seeds of destruction were embedded in Islam as a political ideology.[28] These depictions of Islam do not distinguish between the interpretation of religious principles and a political agenda; they were compounded in the early stages of post–9-11 counterterrorism discourse by statements from at least two well-known Christian leaders, Jerry Falwell and Franklin Graham, which openly equate Islam with evil and destruction. It is the labeling of Islam as a destructive religious ideology and its corresponding identification with Muslims as being imbued with a "terrorist" psychology that is perhaps the easiest to locate, since it emerges from various comments by well-known religious leaders as well as generally in the policies enacted and enforced by the Bush Administration. Here are some quotes from several of these religious leaders and public officials:

- Rev. Jerry Falwell: "The Prophet Muhammad is a terrorist."[29]
- Southern Baptist Pastor Jerry Vines stated that Muhammad was a "demon-possessed pedophile" and that Islam teaches the destruction of all non-Muslims.
- Rev. Franklin Graham, son of Rev. Billy Graham, called Islam "a very evil and wicked religion."
- Pat Robertson, on Muhammad, "This man was an absolute wild-eyed fanatic. He was a robber and a brigand. And to say that these terrorists distort Islam, they're carrying out Islam. I mean, this man was a killer. And to think that this is a peaceful religion is fraudulent."[30]
- Lt. General William "Jerry" Boykin, U.S. Armed Forces: "We are a Christian Nation leading a war against Satan."[31]

When these quotations, all articulated after September 11, 2001, are considered collectively, then the equation of Islam or Muhammad with evil religious ideology conspicuously becomes the justification for the War on Terror, with all of its derivative policies and targets. Thus, it is unsurprising that public and social discourse across North Atlantic societies followed the lead of U.S. government officials and religious leaders. It is no coincidence that the 2005 bombings in London evoked a similar response from Prime Minister Tony Blair. Even as leads to the culprits were first being searched, and not yet sufficiently demonstrated, Blair urged British Muslims to "confront the 'perverted and poisonous' doctrines of Islamic extremism in their midst, if necessary by excluding or deporting the religious extremists who foment it."[32]

The state's identification of all Muslims as terrorists was best illustrated through the aforementioned PATRIOT Act. Under the authority of then Attorney General John Ashcroft, thousands of Muslim men—unless they had been naturalized—were required to register with the INS beginning December 2002, on the suspicion of having knowledge of or being associated with terrorists by reason of their religion. The categories of "enemy aliens," "enemy combatants," and "suspected terrorist" have become commonplace in the days since 9-11. Since October 28, 2002, the last category had been used to detain 2,000 people. The term "enemy aliens" had been used to hold 598 Taliban and Al-Qaeda detainees at Guantánamo Bay U.S. Naval Station. None of these detainees were prisoners of war.[33] The term "enemy combatant" was used to indict and convict several American citizens, including John Walker Lindh[34] and José Padilla. The same term, "enemy combatant" was to be used to detain José Padilla "until the end of the hostilities," according to a District Court judge, although the judge overturned Attorney General Ashcroft's decision to deprive him of the right to meet his attorney or review the evidence against him.[35] Yasser Hamdi, an American citizen, was subjected to the same treatment on the same grounds. The claim that the Bush Administration has been treating most Muslim men as if they are, de facto, terrorists was substantiated not only through the reawakening or invention of categories of "enemy aliens" and "enemy combatants," but myriad other events. These include the night raids on Muslims in graduate student housing at the University of Idaho;[36] the mass round-up of Muslims in Lackawanna, NY;[37] the mandatory registration of all Muslim immigrants in the U.S. through the passage of the National Security Entry/Exit Registration System (NSEERS);[38] the mandatory updating of all entries by U.S. universities in the Student and Exchange Visitor Information System database[39]; the courtmartial of John Yee, a Muslim Chaplain in the American Army for espionage[40]; and the stripping by the U.S. Federal District Court of the authority of the federal judiciary to hear challenges from prisoners in Guantánamo Bay.[41] Needless to say, Ashcroft's successor, Alberto Gonzalez, hailed as the "architect" of the bastion of extra-Constitutional law, Guantánamo Bay, and the chief defender of the use of torture and "extraordinary rendition" (the outsourcing of torture) to extract "confessions" from Muslim men—from the U.S., Iraq, and throughout Europe[42]—has only compounded the association of terrorism and anti-Muslim sentiment. These events have been augmented by a proliferation of the Federal Bureau of Investigation's interactions with Muslim religious communities throughout the United States, in which numerous Muslim worshippers and imams have been solicited for information, often under threat of deportation or having needed immigration papers withheld.[43] There is a direct cause for this identification; in May 2002, the U.S. Attorney General's office received permission to relax the strict guidelines on domestic spying that were once imposed by the FBI upon itself.[44] This explicit authority awards the FBI vast expansive powers to monitor and investigate political rallies, the Internet, religious services in order to catch "potential" terrorists and prevent "potential" terrorist attacks. This authority is technically indiscriminate; however, a perusal of media articles reveals that this authority appears to be predisposed to spy on Muslim social, religious, and political centers.[45]

But December 2002 was not the first time that Muslims became the targets of the state's enmity. Muslims had been the target of hostility in multiple arenas in the North Atlantic for decades before September 11. As Rashid Khalidi and others have demonstrated, European and American policy toward the Middle Eastern world in the twentieth century has been dominated by the agendas of imperialism, oil, and the Cold War.[46] These policies were almost always to the detriment of residents, Muslim or Christian. On social fronts well before 9-11, examples of anti-Muslim focus abounded: France and Germany have experienced long-standing tensions between its "native" inhabitants and its Muslim residents, surfacing in ethnic clashes and government policies insisting on assimilation of its Muslim population, at least through outward symbols.[47] France has prohibited the hijab in public institutions since 1994; in 2004, the policy was extended to prohibit the public expression of religions across the spectrum. However, while French officials have habitually refused to allow schoolgirls or teachers to wear the hijab in its public institutions, they have notoriously been surprised by challenges to the "secular" law from unanticipated groups, such as from the nation's tiny Sikh minority, which took affront at the idea of removing turbans in public.[48] Recently, Catholic chaplains were barred from wearing their cassocks in French schools as part of another effort to apply the legal ban on religious symbols to all faiths.[49] In Italy, a ban on wearing the hijab for the national identity card recently led officials to strive for consistency by refusing a national identity card to a Catholic nun unless she took off her habit for a photograph.[50] A similar theme has surfaced in Germany, which prohibits Muslim women from wearing the hijab in public schools, but until recently, allowed Catholic nuns to wear their habits when they stepped into the classroom.[51] The clear surprise of French, German, and Italian officials in these encounters affirms that the "secularist" laws were aimed at Muslims.[52]

After September 11, 2001, anti-Muslim sentiment rippled throughout Europe in the form of restrictive immigration and citizenship laws. In evidence in Germany for decades, such laws have now become commonplace in England, Denmark, and the Netherlands. More recently, England explicitly repealed its long-standing policy of multicultural tolerance on the grounds that not all cultures can be equally tolerated;[53] it has also increased free speech restrictions against mullahs who are thought to "promote jihad." It has also promoted a United States–like erosion of privacy laws for the ostensible purpose of preventing terrorism. Recently, Holland's public anger against (mostly Muslim) immigrants was expressed vividly in the near-repeal of the citizenship of a prominent Dutch-Somali politician and "ex-Muslim," Ayaan Hirsi Ali.[54]

A number of North Atlantic nations have either passed legislation or endorsed "codes of conduct" that discourage "practices" associated with "Islam." Over the last twelve months, several villages in Canada—a traditional bastion of liberal tolerance—have passed a "Code of Conduct" in which they "recommend" behaviors such as refraining from stoning women, covering their faces (except during Halloween), burning women with acid, circumcising them.[55] Similarly, Italy's government has passed a "Charter of Values" in April 2007, which specifically asks Muslim (men?)

to refrain from polygamy and women from covering their faces in public.[56] It is interesting that in neither of these "religion- and culture-blind" policies is there any mention of refraining from domestic violence "North Atlantic"–style, that is, through the use of alcohol and fists, or guns.[57] Culturally, the population at large took its lead from a state-led fear of Muslims as seen in the attacks on men and women of various backgrounds, because their headgarb and long beards reinforced a public fear of "terrorists" who dress similarly.[58]

As the above examples show, such anti-Muslim sentiment manifests itself in three primary forms: (1) immigration; (2) codes of conduct; and (3) political and cultural representation. They also point to the effect of the War on Terror on the prevailing social and cultural climate in North Atlantic societies, which enables by a now ubiquitous association between Islam, evil, terror, irrationality. In short, Islam is not only incomprehensible, but the language of evil and terror clearly evoke the vocabulary of madness and insanity, while at the same time rendering Arabs, Muslim or otherwise, into a coherent population of people to be afraid of persons who are not only different from "us," in the Western, global cosmopolitan, liberal, capitalist world, but ultimately unlike us in a fundamental, ontological way. This population, by being grouped together and distinguished by a label that is at best only remotely true and at worst, suspect in a range of ways (Muslim), is "racialized," without ever explicitly named as such.

Culture, Heterogeneity, and the Foreigner: Unruly Women

It is no surprise, then, that perceptions have shifted considerably such that Muslim women and children are also increasingly under suspicion as potential terrorists, and similarly persecuted. One example occurred in March 2005, when the FBI detained two female Muslim teenagers from Queens, NY, on suspicion of being potential "suicide bombers." Initially detained for different reasons, the girls encountered each other for the first time while being separately escorted to immigration facilities in Manhattan. FBI agents were alerted to Tashnuba Hayder five months earlier when her parents, Muslim immigrants from Bangladesh, reported that she had run away. Fearing that Tashnuba would elope with a stranger in Michigan, her parents trusted the local police to find her. They canceled their request after she returned home voluntarily. Five months later, FBI agents searched Tashnuba's room and computer.[59]

After an initial interrogation, and on the false pretext of an immigration violation—her mother's—they detained her at the United States Citizenship and Immigration Services (USCIS) offices in Manhattan. The FBI was concerned by Tashnuba's religious fervor, apparent in her propensity to listen to sermons by fundamentalist imams over the Internet, her chatroom comments about those sermons, class notes from a discussion on the religious ethics of suicide, and perhaps most symbolically, her decision to observe full purdah, or what has been commonly described as "full Islamic veil." Their suspicions increased when Tashnuba and her government escorts encountered Adamah Bah in front of the USCIS building at 26 Federal Plaza. Adamah, who wears the hijab, was originally detained because she missed a USCIS appointment in order to go on a high school field trip to see Christos' "Gates" exhibit in Central Park. During their encounter, Tashnuba Hayder and Adamah Bah reportedly acknowledged each other with an unspecified "traditional Muslim greeting," most likely "salaam aleikum."[60] That greeting, combined with their orthodox dress, were the basis of the FBI's concern that the teenagers might be collaborators as "potential" suicide bombers in a terrorist conspiracy.[61] Both teens were sent to a detainment facility in Pennsylvania without access to lawyers or parents, where they were subjected to constant interrogation for seven weeks.

Hayder and Bah joined thousands of Muslims in being the targets of suspicion, harassment, and persecution. These women, like their male Muslim counterparts, were met with hostility, suspicion, and extreme harassment because they transgressed a prevailing cultural and political regime that might be best described as "Western" secular liberalism.[62] But their "crimes" are not the ones for which they were detained or arrested. Rather, their common infraction was their conspicuously heterogeneous comportment—openly subscribing to a particular mode of being designated as "Muslim" or "Islamic" culture. This breach can be seen in explicit practices that are thought to contravene the fundamental ethos of liberal culture, namely that of political secularism.

To return to a theme from chapter 3, cultural difference is an ages-old category that has been used to justify colonial exploits and imperial conquests, as well as advocating for policies of "multicultural tolerance."[63] The irony of the concept of cultural difference is that it almost always presupposes that the culture from which one speaks is the baseline by which all others are to be compared. It is probably not surprising then, that all other cultures are viewed not in terms of how, but whether, they measure up to "ours." Americans never ask, for example, whether there is a "little bit" or "a lot" of religion in the public sphere, but whether there is or there isn't religion in the public sphere.

Heterogeneity, then, is a comparison not of quantitative, but qualitative difference, and unsurprisingly, differences that are perceived to be qualitative are much more threatening than those of degree. In this context, we can see that the threat of the foreigner or of heterogeneity is not a natural one, but it is one that becomes endemic in the ideology of a shared cultural or political ontology,[64] which appears to be the prevailing framework by which culture and differences are discussed in the current world. The "difference" of a culture is hypostatized into "strangeness" or foreignness synechdochically, that is, through some practice(s) that have caught our attention, regardless of whether they are widespread. These practices become the stand-in for the *strange* or *foreignness* of the "entire" culture. The focus on the practice, in combination with what it is thought to (mis)represent and other practices with which it is (mis)associated, raises its status to the level of extreme threat. As I discuss in chapter 3, the *Oxford English Dictionary* lists multiple definitions for the term "strange." Among them are the usual definitions of the character of someone who is from a place "other than one's own," or whose customs are foreign or alien. But there is one that is especially telling: it pertains to people who are considered strange. Such people engage in practices that are not only unfamiliar, but they themselves are understood as "cold," "distant," not affable or encouraging, aloof, "unfriendly." Moreover, the action ascribed to a strange person is that he (or she) is uncomplying or willing to accede to a request or desire.[65]

The shift in judgment from alien to uncompliant is an apt transition by which to understand a "strange" cultural practice such as the hijab as an "unruly" practice. The purdah and the hijab are among those conspicuous practices that appear as an affront to a rational, reasonable, Western liberal American culture. Scholars such as Lila Abu-Lughod and Saba Mahmood, whose research is on the hijab, point out that public discussions about the hijab or the burqa are nearly always discussed in terms of "liberating" or "saving" Muslim women, whether from Muslim men or oppressive rule generally.[66] As Gayatri Spivak points out unsentimentally "White men are saving brown women from brown men."[67] The perspective to which Mahmood, Abu-Lughod, and Spivak refer indicates a condescending disapprobation of the practice of the hijab and women who engage in it, which is akin to the an ages-old colonialist view of "natives" as backward children who must be educated and shown the "path to right reason."[68] I think this view is still highly prevalent; however, there is also another facet involved in the aversion to the hijab. This view still holds that this practice is irrational; however, it emerges from a fear of the "culturally" strange or different—read as uncompliance, a deliberate uncooperativeness, and defiance in the face of right reason. Purdah and the hijab are among those conspicuous practices that appear as an affront to a rational, reasonable, liberal American culture.[69] In the language of liberal political thought then, those who emerge from cultures that are "radically heterogeneous" are the irrational, and part of the "unruly" that threatens the state.

In what follows, the most frequent symbol that I will explore concerns the hijab or some aspect of purdah,[70] although offensive practices can also include growing long beards for men; reading the Qu'ran; listening to sermons by fundamentalist imams; open religious worship; association with other openly devout Muslims; and political speech that expresses dissent by reference to Islamic tenets. The hijab, or purdah, are signifiers of the unruly; more precisely, taken in conjunction with other symbolic gestures or practices like those listed above, they become proxies for a fundamental challenge to secular-liberal culture. As such, the hijab becomes the focus of suspicion, fear, and regulation. The "unruly" symbol becomes the "lightning rod" that must be grounded.

In conjunction with other gestures of Muslim devotion, the hijab or purdah indicate a threat to a larger regime. There are also other, more violent acts—hijackings, bombings, mass murder, insurgencies—which, especially in a post–9-11 political discourse, have come to be understood as gestures of Islamic piety. While the latter set of practices should be treated on their own terms, they are often lumped together with the former set of gestures that represent Muslim piety. Similarly, all adherents of Islam, violent or nonviolent, secular or pious, are indiscriminately associated as "threatening" and dangerous. These conflations form the basis of their public representation as a threat or a potential insurgence to a dominant discourse or regime. In turn, this threat prompts a political or sovereign response that will manage, suppress, or force out the potential threat so that it does not upset or overturn the existing regime. This taming appears "natural" or "logical" so as to conserve the prevailing order.[71]

In this way, the hijab has become the focus of suspicion, fear, and regulation; it comes to represent the threat that must be managed, tamed, or ousted from the polity. The hijab, and its more extensive counterpart, the niqab or full purdah, have long been considered strange and confusing practices in the non-Muslim world. It was the focus of nineteenth-century art representing the exotic East, as well as the subject of both polemical and relativist commentaries. It is fair to say that in the non-Muslim world, the hijab is a poorly deciphered practice. Consequently, it becomes a placeholder for the fears, concerns, and moral condemnations that we—those in the non-Muslim world—hold for other seemingly undecipherable beliefs and acts ascribed to Islam and Muslims, ranging indiscriminately from the intimate integration of religion with political life to suicide bombings to jihad to terrorism. And so, as the practice of the hijab is filled with myth and meaning by a Western cultural discourse, its heterogeneity transgresses the shared ontology of liberalism.

I now want to explore some aspects by which the veil is rendered "unruly" in relation to the liberal political framework. Consider a recent incident, in which the hijab and niqab have been the topic of a controversy in England. Jack Straw, Labor Party politician and Leader of the House of Commons, expressed a preference for Muslim women who veil to remove the hijab in his office so that he might be able to read their expressions and thus, to enhance communication. Straw's position reveals several interesting messages about liberalism: The first message is that mere verbal exchanges are inadequate for proper public communication. This point betrays a fundamental premise of liberalism, namely that words—spoken or written—are the sole currency of this political framework. Law, communication, contracts, commitments are all thought to take place (officially) through the medium of verbal or written language, and not facial gestures, bodily comportment, intonations, pitch, or other features of discourse, which relay nonverbal messages that accompany and augment the verbal message, and allow the listener to make more informed judgments about the meaning of another's words.[72] Second, this point is more revealing of the cultural divide between two parties, that such "modes of cheating" become necessary to understand the message being imparted by one's interlocutor. When two parties are from the same background or share a history, then the exchange of words carries much more that is hidden behind them: an implicit understanding of norms, procedures, protocol. By extension, then, the idea that words can carry our messages fully points to a second tacit premise of liberalism— namely that liberalism is fundamentally meant to accommodate those who emerge from similar or identical cultural contexts, such that words become not a way to articulate *fundamental* difference, *but a shorthand by which to communicate variations of those ideas, norms, and procedures that are mostly shared.*

Another message is that the veil transgresses a fundamental value of political liberalism: transparency or publicity. In hiding the body and the visage of its wearer, the veil becomes troublingly conspicuous, since one appears to be guilty or have something to hide.[73] In the cultural and psychological contexts of secular public comportment, one cloaks or masks for a range of reasons, but very few of them have positive connotations. By extension, couture (*sic*) in the liberal world shares this norm: generally, less is more. Subscribing to this rule of dress suggests evidence of a shared culture—if not a shared rationality. The hijab and niqab bypass this assumption altogether, aesthetically but also politically. Concealment in dress tends to be taken as a sign of an excessive modesty, climatalogical necessity, or external duress from illegitimate sources. And so, it would seem that Straw's preference for the removal of the veil is indicative of a more general preference within liberalism for the elimination of fundamental differences. His supposed problem with the veil is rather a discomfort, I would suggest, with dealing with persons who appear to be fundamentally unlike him, and thus, the request for unconcealment or transparency.

In contrast, the proper mode of liberal comportment is supposedly that of openness or transparency.[74] The success of liberalism depends on the public communication or the public promulgation of law. Publicity represents the proper comportment of a nation-state; it also infuses the character of liberal citizenship. The ideal of publicity reflects the mutual trust that one's own or another's intentions will be ascertainable and comprehensible—whether through a public communication or a shared culture. John Rawls offers a remarkable passage about public communication, which might help to shed light on the veil's seeming affront to liberalism. By publicly declaring one's comprehensive doctrine,[75] one communicates to others who are different that one still shares a political culture with them. As he says, "The aim of doing this is to declare to others who affirm *different comprehensive doctrines* that we also each endorse a reasonable political conception belonging to the family of reasonable such conceptions . . . In this way citizens who hold different doctrines are reassured, and this strengthens the ties of civil friendship" (my emphasis).[76] Rawls articulates an important condition of successful public communication: it implies a shared understanding of the parameters and distinctions between public and private values. It is only on this ground that a mutual understanding—and a mutual trust—is possible. Even the most famous "veil" in Rawls's writing is predicated on this ground. The "veil of ignorance" is a hypothetical measure, conspicuous in its deliberate attempt to prevent us from knowing the particular details of the situations of our fellow citizens and ourselves in order to help us arrive at a set of "enlightened" ideals.[77] But the success of the veil of ignorance depends on *already having a shared culture of reason*. If I am to trust that you will treat me equally and reciprocally, then I must trust that you are rational like me, reasonable like me (both of which presume some overlap between our respective worldviews and understandings), and are willing to communicate with me in order to arrive at a transparent set of goals.

The hijab, perceived as an expression of religious faith, departs from another central tenet of liberal culture: the distinction between public and private values.[78] Liberal public comportment requires one's comprehensive doctrines to remain private or to be encapsulated and expressed at certain times and certain places. The hijab remains troublingly conspicuous in this context, since its appearance signifies an expression of Islam. And so, *as a public ascription to Islam, the veil becomes an antagonistic symbol of this incompatibility.* Like many other cultural practices, the practice of hijab metonymically represents all of an "outside" world's impressions—the most predominant or the most negative[79]—of a particular culture.[80] For many decades, but especially over the last two, the hijab has stood in for the worst, nonrepresentative, but most notorious practices of all of "Muslim culture," ranging from polygamy, sexual slavery, terrorism, suicide bombings, the systematic oppression of women, political repression, female genital mutilation, and perhaps the worst of all—the stark refusal to accept certain quintessential principles of Western liberalism.

I want to suggest one more way in which these synechdochic impressions of the hijab are highlighted in an even more negative light. This occurs when the worst of the unfamiliar culture is juxtaposed against the ideal version of (our) familiar one. In this comparison, the latter culture is most often seen in a positive light. Thus, the above catalog—pertaining to the schematic, negative impressions of "Muslim" culture—is often compared to the "best" of liberalism, in its egalitarian, nonpatriarchal, "freedom-embracing," peace- and order-loving, cooperative, and individualistic version. Unfortunately, this comparison, inaccurate though it may be, is not infrequent. Such a comparison is implied, or often stated outright, in statements by military officials, political figures, and scholars alike.

And so the veil is antagonistic, and it raises the question of rationality on a general cultural level. Furthermore, if veiling symbolizes a religious-cultural regime that is understood as inherently incompatible because of its inability to separate religion from politics, *then it also confounds some of the basic beliefs of liberal feminism.* We saw two examples of these comparisons in the analysis of Islam by Huntington and Rawls. However, they are joined by feminist scholars ranging from Daly to Susan M. Okin. Here are three excerpts of Okin's position on purdah, as published in her 1997 essay, "Is Multiculturalism Bad for Women?"

> [M]any culturally-based customs aim to control women and render them, especially sexually and reproductively, servile to men's desires and interests. Sometimes, moreover, "culture" or "traditions" are so closely linked with the control of women that they are virtually equated . . . Thus the servitude of women is presented as virtually synonymous with 'our traditions.'[81]

> Moreover, it is by no means confined to Western or monotheistic cultures. . . . Many such practices make it virtually impossible for

women to choose to live independently of men, to be celibate or lesbian, or not to have children.[82]

Those who practice some of the most controversial such customs—clitoridectomy, the marriage of children or marriages that are otherwise coerced, or polygamy—sometimes explicitly defend them as necessary for controlling women, and openly acknowledge that the customs persist at men's insistence.[83]

Okin claims that Western and non-Western cultures alike are guilty of oppressing women; yet her examples are restricted to "non-Western" practices. According to her, they occur more consistently than potentially oppressive "Western" practices, and indeed are far worse than anything that women in the West suffer. Indeed, she argues that women in the West are guaranteed many more of the liberal freedoms that men have, are not explicitly devalued as women, and are not restricted in life's ambitions to the domestic sphere. She points to oppressive practices among Muslim families in France, the inhabitants of Mali, and Orthodox Jews in the mountains of Yemen; in some cases she points to the analogous oppressiveness of the hijab and polygamy or clitoridectomy. Of course, one wonders whether she has taken into account class differences among women, which require working-class and poor women in all cultures, West and non-West, to find work outside the home. One also wonders what the supposed substance of liberal freedom is to which women in the West are privy.

The problem here is the gap between the ideal and the practice. Many comparative analyses tend to juxtapose ideal liberalism with actual practices that have occurred and that some in the West oppose. The juxtaposition tends to be incongruent. That is, rarely do scholars offer a comparison between liberal-Christian ideals with Islamic ideals in their myriad varieties or between the oppression of women in the North Atlantic with the oppression of women in specifically Muslim contexts. Thus, for those scholars, it raises the question of whether women who veil—who subscribe to this religion—are themselves rational and/or reasonable. It also raises the question of agency: 'Can these women "possibly" be doing this of their own accord? Surely, they must be subject to external constraints or pressures.'

Viewed from the perspective of what have traditionally been liberal feminist struggles, one conceals as a response to coercion from a patriarchal authority or in submission to attempts to control one's sexuality. Since in the West, feminists fought these battles decades ago in the context of bloomers, corsets, and periodic sexual revolutions, such submission is understood as having been imposed by an external authority, or as the consequence of an acquired false consciousness. There are numerous feminist commentaries that judge the hijab and niqab as equivalent to practices that systematically control women's sexuality and/or violate human rights, such as "rape, forced prostitution, polygamy, genital mutilation, the beating of girls and women . . ."[84] As Chandra Talpade Mohanty points out, such a description makes an unwarranted leap from the practice of veiling to the automatic assumption of its oppressiveness. In such an overgeneralization, "[I]nstitutions of purdah are . . . denied any cultural and historical specificity, and contradictions and potentially subversive aspects are totally ruled out."[85]

The problematic character of the veil, as we saw in Susan Okin's quotations above, lies in the assumption that women would not wear the veil unless they were being coerced, under false consciousness, or reacting to other oppressive circumstances.[86] From the vantage point of the French state or liberal feminists, the concern is that women who veil are prevented, indeed preempted, from the possibility of realizing their true, authentic, and ideal selves.[87] Yet, as numerous scholars have illustrated, there are more and more examples of women who undertake the veil in order to signify their political resistance to Western imperialism, or to signify their decision to illustrate their piety publicly—in defiance of the wishes of their spouses or larger family, or as one among many options that they have chosen as they navigate their life circumstances as women outside the non-West do generally.[88] The troubling element of this picture is not the veil or Muslim women who wear the hijab, but how the veil, along with the notion of agency, is constituted by the Western liberal framework.[89]

The practice of veiling—as popularly understood—challenges the concept of autonomy that is predicated on the twin notions of "negative" and "positive" freedom that undergird Western liberalism.[90] In this model, freedom—understood as the absence of constraints, or the positive realization of one's self, respectively—relies on a concept of autonomy that is predicated on a fully formed, self-subsistent subject. And so, over the last thirty years, Western feminists question why women would veil. As seen from this perspective, the practices of purdah and the hijab seem antithetical to the ideal of freedom and autonomy: because we understand it to be worn from a religious imperative, because it appears as a shroud that hides women from the eyes of men, because we believe that it reinforces sexist, misogynist, patriarchal relationships between women and men, because it reconstitutes an oppressive sexuality for women.

Seen only through the telescopic lens of an unchanging liberal perspective grounded on the constancy of a fully formed subject, the messages of veiling are unreadable, except in certain—usually unflattering—ways.[91]

But another look at the practice of veiling, as several anthropologists have presented, reveals a manifold of signals and messages. For each woman who veils, her reasons extend beyond something as simple as a voluntary choice, or an expression of piety, or a stance of resistance. If we were to understand veiling as a part of a set of customs and decisions that are negotiated in relation to one's ever-dynamic circumstances, then we would see the hijab in a markedly different light. A perusal of the literature on the hijab suggests a range of contexts that are more nuanced and textured, suggesting a kind of autonomy that is located in multiple contexts, circumstances, and competing factors.[92] The literature points to women who have converted to Islam and have decided to wear the hijab, even against the wishes of their spouses; it also shows some among this group who find the chador or niqab liberating from prying gazes; it points to women who have made a strategic decision to wear the hijab in order to negotiate more personal and professional autonomy from elders and family, or to invoke a stance of political resistance to a national administration rather than a symbol of religious commitment. Moreover, for every woman who wears the hijab, there are as many messages about her sense of color, style, and fashion coordination as about her ethnic origins, political commitments, and class status.[93] Consider Frantz Fanon's discussion of Algerian women who veil in *A Dying Colonialism*. He points to the usefulness of the veil in an anti-colonial political resistance, for example, in concealing ammunition or other subversive materials for the Algerian Nationalistic Front, as well as in resisting Western feminist readings of an Algerian woman's body as something to be revealed.[94] This analysis of the veil's multiple functions reveals its complexity: it can serve as a symbol of modesty as well as a potential threat. Chandra Mohanty points to a similar complexity when she discusses the different motives that middle-class Iranian women might have to veil during the 1979 revolution (to oppose the stance of Western cultural colonization and to show solidarity with their working-class sisters in the face of the ban on veiling), as opposed to the Iran of the last several decades, where veiling has become mandatory under an explicitly Islamic government.[95]

Our understanding of veiling might become more accurate were we to change two elements of our approach to the veil. First, we might begin—as postcolonial feminist scholars have beseeched us—by locating the political import of the veil within the specific historical, political, and social context in which a woman engages in the practice.[96] Second, we might take the perspective that the subject is constituted through and by various practices and contexts. Saba Mahmood suggests that "[n]orms are not only consolidated and/or subverted . . . but performed, inhabited, and experienced in a variety of ways."[97] This position challenges the idea, first, that subjects are fully formed; it also challenges the idea that the contexts in which one finds oneself are either fully formed or ideal or completely independent from the subject in question. When we begin with such flawed assumptions, it is much easier (if always erroneous) to assume the Kantian position that a moral decision can be uniform and unchanging from person to person, and thus, that there is something wrong with a woman who makes different choices than oneself.

The picture of veiling reveals itself somewhat differently if we begin from the position initiated by Mahmood, that subjectivity is dynamic as are the contexts in which one finds onself. Moreover, if we were to reject the premise that there is ever an "ideal context" or vantage point from which to make choices, then we might understand various practices as responses to the situations in which one finds oneself. From this vantage point, the practice of veiling expresses a dynamic agency, a challenge, and even resistance within the context of any version of "Muslim" culture at any given moment.

Second, it is important to disarticulate any given cultural practice from the "totalized" picture of the culture with which it is associated, or at least to disconnect the seeming causal relation between any given culture and a practice that is associated with it.[98] It is not necessarily "Islam" that requires (all) women to veil, nor which "produces" terrorists and suicide bombers, in the same way that it is not "American culture," which produces divorcees and "sexually loose women." In the former case, it might be a national law, one's immediate family, one's community that exert a (coercive) pressure. In such a case, by focusing on the practice rather than on the source of coercion, we tend to become distracted and miss the point. The veil serves as a lightning rod for a myriad of discontent about autocracy, theocracy, patriarchy—all of which can and should be rightly criticized—but the practice of veiling occurs in a range of contexts that can also be not coercive. If we were to begin to understand a practice by locating it within the context in which one engages in it, then the picture of veiling—indeed the reasons by which one engages in any given practice—might be seen in a more textured light.

And so, in an important sense, the reasons by which one might argue that the hijab, purdah, or niqab are practices oppressive to women are not particularly important, because it is not the oppressiveness of the hijab itself that renders it threatening. Early in this chapter I contended that pluralism in the context of North Atlantic/Western Liberal societies is much more limited than is acknowledged. One premise of this contention is that the "internal" cultures of these countries, whether Holland, Turkey, or the United States—as unique and as different in terms of the particular liberal paradigm to which they may be committed—are nevertheless homogenous in some fundamental way. They subscribe to

106   *Toward a Political Philosophy of Race*

the above set of commitments and their attitude to the dominant counter-paradigm of "Islam" and "Muslim culture" is similar, if not identical. This might be because their collective cultural identity as "Western" has been formed through an oppositional relation to "Islam" that stems back as far as the Crusades. Another premise is that the range of differences that are "tolerated" or "accepted" are minimal, and often limited to consumer, aesthetic, and culinary preferences, rather than to cultural values that depart from the basic latent (homogenous) religious/moral principles on which their culturally "diverse" "liberalism" is grounded. One primary example of such a latent moral principle of liberalism is that public secularism is in practice a quietly ubiquitous Christianity, whose often subdued artifacts, traditions, and holidays meld with a public and governmental self-understanding of "religious neutrality."[99] Another premise is that variations in individual comportment are accepted insofar as these variations are shallowly aesthetic. Liberal cultures appear to pride themselves on "tolerating" fashion difference—from dashikis, "punk" aesthetics such as tongue- and navel-piercing, hair dyed in shockingly bright colors, and now in the light of the current popularity of Bollywood—bindis, saris, henna tattoos, and nose-piercings. Yet, aesthetic choices such as long beards and the hijab, which evoke not consumer aesthetic preferences but possibly distinct non-Christian religious affiliations attract much more (hostile) attention,[100] especially after 9-11. Even though we have seen examples of the limitations of a "nondenominational" pluralism throughout North Atlantic societies,[101] not a single "North Atlantic" nation has contested the wearing of wigs (as worn by Orthodox Jewish women for the same purposes as Muslim women), headwraps (as worn by Nigerian women), or Sikh turbans or head coverings (as worn by men and women), the covering of women's hair in Hindu temples or orthodox Catholic churches. Even when they might be assumed to be patriarchal impositions, they rarely come under as much fire. I think, in part, this is because the faith or culture that these represent are not considered threatening in the way that Islam is. Part of the hijab's troublesomeness emerges from the mistaken induction that Islam, as a faith-based culture, can—and does—"produce" terrorists, polygamy, suicide bombings, and oppressed women.[102] Moreover, the hijab disrupts those of us who live in the Western secular-liberal world, because it appears as a conspicuous expression of support for a culture *that is incompatible*[103] *with liberalism*—because it denies the separation of politics and religion.

Indeed, we may begin to understand why Tashnuba Hayder and Adamah Bah become targets of suspicion by the FBI, when we consider the threat that these girls appeared to present. By wearing the hijab (in one case) and full purdah (in another), along with the propensity to engage in other acts that appeared alien,[104] Hayder and Bah declared their faith in Islam, that is, the same faith that produces terrorists. Moreover, by being Muslim, they ascribed to a belief system that is incompatible with the political and cultural comportment of the West: to procedural, democratic and liberal principles, and *were understood as standing in loyalty with those who have engaged in acts of violence in the name of Islam.*

On this view, the "danger" of veiling to the state—among other symbols of Islam—becomes even clearer. It serves as the public expression of religious faith, a sexuality that departs from a contemporary Western or even feminist model, by presenting an agency that—although not secular or liberal—still does not understand itself as submissive to patriarchy. In conjunction with its conspicuous public expression of support for Islam, as a (unified) culture that refuses to keep separate its religious and political practices, veiling becomes even more transgressive. All of these implications are conflated in veiling as a practice that is now seen as a public—voluntary—expression of resistance to Western liberal feminism, western secular values, and western ideals of freedom.

Conclusion

The veil—as one among many such signifiers—has emerged as a representation of the larger "problem" of "Muslim culture"—namely as the unruly threat to the existing onto-juridical regime of Western secular-liberalism. In the cases of the teenagers, the degree to which they were perceived as potential threats differed, and they were treated accordingly. Adamah's supporters publicly attested to her popularity and leadership skills, and emphasized her social and political assimilation as a "normal" or "All-American girl," with the clear exception of her decision to wear the hijab. She was released after several weeks of public protest by her teachers, fellow students, and parents. The threat presented by Tashnuba Hayder had no mitigating buffers. Besides her "suspicious" religious habits, during her detention, she fiercely argued Qu'aranic interpretations with a secular British-bred female Muslim FBI agent. Tashnuba was, in short, unruly. Moreover, under pressure from sovereign authority, she became defiant. USCIS agreed to release her only when her mother offered to be deported, along with Tashnuba and two younger siblings, back to Bangladesh, a country barely familiar to the children.

The unruly—whether represented by Hayder and Bah, or French Muslim women, hundreds of Muslim men in U.S. detention facilities, or thousands of Muslim men and women in England, France, Germany,

Denmark, the Netherlands, India and elsewhere—is the unrepentant embrace of Islam and the challenge to a deceptively tolerant, and ultimately, hegemonic Western secular order, which in fact is hostile to cultural differences that are "strange," and hence, unruly. The political response of that order is to manage the challenge by regulating or eliminating its visible traces in the hopes of pulling out its roots in the process. The so-called "choice" of Muslims to ascribe to a culture that is unreasonable, is somehow in itself an expression of that which must be managed, domesticated, tamed. That the "unruly" must be managed is both reinforced but also held up (alerted) by certain signs that mark the threat. The threat is, unfairly perhaps, taken up to be the representation of a culture, but also necessarily so. And so, the hijab—in conjunction with some or many of these other representations, is rendered such a mark, but itself becomes the naturalized target of the state's hostility. It exists as a sign that Muslims are ontologically heterogeneous. As we saw with Huntington's and Rawls's descriptions, Islam is perceived as a culture whose principles and visual significations are fundamentally transgressive to Western liberal norms. As such, Islam (and Muslims) imply a radical heterogeneity and a cultural ontology so distinct from the prevailing political culture that it (and they) are naturalized under the banner of "irrationality," "unreason," or madness.[105] And those whose disagreements are "cultural," and therefore unreasonable, are thought to be difficult or unruly as a matter of choice.

Even prior to 9-11, the existence of Muslims denoted an unyielding, conspicuous heterogeneity, precluding an easy assimilation or affinity within U.S. society as well as within Western liberal society. The newly illuminated presence of women who are avowedly Muslim in the post–9-11 context is now viewed as transgressive, threatening, and downright subversive. The war on terrorism, contrary to various conservative and liberal claims, extends beyond the prevention of terrorism. More accurately, the war on terrorism is part of a larger defense of Western liberal-secular culture and perceived threats against it. Those whose culture is radically heterogeneous from ours, and thus who don't share in our common liberal-secular cultural comportment are not "entitled" to the state's protection. As the Bush Administration has pointed out about the detainees in Guantánamo Bay, "These people are not like you and me."[106] In the case at hand, their position appears to refer to those whose practices— ranging from the hijab to polygamy to suicide bombings—are seen as transgressing or departing from the common culture that members of a group ought to share, and thus necessarily as irrational or criminal practices. And so, we might better understand the logic behind the preemptive hunt for "potential terrorists," qua enemies: the idea of "innocent until proven guilty" does not apply to those who are "not-like-us" or "not-human-like-us." These "characteristic" marks ascribed to Muslims, denote the perception that this group, in its cultural heterogeneity, is unworthy of the protection afforded "Americans," or to the "true brethren" of our polity—because they do not share our cultural comportment. The implication of this position is that the burden is on the "outsiders," the "foreigners," "to prove" they are one of us, instead of accepting them under the stated conditions by which people are allowed to enter a liberal polity—that is, like us *unless and until* they demonstrate otherwise. Short of this proof, legal protection and dignified treatment will be withheld from those whose culture diverges radically from our common liberal-secular cultural comportment. The cases of Tashnuba Hayder and other "unruly" Muslim women and men are not so random; the state's wrath is directed toward those whose heterogeneous cultural comportment is unbending and defiant, peaceful or otherwise.

In chapter 5, I will explore how the racialization of this "unruly" population is concealed behind "official" procedures that purport to adhere to the "rule of law."—that is, through the second aspect of race as a technology.

5

Producing Race

Naturalizing the Exception
through the Rule of Law

"The "alien" is a frightening symbol of the fact of difference as such, of individuality as such . . . The danger in the existence of such people is twofold: first and more obviously, their ever-increasing numbers threaten our political life, our human artifice . . .[1]

Introduction

In prior chapters, I identified some of the discursive mechanisms by which Muslims in the United States are understood as the most recent outcaste group. I suggested that several traits have been ascribed to Muslims since 9-11—traits that, when combined, form a powerful indictment of Muslims as an exception to the universal race of (rational) human beings. These traits took on a singular potency when understood as part of an effort to create a new pariah. Through them, Muslims have begun to be depicted as a new race—an evil and less rational race.

I have discussed the identification of Islam with terrorism and the destruction of non-Muslims more generally as forms of inscribed cultural specificity. And as I have discussed already, significant cultural difference—seen as a *threat* to other reasonable and hence law-abiding members of the polity—is understood as holding the potential for criminality, that is, the "unruly." In the case of Muslims, the actions of the group of nineteen on 9-11 have become a synechdoche for the "nature" and unique cultural practices of all members of that ethnic and cultural group. And thus, this synechdoche reinforces the perception of the entire group as engaging in a set of culturally heterogeneous practices that emerge through their affinity for another tradition or "another" God, and thus, another law than the culture, which binds us as a community. Hence, these practices are seen as profane or criminal practices, in other words, as transgressing or departing from the *common culture that members of different groups should share.*

In what follows, I explore the (second) way in which race functions as technology: by transforming the "unruly" into a set of "naturalized" procedures by which a racialized population is produced. In chapter 4, I catalogued numerous laws and legal actions taken by the U.S. government and other states to target Muslim men and women as terrorists, enemies, criminals, and other kinds of threats to society.[2] That there have been so many criminal, immigration, and "cultural value" laws directed against them suggests that they are easy and obvious targets for outcasting, in large part because of the widespread suspicion that was exacerbated through numerous sources and cast upon them.

As I discussed in chapter 1, juridical productions of race occur by concealing this function behind a more "official" function. In this case, I argue that the creation of "exceptions" to the rule of law is part of the process of racializing a population. Race is not produced—a population is not racialized—through the creation of "exceptions" alone, but functions together with a series of other political operations, such as those discussed in chapter 4, as well as others that I discuss in ensuing chapters. In this chapter I wish to focus on the status of outsiders—as immigrants— because I believe it is a crucial substantiation of the exception narrative as mentioned above. Their identification as immigrants facilitates the indictment of certain outside populations as outcaste or evil races. There are two aspects of a group's status as immigrants: one is the *association* of immigrants with *outsiders* or the "not quite one of us," through phenotypical and cultural differences. The second aspect is that of their nebulous status as immigrants, namely a population who is not-quite-one-of-us; both traits hearken back to the discussion of strangeness from chapter 3. What is important to take away from these "characteristic" marks of immigrants, however, is a crucial perception that enables the recognition of this group in its cultural heterogeneity *as being unworthy of the protection* afforded by a reading of Constitutional rights as *human rights*. Once we ascribe the prior interpretation to a given group, then we might better understand the logic behind the preemptive hunt for "potential terrorists," qua enemies: the idea of "innocent until proven guilty" does not apply to those who are "not-like-us" or "not-human-like-us." I want to explore this concealed racial logic and how it is reconciled with a self-understanding that procedures and the rule of law are being "strictly" followed.

Exceptions and the Rule of Law

As I discussed in chapter 2, the phenomenon of outcasting select popu-lations has often been understood as a consequence of the hypocrisy of liberal democracies. The accusation of hypocrisy emerges when a liberal democratic nation's claim to extend rights equally to its entire popula-tion is shown to be untrue, or when equal treatment for certain popula-tions is rescinded in the name of some urgent political concern. Developing the example of populations that are loosely recognized as Arab or Muslim in post–9-11 United States, I argue that such a practice is not hypocritical but rather an intrinsic element of American liberalism; the United States can understand itself *consistently* as aspiring to the lib-eral democratic project of equal treatment and protection of its mem-bers, even when simultaneously marginalizing or ostracizing certain populations within its midst. The consistency of these two practices might be usefully understood as a long-standing mode by which certain ethnically, culturally, or racially conspicuous groups—seen as a threat to a national population that understands itself as internally united, stable, and secure, *but for this group*—are outcasted politically and legally. In the context of the political and ideological framework of the United States, which takes its lead from classic liberal political philosophy, this practice is not necessarily a self-conscious one, but rather one that depends on a dual interpretation of the term "person." Such a dual interpretation in turn corresponds to a vacillating interpretation of constitutional protec-tions. Ultimately, the promise of equal protection is extended to all resi-dents of a polity, as long as they are seen to qualify for membership—not in the polity—but in the set of human beings we call "persons." Even if human rights can conceptually be reintroduced for minorities by special law, this avenue becomes a fruitless avenue of appeal, when the condi-tion of human rights—namely that they be universally extended to all members of the same class is rendered null through the creation of ex-ception populations, as I will discuss further.[3] The notion of exceptions, which Hannah Arendt uses to describe the social perception of the pariah, seems to be particularly insightful here. Arendt discusses excep-tions as the method by which members of an outside group can assimi-late into a dominant group—namely by showing oneself to be superior in some trait valued by the dominant group.

In what follows, I want to consider an exception in the following way: as the avenue by which one group is seen as inferior in some respect in comparison to another group, dominant or minority.[4] The practice of creating exceptions, as the state has been able to do most recently with Muslims, be they immigrants, potential terrorists, or enemy combatants, seems to be an intrinsic impulse of societies that wish to reconcile the formal adherence to the principles of liberalism with the fear of extreme cultural heterogeneity in the name of defending rational values, security, and eradicating the threats to freedom within our midst. Considered in this way, the "exception," understood is a particularly powerful weapon in selectively realigning the boundaries of universal human rights.[5]

How does the ideological self-understanding of American liberalism remain consistent with its promise of universalism while constituting exceptions to the society whose members will be awarded full legality and protections? Dialectically speaking, it is only possible to recognize the set of members who are granted rights when we have a clear idea of who is excluded. Liberal political philosophies tend to offer a catalog of interests and characteristics of those human beings who are intended to be the recipients of natural or inalienable rights. John Locke, for example, refers to "reason" as the intellectual faculty and condition by which men know which rights are inalienably theirs. Reason, combined with the need to protect property interests, forms the basis of the argument for the Lockean social contract.[6] The extension of rights in classical liberal thought is neither universal nor inalienable, as feminists have long argued. The circle of membership—the set of individuals who are recognized as citizens and for whom the promise of *rights is indeed universal and inalienable*—often depends on the attentive and obedient subordination of women (in the household, as free labor, mothers, sex partners), and of slaves (who for Locke have been granted their lives in an altruistic gesture by their victorious vanquishers, after a war of aggression has been fought), etc.

And those who are excluded, are excluded "justifiably"—either because their proper roles preclude them from claiming citizenship or rights, or because they have forfeited their rights by misbehaving (i.e., criminals), or because they are not entitled to claim rights because they do not qualify by virtue of some set of political, social, or ontological reasons. In other words, liberalism's promise of universal and alienable rights is often intimately connected to the justified exclusion of some population, that is, an "exception" population.[7]

And so, the state understands or constitutes certain ethnically, culturally, or racially conspicuous groups as not quite capable of engaging in political interaction, or not eligible for "citizenship," the standard trope denoting "full rights and membership in a polity." In a contemporary liberal society such as the United States, this mode of self-understanding involves the selective awarding or privation of certain rights and protections that are normally afforded to citizens and noncitizens alike; it does so by vacillating between an understanding of rights as political (and thus afforded primarily to those who are full members or citizens) *or* universal (and thus to be extended to individuals in a polity, regardless of their legal status in the polity).[8]

But liberal polities do not engage in a self-conscious creation of exception populations; rather the creation of "exceptionalism" is justified through recourse to certain already given understandings of what constitutes reasonable values. This is often a self-referential and circular move, since the question of reasonable values is precisely always what is under scrutiny in debates between heterogeneous populations.[9]

The American state's justification of the exclusion of certain populations is necessary—for several reasons: First, by continually redrawing the boundaries that circumscribe the set of members who are entitled to the liberal promise of "full, equal, and universal treatment," the state can emphasize and promulgate to members and nonmembers alike the import of its protections. If we were to extend the economistic argument that the value of a good increases in proportion to its scarcity, then it would make sense to say that equal and universal treatment can hardly be recognized and valued unless it was understood to be acquired through difficulty. Otherwise, the truly "universal" and equal treatment of all individuals would be transformed into a ubiquitous, transparent material that enveloped everyone, like air. Second, it is only by identifying an enemy or stranger that a liberal polity can understand itself and its function— the collective and collaborative function of maintaining an internally united, stable, and secure society. And so, the selective criteria by which "members" are constituted enables the state to mark certain populations as insiders, and others as enemies. And thus, by engaging in a selective extension of rights, the state is able to legitimate its inconsistent treatment of different populations while appearing to conform to its supposed promise of universal and identical treatment of all human beings.

Carl Schmitt's discussion of the political, whose existence is predicated on the distinction between friend and enemy, illuminates this point. According to Schmitt, the political is essentially defined through the identification of those who are considered an enemy.[10] An enemy does not need to be evil or ugly, and can even be an economic partner. "But he is, nevertheless, the other, the stranger; and it is sufficient for his nature that he is, in a specially intense way, existentially something different and alien, so that in the extreme case conflicts with him are possible."[11] Thus, an enemy, because he is precisely what the polity is not, is necessary to engender a collective self-recognition.[12] The enemy, for Schmitt, is what the polity understands itself against. The case of Muslim immigrants enables the self-recognition of the U.S. as an internally united population, whose identity can only be understood through the ostracization of the "enemy" within its midst—that population, which is not only culturally heterogeneous, but appears to constitute a threat to the self-preservation of the polity.

Why must the enemy be internal? Is it not sufficient for internal self-cohesion for a polity to regroup against an external enemy, as Schmitt implies?[13] Of course, it is certainly possible for the latter to occur. But the creation of internal enemies can be a tactic by which sovereign authorities can regulate potentially "unruly" or threatening populations by re-orienting other subpopulations to understand them as a threat to "themselves."[14]

Schmitt's reading of the dynamic between the polity and its enemy is especially astute. However, I wish to go one step further, and suggest that the polity must set the enemy outside the law that pertains to members of that polity in order to continually reinforce this recognition. And this is why the concept of "exception" plays a crucial role in the creation of an enemy group—particularly in a liberal context, where rights are considered the inalienable property of all human beings. The ethos of such universalism is important precisely for its promise of eliminating the capacity to find new groups to marginalize. This is why the notion of exception is crucial to the creation of new outsiders and insiders, that is, because it can explain and justify why rights thought to belong to all human beings should be withheld from some group. The strength of "exceptionalism" lies in showing why the group in question does not meet the requisite criteria for protection by the state. In the case of Muslims—as once was true for Black Americans[15]—they are seen to be not sufficiently human, or if human, then not sufficiently manageable by a dominant political authority or dominant social group to be extended the necessity of human rights. Here, the term "enemy" refers to that group that must be cast out by being marginalized and deprived of the protection of the state. And thus, the enemy represents that group that constitutes an "exception" to the population that the state ostensibly exists to protect.

An "exception" is typically understood as a deviation from the standard. On this reading, we understand the enforcer of the law to be either hypocritical or inconsistent. But what if we were to understand the "exception" as an intrinsic element of the standard *qua law*, as does Giorgio Agamben? For Agamben, the basic expression of sovereignty simultaneously circumscribes the polity, those who will be acknowledged and subject to the law, as well as those who will be forced outside those parameters.[16] The latter group does not "incidentally" become the exception, but rather is intrinsic to the instantiation of the former group, in other words, the group who will be included or protected.[17] Exceptions are intrinsic because they enable sovereign authorities to manage and secure their own claims to power. That is to say, through the creation of potential vulnerability for all populations, sovereign authority gives an incentive to them to avoid being targeted, by being able to focus on another group as a scapegoat. The concept of exception—understood as a "routine exclusion"—enables us to understand how certain subject populations can be marginalized or eradicated as a matter of fact or procedure. If the American state convincingly renders Muslims a new race of "evildoers" with an inherent psychology of terrorism,[18] then it can constitute Muslims as some kind of "exception" population, a population that is simultaneously subject to the law, but not entitled to its protection. As Agamben points out, "It is literally not possible to say whether the one who has been banned is outside or inside the juridical order."[19] As a result, the vulnerability of such a subject in relation to the sovereign renders it possible to be eradicated or marginalized without such destruction being seen as a "sacrifice."[20] By extension, then, exception populations can be abandoned as a matter of "unexceptional" practice. But this creation of exceptions is not particular to immigrants or to Muslims. Agamben's analysis suggests that Michel Foucault is correct to claim that the modern state is, at bottom, a racist one, in that it is its agenda to distinguish and compel one population to live from another population's mandate to death.[21]

Constitutional Rights: Political? Human?

Drawing upon some of the above political frameworks by which enemy populations are understood, I wish to apply the concept of "exception" to the American political and legal context. Exception populations are instantiated and demarcated from a core polity through a dual interpretation of Constitutional protections as political and human rights. In this reading, it seems that the normative significance of the universalism of "natural" or "human" rights can be retained while extending them to select groups, and depriving others of them. Thus, by reading the Constitution as a document that enumerates those rights extended to individuals as human beings, but by offering this reading only to its citizens, the state *de facto* insists upon a second meaning of constitutional protections that illuminates them as political and, hence, selective rights, which can be extended only to "friends," and not enemies, which corresponds to a distinction, simply put, between "us" and "them."

The ambiguous status of Constitutional protections as both political rights and human rights is concealed during times of peace by the generally indulgent extension of a bulk of these protections to citizens and (legal) noncitizens alike.[22] This ambiguity refers directly, if implicitly, to the question of how to understand the figure of the immigrant. There are several parts to this story. The first part of the story is about immigration as read through the history of American immigration law. The status of immigrants in American legal history is crucial to understanding how pariah groups are created and exceptions are legitimated, because immigration law confirms that arriving outsiders ("aliens") will be generally viewed and treated with suspicion, because of their ethnic and cultural dissimilarities, and distinct geographical origins, from the general American population. The current moment deals with Arab immigrants of Muslim origin, but it resembles in important ways the treatment of other ethnic groups who arrived from the mid-nineteenth to the end of the twentieth century—the Chinese, Sikhs, Mexicans, Irish, Italians, Slavs, Pakistanis, Indians, among countless others—for whom inclusion in the national political imaginary was often an arbitrary and elusive process, and coincided with a concurrent outsider status.

One of the concerns about the way that (mostly male and primarily Muslim) Arab immigrants are currently being treated by the Office of Homeland security is that they are not being extended the general Constitutional protections that are considered "inalienable" for American citizens and often indulgently extended to immigrants during times of relative domestic peace. This division between the Constitutional rights extended to American citizens and those most often arbitrarily extended or withheld from immigrants has its origins in the development of American immigration law.[23] Through a set of strategic administrative and legislative moves beginning in the late 1800s,[24] immigrants became subject to a body of law and to a mode of treatment that is separate and mostly distinct from the rest of American and Constitutional law.[25] These moves enabled the cementing of certain norms in immigration procedures: not required to be extended to immigrants were various rights implied under the Constitution: the writ of habeas corpus, the right to due process, routine judicial review, the right to an advocate or an attorney.[26] There is an enormous burgeoning literature begun well before 9-11, authored by liberal and communitarian scholars from various fields, which debates whether rights such as those listed above should be rights of membership rather than fundamental moral claims due any human being.[27] While I cannot possibly treat this literature adequately here, it is *the fact of the debate* that is of central importance to the argument here.

The tension over whether rights are political or human (universal) emerges from the central question of liberalism, namely that of how "membership" should be understood. The narrowest interpretation of this question is that membership is based on claims to legal recognition by the state. The broadest interpretation is that membership is based on a community of human beings. Membership then connotes at least two different sets of individuals, and possibly many more. But more fundamentally, the tension over the meaning of membership stems from whether it is being read from the "inside" or from without. Kunal Parker terms the former reading of "membership" as a liberal "insider" narrative about citizenship, in other words, one that rests on the uncritical (and mistaken) premise that "members" of a group have the right to exclude or deprive "outsiders" of citizenship rights.[28] Read from the "outside," of course, that is, as pertaining to all human beings, membership would lose its central import, since it would of course render all rights as human rights, to be awarded independently of legal status.

Yet, Hannah Arendt recognizes the central problem of securing rights as human rights. She points out that the recognition of one's human rights is *predicated not on one's status as human, but on one's recognition as a member of a polity.* One must be afforded some vehicle by which to mediate between oneself and the state. It is that recognition upon which the rhetorical discourse of human rights is predicated—namely that human rights are to be accorded to all human beings under any and all conditions. And it is this premise that is betrayed in the absence of national rights:

> If a human being loses his political status, he should, according to the implications of the inborn and inalienable rights of man, come under exactly the situation for which the declarations of such general rights provided. Actually the opposite is the case. *It seems that a man who is nothing but a man has lost the very qualities which make it possible for other people to treat him as a fellow man.* This is one of the reasons why it is far more difficult to destroy the legal personality of a criminal, that is of a man who has taken upon himself the responsibility for an act whose consequences now determine his fate, than of a man who has been disallowed all common human responsibilities.[29]

In this excerpt, Arendt challenges the very assumption of international human rights that is often accepted uncritically in the contemporary world. Arendt draws on Edmund Burke's point that even savages are accorded human rights, but unless there is a state that recognizes and guarantees them, they remain ineffectual, indeed nonexistent. And here, I would go one step further than Arendt: It is not only the absence of political rights—but the *absence of the dual recognition that political rights are human rights*—that renders the distinction between human being and animal collapsed, such that one becomes a political and legal nonentity.[30]

> The conception of human rights, based upon the assumed exis-
> tence of a human being as such, broke down at the very moment
> when those who professed to believe in it were for the first time
> confronted with people who had indeed lost all other qualities
> and specific relationships—except that they were still human.
> The world found nothing sacred in the abstract nakedness of
> being human.[31]

To be human is meaningless within the context of a polity if it is not
accompanied by certain political protections. And thus human rights can
only be secured through the recognition of one's political status as a
member of a community. The absence of this dual recognition, then, is
especially devastating for the figure of the immigrant.

The case of the American treatment of Muslims is consistent with the
history of its treatment of immigrants. In the American context, Constitutional rights are often read either as human or political (membership)
rights. Yet, the distinction between human rights and political rights
emerges *not only* from the Arendtian point that one must be recognized
in the latter, that is, as a member, in order to receive recognition of one's
human rights. It also emerges from the ambiguous reading of the central
category of individuals to whom rights are thought to be extended: persons. In the standard legal literature, the debate over whether immigrants should receive certain rights of due process and equal protection
is thought to rest on the category of "persons," a term constantly present throughout the U.S. Constitution.[32] The powers and equal protections of the Constitution are most famously defined as applying to "any
person" within the territorial jurisidiction of the United States, as seen in
Amendment XIV.[33]

But this debate emerges from another source as well: the central ambiguity over the meaning of the term "person." As Charles Mills points
out, this category, of central importance in the philosophical literature,
emerges in challenge to the world of rank and ascribed status, as a way of
denoting the central equality of human beings.[34] As a conceptual category, the term "person" has ambiguous dual meaning—one that refers to
both a legal as well as an ontological status. How this term is read connects back to the distinct ways in which membership can be construed—
from the inside or outside. From the former perspective, "person" is a
legal category whose recognition is cemented by the set of laws that liberal institutions uphold and promote. Thus to be a citizen is to be a
"legal person," and thereby an "official" member of a polity, distinguished from the "unofficial" or "illegal" denizens of a polity. From
the latter, that is, "outsider's," perspective, a "person" is an ontological

category, which entails automatic legal recognition. On this reading, then, Constitutional rights are human rights, which must be extended to all who live within the polity—"members" or not.

However, there is a third dimension that attaches itself to this dual reading of "person." It is a dimension that neatly connects to the ambiguous and shifting reading of Constitutional rights as political or human. The question of whether to grant rights as human rights or political rights depends not only how the term "person" is read Constitutionally, but on whether to read the person in question—in this case, the figure of the immigrant—as merely a human being or as a legal person also. The condition of reading the immigrant in the latter sense requires that they satisfy the crucial criterion: not only must they be "human," but they must be "human-like-us."

Heterogeneity in this case is expressed through the existential status of the immigrant, who lives neither inside nor outside the polity, but hovers on the edge.[35] To clarify, the figure of the immigrant expresses existential heterogeneity through simultaneous or vacillating allegiances to multiple cultures, conventions, nations, or territories. Such plural affinities preclude the immigrant from fitting neatly and easily into the conventions of the society into which he has immigrated. This renders him undependable, an uncertain ally in the quest for the unity, conformity, and stability of any given society, especially during times of crisis. For the dominant "rational" society, then, cultural heterogeneity—in the figure of the immigrant—is again interpreted as the existential inability to live neatly within the community, that is, the inability to be human-like-us. Thus both existential and cultural heterogeneity are perceived as potential threats to the internal stability of a society. And this combination, in turn, renders new immigrants particularly susceptible to being identified as the new enemy.[36]

The most obvious evidence of this reading emerges from the history of the plenary power doctrine with regard to immigration law, which grants it "a unique immunity from judicial review."[37] In 1891, Congress made the deliberate decision to allow the federal administrators final decision-making power over immigration law.[38] This decision cemented an opinion written several years earlier by the Supreme Court in *Chae Chan Ping v. United States*.[39] The Court states that the federal government is allowed full and absolute jurisdiction to prevent the entrance of immigrants. Known as the origins of the plenary power doctrine, this authority is expanded by the Court several years later, allowing the federal government full jurisdiction to "expel or deport foreigners who have not been naturalized."[40] The implication of these decisions is that immigration law is not automatically subject to judicial review, and thus may develop

independently of Constitutional law. The separate development of these
two bodies of law, Constitutional and immigration, engender the development of two distinct frameworks of recognizing political subjects.
Michael Scaperlanda argues that the recognition of immigrants has vac-
illated between the "personhood" and "membership" models.[41] The first
model treats petitions put forth by immigrants within the context of the
Fourteenth Amendment and due process concerns. Full constitutional
rights are accorded to those deemed full and proper "persons," in this
model. The second model, namely that of membership, treats the concerns of immigrants in terms of whether they are due any of the rights
that are accorded to members of the nation-state. As Scaperlanda points
out, for much of the last 130 years, the Congressional plenary power doctrine has rendered immigrant law, and the political, social, and economic security of immigrants virtually nonexistent. The models that the
courts have used to render immigrants not a part of Constitutional concerns or of "personhood" doctrine have varied, but their consistent results have undermined the legitimacy and consistency of their presence
in the American political context.[42]

By contrast, the struggles faced by immigrants and aliens were considered part of the problem that the U.S., as a sovereign nation, had to
face—to regulate and control who passed through and stayed within
their borders. As foreign nationals, their status was subject to the whims
of federal administrators and immigration officials. Their political status
was further compromised, as Scaperlanda points out, by the shift in judicial attitudes around the Chinese Exclusion case,[43] which entailed that
immigrants were no longer automatically seen as being entitled to the
rights of personhood that citizens could take for granted.[44] The implication of these two events was that rather than being included in the American racial conversation, (non-White) immigrants generally, were seen as
non-American—foreign—races, having no claims to the set of concerns,
characteristics, or rights that American "races" did.[45]

As such, Gabriel Chin argues that immigration law is the last stronghold of racial segregation in the United States, owing largely to the
Court's attitude that "aliens of a particular race," may be excluded or removed from the U.S., and have no constitutional rights when seeking admission to the U.S.[46] Further, the Justice Department, one of the venues
through which immigration law has been made, has argued that "citizenship" could be withheld from immigrants by reason of inadequate
habits, culture, or the "deficiency" of race. Referring to Chinese immigrants, the Justice Department insisted that color-blindness did not
extend to aliens: "[T]he Chinese are a people not suited to our institutions, remaining a separate and distinct race, incapable of assimilation,

having habits often of the most pernicious character . . . a people of such a character and so inimical to our interests as to require that their coming shall be prohibited."[47] In effect, then by holding that Congress had an absolute power to regulate immigration, a power not articulated in the Constitution, and one that is not subject to judicial review, the Court effectively holds that immigrants are unworthy of the status of "legal person," and hence unworthy of ostensibly "inalienable" protections such as the right to judicial review. This reading of both the immigrant and the Constitution is echoed by Charles Mills, when he astutely points to the implicit presence of non-Whites as crucial to the reification of (White) persons in the Racial Contract of the liberal polity. Labeling them subpersons, Mills says, "Subpersons are humanoid entities who, because of racial phenotype/genealogy/culture, are not fully human and therefore have a different and inferior schedule of rights and liberties applying to them. In other words, it is possible to get away with doing things to subpersons that one could not do to persons, because they do not have the same rights as persons."[48]

Whereas Mills argues this point with regard to raced persons generally, others such as Natsu Taylor Saito illustrate the double standards of liberal protections with specific regard to immigrants. Speaking with regard to Asian immigrants and their continual depiction as non-American, un-American, and "foreign," Saito suggests that the "identification of those that race as foreign must be understood as part of the larger process of maintaining our particular social, racial, and economic hierarchies. Matters of citizenship and foreignness—who is a member of this polity, who should be allowed to live here, who should pay which social costs, and who should receive which benefits—are . . . closely tied to deeply held beliefs about what it is to be an American and what America should be."[49] And yet, the absence of an explicit confession on this front, seems best explained by Alexander Bickel, "It has always been easier, it will always be easier to think of someone as a non-citizen than to decide he is a non-person."[50]

In the American context, that is, as understood through the ethos of immigration law, *one can only be recognized as a legal "person" or a member of a community when one is not merely human, but "human like us."* The message of the American polity is that while Americans will be afforded political rights as if these are human rights, but *non-Americans, because they are not-yet-human-like-us, will, at least until such time as they become American,* be granted human rights only as political rights.[51] That is to say, until such point as membership is afforded, one can only be construed as an enemy, or that "Other" *qua not-yet-human-like-us* to whom, therefore, we have no obligation to extend human rights. Hence, Constitutional rights are understood as natural rights only for members of the American polity. Here we see an instance of how a category is instantiated through sovereign power, which simultaneously becomes "exceptionalized": the sovereign protection of the state is extended to "all persons," but the question of who is fit for "personhood" is continually and implicitly modified and reconstrued to reproduce certain fundamental divisions between populations.

These divisions are predicated upon a distinction between nonpersons (the enemy or the stranger or the foreigner, per Schmitt) and persons (the set of individuals who constitute the polity). And here is where the tension of liberalism is necessary to continually reproduce its self-understanding as maintaining the promise of universal rights: Under this view, every human being is potentially eligible for recognition as a member of a polity, as long as he/she meets the (fairly rigid—and constantly changing—set of) criteria by which member qua person is defined. And by implication, one can reside in a polity, one can even participate in many practices that citizens do, but one can not be a full member of the polity—entitled to full protections and rights—unless and until one fully meets the criterion of what it means to be human. Short of that moment, one can be understood in various modes that fall short of the definition of human being: stranger, alien, enemy—but most importantly, as "an exception" to the set of individuals in this polity that we call citizens. That is to say, whatever "it" is, it is not "one of us," and therefore we are not obligated to award it Constitutional protections or rights.

Thus, the effect of the stark division between the set of rights afforded to members versus nonmembers is to reinforce the collective self-recognition of a national political imaginary for a set of core constituents who were continually informed that they "are lucky enough to live in a country that believed in democracy and freedom."[52] The right of freedom, in this trope, often implied that it was a human right that human beings in other countries are not lucky enough to be afforded . . . but what is omitted is that other human beings who were not lucky enough to be natural-born American citizens, or given the correct political times and circumstances—to be "naturalized"—are also not lucky enough to be extended this protection by the American government except by fiat and selective discretionary judgments during times of international instability. Non-American immigrants are susceptible to the urgent drawing of lines between friend and enemy, which, at least juridico-politically, occurs primarily through the suspension of procedures that are normally utilized to ascertain the grounds for indicting someone of a crime, or of judging him guilty of one.

The process of "nationalizing" the rights enumerated in the Constitution, and thus correlating the extension of human rights with the condition of citizenship, effectively elides the issue of whether human rights can ever logically and consistently be considered merely political rights, and whether political rights can ever be justified as less than universal human rights. But what we do know is that this elision also creates the opportunity to turn *any given group—natural-born or immigrant—into an enemy population*. By insisting upon the enemy alien *exception*, the Attorney General's office has returned the American political stage to a pre-Reconstruction era whereby human rights will only be given to those deemed human like us, and those deemed not-quite-human-like-us— whether for just or unjust cause (we will never know since their causes will no longer be stated or heard, much less tried, publicly) will be deprived altogether of the moral claims and rights that are thought to be granted to all human beings in a liberal context: respect, dignity, and recognition. And so, how have Muslims, in the American public mind, become the new exception population? Muslims, following the argument of Agamben, constitute the newest population whose status is that of "bare life" in the American discourse, because they are not-American and (simultaneously) not-yet-human-like-us. And so, they are not worthy of being American, the sign of which is being extended Constitutional protections on the ground of moral claims, that is, as human rights. This ambiguity refers directly, if implicitly, to ambivalence over how to understand the figure of the immigrant. The immigrant's nebulous status, as one of "us" in that he is human, but not (or not yet) human like us, seems to facilitate the distinction between friend and enemy during times of crisis. Again, it is not just cultural difference, but cultural difference perceived as a potential threat that seems to legitimate the generally popular trend of stripping a new group of political and legal protections, as in the case of immigrants of Arab descent or Muslim faith.[53] The moment constituted by the two years after 9-11 has facilitated the current Administration's promulgation of a crisis situation extreme enough to legitimate the *ad hoc* legal distinctions such as "terrorists," "enemy combatants," and "evildoers" versus "Americans," "citizens," and "friends" in direct reference to Muslims.

Conclusion

It is, on one level, a historical commonplace of liberalism that the promise of equal protection has been not extended universally. But the rationale of these "commonsensical" exclusions as "mere" exceptions to the American Constitutional promise of equal treatment and universal protections of all persons within their borders, raises deep suspicions.

The transhistorical constancy, the consistent presence of exceptions within the political and legal history of the United States, compels the urge to ask whether these exceptions really are unwitting, happenstance, or accidental. I suggest instead that exclusion is an intrinsic element of American liberalism, emerging from the impulse to circumscribe and valorize the liberal subject as a privileged member of that polity, granted a treatment that, incredibly enough, is considered elite, and is one for which few are eligible unless they can meet a rigorous and stringent set of criteria. The criteria in question revolve around the reproduction of a set of implicit values and at minimum, the cultural appearance, of those who constitute the full-fledged members and who author the laws of the liberal polity. Through this lens, exclusion is intrinsic to the maintenance and reproduction of liberal values and practices. The figure of the Muslim immigrant is a precise threat to the cultural homogeneity (or limited heterogeneity) and political unity of the liberal polity. But since the self-understanding of American liberalism is at variance with the above description, the method by which such divergence is reconciled is through a vacillating interpretation of the concept of the "person" at the center of that quintessential document of American polity—the U.S. Constitution. There, through the judgment of the Supreme Court, the liberal "person" is sometimes understood as an ontological category and at others, a normative one. This selective, always convenient, interpretation corresponds to a selective interpretation of the nature of the rights thought to ground a liberal polity—sometimes these rights are thought to be inalienable for everyone, and other times, they are thought to be so for members only. This reading of the intrinsic exclusionary impulse of liberalism has often been recognized by various liberal theorists as a necessary, justifiable, impulse. It is one that is embedded in a worldview, as Kunal Parker points out, which leaves the burden of proving that one is worthy of membership on the claimant—always already the "outsider," rather than insisting that exclusion is not a rational impulse. In this logic, the burden of proving the legitimacy of exclusion from a polity should rest on those who wish to exclude, in other words, on the "insiders."

In many ways, the increasingly restricted movement of Muslim immigrants and increasing erosion of the civil liberties and protections of Muslim Americans bears an uncanny resemblance to Hannah Arendt's description of the treatment of Jews by various European states prior to the onset of World War II. Arendt points to statelessness as that condition in which the country of one's origin will no longer claim members of a certain (ethnic) population as one's own, disenfranchising them entirely, and thereby casting them astray and leaving them in the position of having to appeal to the mercy of another nation for protection. Her analysis describes the reluctance of other nations to claim the unwanted as their own, and unwillingness to extend them active economic or legal protections, leaving them in effect "undeportable."[54] The stateless, as Arendt points out, were constituted by minorities who could not claim membership in a nation on the basis of origin or blood, thereby requiring a "law of exception" to guarantee them both recognition and protection in spite of their "insistence" upon claiming a different nationality.[55] On such grounds, the law was transformed from an instrument of the state to an instrument of the nation, thereby rendering human beings members of ethnic groups rather than members of polities, in others words, citizens.[56] Statelessness becomes evident through "denationalization," and through the constitutional inability to guarantee human rights to those who have lost "nationally guaranteed rights." The final evidence of statelessness—and this seems to be the consequence of the first two moves—is that the claim to "inalienable human rights" becomes a demonstrably empty one.[57]

It is difficult to apply fully all the elements of Arendt's understanding of statelessness to Muslims. It is certainly the case that the "denationalization" of Muslims is a post-facto phenomenon, one that appears to have gained momentum as diasporic Muslim immigrants have found themselves under increasing scrutiny by immigration officials. This scrutiny, along with the absence of judicial review, has led to the deportation of scores of immigrants to their "countries of origin" without warning, welcome, or community.[58] The phenomenon of denationalization appears to be closely linked to the American attempts to reinforce an "outsider" status for Muslims in the United States by constructing a certain descriptive conflation of Muslims with terrorism, namely by perpetuating a position that Islam is a religion that should be suspected as embedding certain seeds of terrorist psychology.[59]

The plight of Muslims in the United States is distinct from that of European Jews prior to and during World War II. However, Arendt's discussion of statelessness has a certain resonance with various events in contemporary American political discourse.[60] The more important implication of Arendt's analysis of statelessness is its fundamental implication of rightlessness.[61] The Bush Administration has, according to certain political observers, planned its next round in the war on terrorism to resemble yet another stage in the creation of statelessness and rightlessness not only for immigrants but even for the natural born.[62] The powers of the PATRIOT Act and successive policies are only possible in a social and political milieu where, as Arendt points out, rightlessness has become the order of the day, and the distinction between human being and citizen has been eradicated. It is a milieu that foreshadows totalitarianism as a condition where the distinction between the public and the private no longer exists, because the possibility of action, of difference, through the right of freedom, has been sharply restricted by the state. Such possibilities occur in a world where "exceptions" are routinely made in the extension of "human rights" to all members of the human class, through the irrationalization, inferiorization, and delegitimation of certain persons based on ad hoc differences—by creating "an illusory line between alien and citizen,"[63] and enemy and friend.

Is there a remedy to the exclusion that is the counterpart to the rhetoric of American liberal universalism? The intrinsicality of exceptions might imply that such a solution is impossible; however, I think we do not need to be so pessimistic. Part of the reason behind the continual repetition of "exceptions" is that they are seen as accidental; that is, their intrinsicality is concealed behind the superficial, if conspicuous, rhetoric of "equal rights." If we can crack open the facade and consider the creation of "exceptions," as a long-standing tendency of American liberalism, rather than a series of isolated accidents, then we can minimize or even anticipate this tendency by looking for warning signs. In so doing, we may be able to avert or head off the creation of potential scapegoats. In other words, a lasting solution requires a change of perspective. Any time a catastrophe occurs is tragic. If it happens repeatedly, then the tragedy becomes continual and repetitive, and there appears to be no end in sight. However, if we recognize this tendency as part of a systemic pattern that occurs on a regular basis, then we might be able to find a solution. Solutions to the problem of "intrinsic" exceptions can only occur by changing the way we understand such events, and deeming them unacceptable, and searching for an extensive reconfiguration of the United States' political framework—one that addresses and rectifies the procedure by which political recognition is awarded by the state, that is, the vehicle of membership. Short of a change in perspective and a new framework, this remedy—and the fulfillment of the promise of liberalism—that remedy remains to be seen.

6

Border-Populations

Boundary, Memory, and Moral Conscience

Introduction

In the prior chapters I discussed some of the events of December 2002, when Attorney General John Ashcroft's office detained male Muslims under the aegis of the PATRIOT Act.[1] Around the same time, and in stark contrast, there was a sudden furor over remarks made by then Senate Majority Leader Trent Lott, who insinuated that segregation might have been a preferred American political condition. Referring to Sen. Strom Thurmond's 1948 segregationist campaign, Lott repeated the gist of comments that he'd made once before, in 1980: "We're proud of it. And if the rest of the country had followed our lead, we wouldn't have had all these problems over all these years either."[2] Rebuttals emerged from various sources across the political spectrum. The right, the far right, the liberal, and the radical left all rushed to express their dismay at Sen. Lott's callous and politically miscalculated remarks. But there was more: in response to Sen. Lott's comments, the varied political factions—in a rarely seen collective, indeed, univocal agreement— declared that segregation, apartheid, and the second-class status of Black Americans was a relic of an unfortunate American past.

As I have argued in prior chapters, liberal polities tend to search for scapegoats who can serve as the latest enemy as a way of managing their populations in the interests of long-term goals.[3] In this chapter, I develop my argument from the last part of chapter 2. The outcasting of new "enemy" populations is augmented through the conspicuous cooptation of a long-standing outsider as part of the core dominant political imaginary. This tendency has reasserted itself most recently in the striking contrast between the treatment of Muslims in the United States and the sudden "welcome" of Black Americans as part of the core American polity.[4] What accounts for such a disparity in the reception and treatment of these two groups? Although this incident occurred nearly three years ago, the answer to this question can only be adequately articulated well after the moment of emergency in which the phenomenon first became conspicuous. Once located legally, socially, and culturally outside the periphery of the American polity, Black Americans have now been reconfigured as what I will term a "Border-population." As such, they are located on the periphery itself, which distinguishes insiders from outsiders. And so, like any border, the political and rhetorical positioning of this population now serves to protect the "internal boundaries" of a nation, as Johann Fichte calls them, and is crucial in facilitating a recognition of the significant divide between the core populace and those who stand squarely outside the symbolic boundaries that unite the populace.[5] But in this role, Border-populations function as more than merely a wall dividing "insiders" from "outsiders," or "we" from "them." They also serve[6] as the historical memory and institutional moral conscience that facilitates the American state's capacity to create the newest population of outcastes, namely Muslims in post 9-11 political context.[7] As a moral gauge, a Border-population's reactions (or absence of a unified reaction or referendum) are used by the state and/or inner populace to justify the outcasting of another group as legitimate. Such a transformation of the symbolic position and place of outsiders[8] to "Border-guards" and Moral Gauge—is neither an incidental occurrence nor unique to American politics. The following argument, I hope, will illustrate that *these dynamics are an integral element of any liberal polity.*

The Third Term:
Pariah Populations as a Border-Guard

In chapter 5, I described some of the rhetorical, conceptual, and political methods by which (liberal) polities maintain their self-understanding as consistently extending the promise of equal treatment to all members. The primary method is the selective awarding of Constitutional protections to all (insider) members of their population, while incorporating the necessary exclusion of an "exception population." In the case of the United States, Muslims have been rendered the new "evil" race, and hence the newest exception population.[9] There is another, crucial step to this tendency of liberalism: the mode of identifying the outsider as distinct from the insider can only be firmly cemented through a third term—or in this case—population. In its ambiguous place—as part of but also marginal to the polity—this population distinguishes and mediates the relationship of outsiders and insiders. In this role, it serves as a Border-population, circumscribing the internal boundary that delineates those who exist within it as patriots, citizens, or those who "rightfully" belong in the nation.

For Fichte, insiders—or in his example—Germans (versus other Teutons) are denoted through the existence of internal boundaries, which are represented through language. He says of this group:

> Those who speak the same language are joined to each other by a multitude of invisible bonds by nature herself, long before any human art begins . . . they belong together and are by nature one and an inseparable whole. *Such a whole, if it wishes to absorb and mingle with itself any other people of different descent and language, cannot do so without itself becoming confused, in the beginning at any rate, and violently disturbing the even progress of its culture.* From this internal boundary, which is drawn by the spiritual nature of man himself, the marking of the external boundary by dwelling-place results as a consequence . . . [i.e.] rivers and mountains . . .[10]

In modern times, a similar principle seems to continue the demarcation of "internal boundaries. The specific demographics that unify an "insider" population—linguistic, phenotypical, cultural, ethnic, political or economic traits—might change, but the conspicuous symbolic markers that denote that population stay the same. Typically, this group of insiders is anchored in its status through political and legal recognitions such as the rights of citizenship.[11] Their political security can be augmented through economic security, but it is unnecessary especially if a secure cultural status as "insiders" exists. By a secure cultural status, I refer to the symbolic and widespread popular acknowledgment of their "entitlement" to citizenship and political and social recognition.

In a slight twist on Fichte's principle of national unity, Carl Schmitt points to the unity of the insiders as articulated through the politicization of language. He refers to the "political"[12] as "contained in the context of a concrete antagonism . . . expressed in everyday language" and turning into "empty and ghostlike abstractions when this situation [of friend-enemy grouping] disappears. Words such as state, republic, society, class, as well as sovereignty, constitutional state, absolutism, dictatorship, economic planning, neutral or total state, and so on, are incomprehensible if one does not know exactly who is to be affected, combated, refuted, or negated by such a term."[13] He continues, in a footnote, to insist that "[t]erminological questions become thereby highly political. A word or expression can simultaneously be reflex, signal, password, and weapon in a hostile confrontation."[14] Similarly, I would suggest that the cultural status of insiders is anchored and reflected through the usurpation of certain terms of identity, usually attached with certain normative qualifiers, such as "good Americans," "devout Christians," "patriotic citizens," "caring neighbors," etc. But the most important demarcation of their status as insiders is the coequal presence of two other population groups: outsiders and pariahs.

Outsider populations, which can also reflect a range of differences demographically, can be understood in dialectical relation to insider populations: they are usually politically and legally disenfranchised; subject to harassment as the predominant form of recognition; socially, legally, and politically ghettoized; and used as a reference by which to distinguish those who are core insiders, usually through an implicit or explicit system of apartheid.[15]

Pariahs, on the other hand, take on a very different, and more ambivalent, set of traits than do outsiders—both politically and socially. In part, this is because of the strategic normative and logistically conceptual functions that they serve. Pariahs are, in Hannah Arendt's words, those who have stopped being political outcastes, but are still socially marginalized.[16] In other words, even though a set of "universal" political rights and a formal civil status has been extended to the pariah population, it nevertheless exists in uneasy relation to the insider group.

As Arendt argues, pariahs are one step away from the potential of being completely rightless and stateless; therefore, they are vulnerable to being outsiders, but they are not yet in that role. I think there is an additional step that often comes into play in order to sidestep the potential of becoming a full outsider. This move involves cooperating[17] with a sovereign authority to identify another outsider population. If successful, pariahs can secure their status as Border-guards[18] by instantiating and keeping new outsiders away from the internal boundaries of a polity while simultaneously serving to protect and circumscribe an inside population. In serving as the Border-guards, pariah groups serve an important role in maintaining the logic of liberalism.

The spatial and analogical traits of borders might be useful in order to illustrate why pariahs serve as a Border-population. Physically, borders are meant to divide and separate, to protect by keeping out certain elements while fencing in others. Thus, prisons, gardens, nuclear contaminated areas, and nations all have borders. In these examples, what is being protected or guarded is both "internal" to the border or fences, as well as beyond the border. These examples do not serve as completely suitable analogies because the element that is used as a border is presumably inanimate, and easily differentiable from that which is being protected or excluded. The analogy of border- or prison-guards has more potential because this group is often part of the same group of beings who is being included or excluded.

Spatially, Border-guards form a phalanx around that group of human beings who are elite, privileged, being protected, and yet they are also part of the inside group itself, albeit peripherally. Institutionally (at least in the United States), Border-guards are federal positions, but are among the least well compensated. Thus, they are "formally" part of the polity—as citizens—but are hardly ensconced in its core-echelons. And yet, often, the demographic background and genealogical, ethnic, and class history of the employees who fill these positions are very similar to the group of "foreigners" for whom they are responsible for keeping out of the polity itself—children of immigrants, poor, working-class and minority populations.[19] And so, Border-guards are both part of the inner populace, and on the periphery as well—professionally, socially, ethnically, economically, politically. And it is only by ensuring the exclusion of a more hated, more "undesirable" population that Border-guards can continue to maintain and secure their status on the periphery, marginally within the core-population of citizens, and remain less vulnerable to the policy vagaries and exigencies of sovereign institutions.[20]

Similarly, when a pariah population serves as a Border-guard, their spatial, demographic, but most importantly—their *symbolic*—designation is simultaneously reflected as inside the polity but only on the periphery. There, pariahs can be simultaneously construed as part of the polity, among the "insiders," while remaining on the boundary—*outside* of which the polity can instantiate "exceptions" to the promise of universal and equal treatment to all members of its polity. Negatively, by being cast in this double role, these former outsiders are depicted in the ambiguous light of being neither always part of the "coherent national We" nor always marginal to the polity.

Another way of understanding this ambivalent role is to think of the pariah population as both a subject and authority. As a subject-population, pariahs are always under obligation to obey the law, but without necessarily being awarded its protections.[21] Giorgio Agamben discusses the relationship of sovereign authority to subject populations as one of abandonment by the law. For Agamben, this relationship is inscribed by the compulsion to obey the law while being simultaneously vulnerable to its abandonment.[22] Yet his description neglects the logical and concrete fact that not all populations are constantly in threat of being abandoned. After all, if they were, then Muslim immigrants, White middle-class software engineers, and former United States Secretary of Defense Donald Rumsfeld would all coevally be in danger of being *homo sacer*—the sacred, and sacrificed, human being. Such a possibility is difficult to fathom. Rather, for a population to be subject to the law's authority (and to its abandonment) *an authority is required* (or a population whose authority is reflected within the law) whose whims and dictates are directed toward preying upon that population. This is a more probable trajectory for a population that is already susceptible to being held up as scapegoat by virtue of its marginal status.

How does this authority emerge? Michel Foucault, in his analysis of bio power, points to the widespread set of decisions on the part of the state to inscribe and compel certain populations to live and while allowing others to die.[23] In this lecture, Foucault's analysis of the racist state echoes some of the political and institutional character of the antagonism of Hegel's Master and Slave dialectic. Still, Foucault's discussion elides an analysis of the kind of subjection (*assujetissement*) evinced by both those in subjected-positions and in subject-positions, as he does in *Discipline and Punish*. There, in his discussion of Bentham's panopticon, he points to the self-subjection of those under surveillance in the prison. The self-monitoring of both prisoners and guards enables and facilitates the disciplinary processes—of striving to be the kind of subject who is recognized in a certain singular way in the eyes of the law—to unfold smoothly.[24] And yet, even in the process of "becoming subordinated by power," there must still be *an institution which coordinates, mechanizes, and administers the system which is to be involved, however latently, in the constitution of power and the processes by which bodies, individuals, populations become entrenched in the cycle of power.* As Judith Butler says (of Foucault's and Althusser's discussions of power): "'Subjection' signifies the process of becoming subordinated by power as well as the process of becoming a subject."[25] Butler goes further in complicating the concepts of power (authority) and vulnerability (subject). Of interpellation, that practice named by Louis Althusser whereby one *becomes* that subject who is hailed by an authority, she says,

> The one who turns around in response to the call does not respond to a demand to turn around. The turning around is an act that is, as it were, conditioned both by the *"voice" of the law* and by the *responsiveness of the one hailed* by the law. The "turning around" is a strange sort of middle ground (taking place, perhaps, in a strange sort of "middle voice"), which is determined both by the *law* and the *addressee, but by neither unilaterally or exhaustively.*[26]

And thus, a subject and an authority respond to each other in such a way so as to confirm, transform and/or deflect the full weight of "subjection." Contra Agamben, not all populations are necessarily, immediately, or abstractly in a state of exception, since some authority is required to enable that position of vulnerability. But even a dyadic relationship is too simple to describe the different degrees of vulnerability of various populations. Rather, which populations constitute exceptions, that is, are vulnerable and which are *potentially* exceptional or vulnerable, is a dynamic, shifting, and—at minimum—triadic relation.

If this is the case, then it follows that in a polity, the practical *telos* of any population is to ensure its own protection under the law. Only one part of the population can exercise the option of being the force behind the expression of sovereign authority—and thereby of the instantiation of certain kinds of recognition by the law.[27] What are the options of other populations in light of the assumption *that their practical telos is to ensure their own protection?* I would suggest that it is precisely the fear of being abandoned by the law that compels it to seek out another scapegoat for the law's abandonment. With the presence of another group to marginalize, the pariah population can be better assured of its place on the periphery, and thus of not being (formally) abandoned by the law.[28]

Here is where the role of the Border-guard comes into play. Only by ensuring that another group can be thrust into the extreme "outsider" role, can a Border-guard attempt to move into or preserve their— peripheral, but no longer completely vulnerable—place on the margins of the inside group. On the periphery, pariahs still exist ambiguously in relation to the core-insider population. They share a formal set of rights and recognitions with the insiders, but there is no concrete, political security that would anchor their standing firmly within the "insider group." They remain in large part at the mercy of the sovereign authority (whose primary constituency is still the core-insider population), in terms of the concrete recognition of the rights to which they are formally entitled. And thus, this pariah group still shares certain political and economic vulnerabilities with the core "outside" group.[29] The pariah population maintains an uneasy relation to outsiders because its status/treatment is in some ways not (or no longer) as extreme, unprotected or atrocious as it might be for an outsider population.[30] In light of its *telos*, the potential vulnerability of becoming the outsider—of being pushed outside the gates of the city, impels the pariah group always to attempt to cement its relationship to authority by removing itself from vulnerability, and thus by cooperating with or (passively) allowing itself to be deployed by the insider population to create and maintain a new outsider population.

Pariahs, Border-Populations, and Moral Gauges: The Example of Black Americans

The "integration" of pariahs is facilitated by a sovereign (or the executive) authority, along with the complicity and cooperation of other prominent public (but not necessarily state-sponsored) institutions, for several complicated reasons. The most important reason is the advantage that such an integration, if accepted by a core inside populace as valid, provides for a sovereign authority in constructing and enforcing policies that facilitate the exclusion of another ethnic group as an enemy to the internal coherence and strength of a polity.[31] The outcasting of new "enemies" requires the presence of the Border-population, in its ambiguous role as both insider and outsider, but also as official historical memory and Moral Gauge.

The procedure of co-opting a Pariah population to serve in these functions depends on three steps: The first requirement is the acknowledgement that in the past, other groups had been ostracized similarly, but the outcasting was based on *distinctly different and illegitimate* reasons. Second, the inclusion or depiction of the pariah group in question as part of the mainstream society must occur through a variety of legal, political, and discursive transformations. And third, there must be an agreement—or the conspicuous absence of disagreement, for any number of reasons—by the mainstream society *into which the former pariah group has been included*—that the current steps being taken to manage, control, discipline, or terrorize the new, emerging, outgroup is legitimate. For these criteria, I focus on Black Americans, because this group is the most prominent and longest-standing pariah group in American history, constantly and most often juxtaposed against a nebulous, already-existent White population, which constitutes the mainstream, dominant cultural and political majority population in the U.S.[32]

As legal citizens formally protected by the Constitution, African Americans now mark the boundaries between the inside and the outside of the American polity, and they can be depicted in the public's imagination as having the unique vantage point of being able to judge and evaluate the treatment received by other groups at the hands of the state. This positioning of African Americans stems from their unique history in the United States, into which they were brought as a stateless and rightless population, ineligible for citizenship, undergoing notorious persecution and atrocities, and having the political and social status of chattel. From this vantage point, they can be appointed (informally) as the moral gauge and historical conscience of the actions of the American state towards other groups on issues related to discrimination, persecution, and ostracization. In this case, I believe it is crucial to the success of the state's increasing ostracization of Muslims in this country that Black Americans not only be reconstructed as the current Border-population but, in light of their history as outsiders, as a morally authoritative population that can legitimate this ostracization.

Even before 9-11, the African-American population had been strategically, discursively, and politico-legally deployed in opposition to other— insider and outsider—groups. It goes without saying that Black Americans have certainly been outsiders for much of American history—politically, legally, socially. Much of the scholarly discourse confirms this marginalization, going so far as to understand the entry of new ethnic groups into the U.S. over the last century within the racial dynamics of White-Black political, legal, social, and cultural relations. Thus, new immigrants either "become White"[33] or they become "negroized" as a reflection of their acceptance or outcasting.[34] However, I hesitate to ascribe only a bifurcated dynamic to Black-White relations, because such a comparison would imply that Whites have "become" mainstreamed. This implication is inaccurate insofar as the symbolic importance of the category of "White" is that it reflects an already existent, politically and culturally hegemonic—"White supremacist"—population into which certain incoming groups become mainstreamed or against which other groups are juxtaposed and ostracized.[35] And so, the "White" population must cement and legitimate its ostracization of a new group by showing how a previous group is no longer an outsider and is now safely ensconced in the mainstream public culture and political norms of the dominant group. Black Americans have thus alternately been depicted as pariahs as well as part of the dominant American political imaginary, through several sources of political discourse, such as the state, the judicial system, along with the cooperation of the "respectable," that is, corporate media. This co-opting of Black Americans in turn facilitates, even legitimates, the outcasting of various minority and immigrant groups, as we have seen in relation to different Latino and Asian populations. This contrast depends on the gradual transformation of an old outsider into a pariah. Such a moment (of conferring a pariah status) attains significance only when simultaneously seen in connection with the creation of a new outsider status for another group that has not been previously (or at least not as strongly) identified in this light.

In order to do this, the sovereign authority must illustrate that the ostracization of what was previously perceived to be a pariah group, that is, Black Americans, is an event of the past, and was a regrettable and illegitimate occurrence. The recent public consternation from voices across the entire political spectrum over former Senate Majority Leader Trent Lott's remarks cements the most recent move towards the promotion of

Black Americans to pariah status—namely the unified interpretation that Black Americans should no longer be considered an "outsider" group—politically, legally, or culturally.[36] Another step toward this integration, in other words, the admission or depiction thereof of the pariah group into mainstream society, was initiated through the passage of the Thirteenth and Fourteenth Amendments of the U.S. Constitution, as well as the passage of the 1964 U.S. Civil Rights Act, among other such legal artifacts.

Yet, the political and legal "inclusion" of Black Americans into the U.S. polity has only recently been followed by the attempt to depict them—symbolically and discursively—as a core part of the dominant American Nation.[37] This depiction occurs through the selective and conspicuous awarding of recognition and status to the former pariah group. We see this through the concentrated focus of attention on the appointments of Black Americans in important U.S. Cabinet and judicial positions, as well as through the heightened representation of Black Americans in media, military, judicial, and academic positions. In addition, the extensive support across the political spectrum for, and the current U.S. Supreme Court's upholding of, affirmative action, as well as the key journalistic method of incorporating minority witnesses in media reports are also deployed to reinforce the perception that Black Americans are now part of the mainstream population.[38]

To what extent have these efforts to position Black Americans as pariahs been successful? It is difficult to answer that question with any certitude. There are several recent moments that seem to reflect the new status of Black Americans as pariahs, moments that seem to confirm the responses of many political figures and commentators, who recently, so "bravely" declared Black Americans to be, finally, unambiguously, a core segment of a coherent American population, in the wake of the Senator Lott controversy.[39] Pundits were anxious to provide evidence of the rejection of the institutionalized racial ugliness of America's political and social history, by citing various data that confirmed that African Americans contributed more to the American economy, were garnering more income, and achieving more prominent professional and political status than ever before. But the drive to instantiate a social transformation of Black Americans from outsider to pariah status is seen most vividly through several prominent appointments by the Bush Administration, including those of Secretary of State Colin Powell, National Security Advisor Condoleezza Rice, and Secretary of Education Rod Paige. These appointments, made by a Presidential Administration whose otherwise conservative policies upholding standard free-market economic policies, and judicial and legislative initiatives, that severely disadvantage American minorities, while priding itself on a multicultural openness,[40] seems to confirm, at least symbolically, an overcoming of (destructive) racial-consciousness.[41]

In addition, the visible increase of African-American faces on television and in the workplace also seem to insist upon the social acceptance of Blacks as part of the elite National American "We." For example, especially in the days after 9-11, television and newspaper media were noticeably including the voices of minorities who were not only condemning the terrorist attacks upon the Pentagon and the World Trade Center, but also anxious to confirm that "they were proud of America and to be Americans." This attitude was reflected vividly even on "liberal" television news programs such as CNN, as well as network channels such as CBS, ABC, NBC, and Fox. Another recent symbol of the social inclusion of Black Americans is found in the following: in April 2003, almost all of the 3,900 accredited colleges and universities in the United States[42] filed *amicus curiae* briefs attesting to the necessity of considering race as an important part of the post-secondary admissions process, that is, through some form of affirmative action. Figures not known for their enlightened views on diversity issues, such as the president of Harvard University, Lawrence Summers, were eager to publicly affirm "racial diversity" as a crucial element of any college population,[43] thereby seeming to promote a reflection of the importance of instituting legal educational protections for African Americans. And indeed, the Supreme Court has responded repeatedly and favorably by ruling that race, as one among other criteria of admission, is a legitimate consideration.[44] Such official stances from leaders of educational institutions, popular media, presidential administrations, and high judicial bodies appear to offer a narrative about the assimilation of Blacks into the American nation, perhaps even transforming their depiction in the American eye from outsider to pariah through the creation of particular laws that recognize the status of African Americans as a formerly persecuted minority whose assimilation into the dominant national imaginary has been substantiated through important citizenship rights,[45] such as the 1964 Civil Rights Act; an increasing body of anti-discrimination laws in the form of judicial opinion and affirmative action policies; and official apologies for past harms done to African Americans in this country.[46]

Of course, this supposed integration and assimilation, as viewed through the dominant lens of the popular media, cannot eradicate the fact that male Black Americans constitute a significant number of American troops who are placed in more dangerous positions in war, huge proportions of the American prison population, and Black women and men are still near the bottom of the prosperity ladder. It is a well-documented fact that African Americans are still subject to racial profiling, systemic criminalization through drug prohibition laws, three-strike felony penalties, redlining in housing, mortgages, banking.[47] They are still routine targets of discrimination in employment and college admissions, promotions, gerrymandering of voting districts, and social stigmas.[48]

It is the ambiguity of their place as among the "new insiders" and as still excluded from the concrete protections of the law that their role as a pariah population, and their *telos* in avoiding the complete abandonment of the law—or being the most vulnerable population—still lies. And hence, there is an understandable reason why they serve as the Border-population.

The depiction of a former outsider group as a new addition to the core population is deracialized, through the lenses of patriotism and family loyalty, cultural similarity if not homogeneity; and shared reason. This deracializing occurs in stark contrast to the method of creating the new outsider, whose status as villain is—at the very least—ontologically, if not also phenotypically portrayed. Concretely, we can see some of the former through the general impulse for inclusion that is embodied in the multicolored patriotism that circumscribes "Americanness," that is, through the multihued (but never class-based) representation of "our boys (and girls)" in Iraq, the nondiscriminatory impulse to wave the flag, the repeated testimony of the average Black Americans on television and in print media testifying to the evil of any given Arab-du-jour: Saddam Hussein, Osama bin Laden—regardless of the logic or lack thereof in hunting them down in the "War on Terrorism." This deracialization of Black Americans is conjoined by a simultaneous racialization of Muslims through the parallel condemnation of Islam and terror as synechdochic elements of most "Middle Eastern" persons.

Augmenting the role of Border-population is the role of "Moral Gauge." As mentioned above, this role emerges from and reflects the historical past of a population that has itself been ostracized in various ways. The collective experience and self-awareness of this population, as well as the external acknowledgement of its past, combine to place this group into something of a superior moral position, and thus enable this population and—especially its various leaders—to weigh in on a subset of public controversies as legitimate moral authorities. Black Americans have been thrust into the role of moral gauges in various instances, precisely on the grounds that the history of persecution and suffering undergone by this population places it in the unique and well-suited position to offer authoritative opinions and judgments about the moral status of the conditions and treatment that other groups might receive. Several examples come to mind. In November 2003, the Massachusetts Supreme Court ruled that gay and lesbian couples could not be preempted Constitutionally from the right to marry.[49] This ruling induced widespread debate nationally, causing comparisons to anti-miscegenation laws (which were institutionalized among many states until the latter half of the twentieth century), which were designed to prevent couples of different races from marrying. Media and presidential political candidates—on both sides of the issue—sought the authoritative weight of Black churches in both the northern and southern United States to support their positions. Leaders of Black churches and Black politicians and intellectuals hastened to weigh in on this debate. Leaders of synagogues, White Episcopal and Baptist churches were conspicuously not asked to weigh in on this issue.[50] With regard to the outcasting of Muslim immigrants, there is certainly no united position held by African Americans; however, the absence of a unified outrage or moral condemnation of such ostracizing is perhaps a telling silence. Moreover, in popular culture, such as among Black social critics and comedians, there was a resonant, if ambivalent, refrain: "Wow, we're bad off, but at least we're not them!"[51] More importantly, this silence or absence of outrage might be understood as a relief that the focus of persecution has taken other targets for the moment. The discourse of "terrorism/terrorists" has taken on a Middle Eastern/ Arab face, thus distracting the American state from the old "enemy" population—Black men and women.

More importantly, the state can point to the increasing integration and social acceptance of the pariah population as a shield to deflect the charges of creating a new outsider in many of the same ways as it has done to prior outsiders in the past. And this "integration"—in the form of widespread support for affirmative action, the increasing visibility of Black Americans in prominent government and media positions, and the "declaration" that segregation and apartheid are, *fortunately*, phenomena of the past—enables the current state to position the Black American population as a qualified moral gauge who would surely alert them by pointing to such events, were such atrocities being practices again or— at the very least—practiced for an unjustified reason.

Furthering State Interests:
Dividing Populations Against Each Other

I am not suggesting that Black Americans have initiated the creation of a new outsider—and certainly no more so than certain individuals may have done so.[52] Rather, they have been placed in this light by certain sovereign—and public—institutions in order to legitimate the creation of a new outcaste group, and in certain instances, that various individuals in this populations have cooperated with the state's agenda. The ambivalent role of a pariah population is intrinsically linked to the role it plays for the state as the historical memory and moral conscience, and the dividing wall they exemplify ensures the ability of the polity to identify itself as united, but also that enables the state to understand its treatment of the "enemy" as justified. As I have argued above, in being placed in this role, the pariah group is anointed in that role as the moral gauge of the political treatment of new strangers—in order to cement certain claims of insider status, while also justifying and legitimating the outcasting of a new population as an "enemy" or "stranger."

But such a move can only happen with the lead/collaboration of the state or sovereign authority, which also has a stake in preserving its own interests. Which interests are those? To maintain its own place as the authority that dictates and enforces law, and selects which groups it will protect and which populations it will marginalize.[53] There are three ways to understand the state's interest in cultivating the pariah status of a group. First, this interest can be explained through the element of hegemony or social control. Such an explanation, perhaps most famously offered by Antonio Gramsci, suggests that the state can reinforce its rule by consent by furthering the interest of subordinate groups. The subordinate groups in question understand their interests are being furthered, thereby realigning their loyalties towards the state, in the event of divided loyalties.[54]

The second reason for the state's interest in cultivating former outsiders in this way, is to enhance a polity's capacity to maintain its self-understanding as consistent with a modern political liberal ideology, one which extends legal protections and rights "universally" while selectively withholding them from a certain group.[55] To the extent that the polity is reminded that it ostracizes populations on a routine basis, it can concede past violations as cases of mistakes or exceptions, thus paving the way for an ethical justification of its latest ostracization (the third reason, below), but also so that it can continually remind the Pariah population of its insecure, ambiguous, status.[56]

The third reason is perhaps the most important: by cultivating and coopting pariahs into the mainstream population, the state can depict them as sharing the dominant *weltanschauung* on foreign and domestic polity. Thus, pariahs as a group can be symbolically rendered the moral sentinel of the legitimacy of certain political, legislative, and administrative actions on the part of the state. If Black Americans as a group, despite their own suffering and the acute self-awareness of the reasons behind it—the inhuman treatment of them as subhuman (or not-quite-human-like-us) and their former political status as illegitimate exception to the universal distribution of liberal rights—are *depicted* as watching without express or conspicuous dissent, while another group is treated in the same vein as they once were, while rights are withheld on the grounds that Muslims constitute an exception to the moral grounds of Constitutional rights as human rights—then the treatment of Muslims as the new outcaste, the new outsider, the new "evil" race can be legitimated, normalized, and accepted by the broader polity even as this polity congratulates itself on being a liberal society that has overcome a racist past.

Concealing and Unconcealing: Multiple Border-Guards and Outsiders

I am not arguing that Black Americans are to be understood as a Border-population across all current political circumstances and in relation to all other social groups. The pariah-outsider relationship can be used to compare groups across national borders and across time. The political/social status held by any given group depends on the group to whom it is being compared and the political context in which this comparison is taking place. In fact, such comparisons may be especially effective in order to reveal the multifaceted lights, moral status, and social connotations that complex entities such as cultural and ethnic groups may hold simultaneously. In this regard, I wish to invoke Martin Heidegger's notions of concealing and disclosing as he describes them in *Being and Time.* Heidegger uses these concepts to discuss the various "facts" that may be revealed to us (*Unverborgenheit*) as "true" at any given time in the context where other facts may have become "concealed" or hidden in darkness (*Verborgenheit*); he does so in order to caution against a monolithic, or uniform received notion of knowledge, history, or truth.[57]

In a similar way, I would suggest that the outsider status that any group may hold (in relationship to another) at any given time may be "concealed" as a differing status is revealed (in relation to another group and another political topic). Incorporating the concepts of concealing-unconcealing would allow us to consider frankly the different (and multiple) degrees of vulnerability that groups can hold in a variety of lights—*without necessarily ascribing that status to them in toto*—in all circumstances, times, and in comparison to all other groups. Such an admission would allow us a much more complex set of possibilities in our philosophical and political analysis. And thus it may be possible (and quite plausible) to argue that at one time—or even currently—Black Americans held an outsider status in comparison to Irish immigrants or certain Asian American groups on the issue of economic mobility or social acceptance in educational and workplace institutions.[58] In chapter 7, I offer the example of Asian Indians as a population who became racialized at the turn of the twentieth century; they did so between a dominant White population and other "pariah" populations such as Chinese and Japanese, and Mexican immigrant groups.

And so, in sum, Black Americans are both part and not part of the dominant group, in this case, the American nation. At times, they are part of it politically, at times symbolically and socially. In this regard, the Outsider-Pariah relationship is neither static, eternal, nor uniform. In other words, the description of outsider and pariah that I ascribe to Muslims and Black Americans, respectively, is one particular status among many that any group can hold at any given time.[59] By transforming previous outsider groups into new pariahs, the state can raise the shield of "plausible deniability" to the charge that new villains and outsiders are being unduly created. When the state can point to a previous legal outsider as now a core member of the polity, in effect enabling an official escape from the status of outcaste, as American society in conjunction with the Bush Administration has been able to do with Black Americans, then it can eschew the question of whether the creation of a new outsider is legitimate—because the dominant former outcaste functions as the official gauge and gatekeeper of such atrocities. Since Black Americans are understood to have suffered most visibly at the hands of the American state as well as private institutions and businesses, but can now be depicted as having been assimilated into the polity, then their supposed assimilation creates an effective tourniquet by which to deny that the atrocity of creating a new pariah is possible—for them, for others, now, or at any point in the future.

Conclusion

It is clear that the outcasting of new enemies requires more than a simple decision on the part of a state. It requires the presence of at least three populations: insiders, outsiders, and Border-populations. In this chapter, my focus was on the role and traits of Border-populations. Border-populations serve as an internal boundary dividing insiders from outsiders, but they also serve as a vehicle for the state to deploy in three ways: (1) as a former outsider and ambivalent (pariah) population that serves to guard and defend external borders against potential "dangerous" outsiders in the hopes of mitigating their vulnerable "outsider" status; (2) a decoy against possible charges that they are unjustifiably ostracizing a new populations; and (3) a moral gauge to justify the creation and persecution of new enemies. Border-populations act neither wholly voluntarily nor are they completely involuntarily deployed in this way. They have an interest in removing themselves from the completely vulnerable position of being the outsiders, and the state has an interest in dividing populations against each other in order to maintain its control over the polity. Moreover, such a role can be served by various populations within a polity, depending on the context.

The potential of becoming an outsider, and thus, abandoned by the law, depends on the existence of Border-populations. Border-populations, thus, are longstanding political and cultural pillars of those polities that wish to maintain the myth of universal and equal treatment of its citizens, while selectively extending those rights in order to help maintain their value. The integration of Border-populations into the polity is required as a means for the insider population to make the claim that the persecution of prior outsiders, such as for Black Americans, is a thing of the past and not a legitimate treatment; simultaneously, insiders, via the state, can impose similar treatment upon current outsiders as "legitimate" because the "terrorist" and "dangerous enemy" status of Muslim immigrants, "confirms" that they are altogether different. The desire on the part of former outsider groups to "get out of the line of fire," combined with the interests of the state to maintain control over its populace, enables cases like the contemporary American one, namely the ability of the American state to deploy Black Americans in the role of the Border-Guard and Moral Gauge in order to justify and legitimate the outcasting of Muslims.

7

Technologies of Race and the Racialization of Immigrants

The Case of Early Twentieth-Century Asian Indians in North America

Introduction

In this chapter I want to apply the framework that I have laid out in the preceding chapters to show how new populations can be racialized. The case in question takes place at the turn of the twentieth century in North America. The people in question are referred to as "Asian Indians," who migrated via Hong Kong and China to Western Canada and the West Coast of the United States. Asian Indians were a crucial presence in the American political scene; at some moments—particularly after the wholesale exclusion of Chinese and Japanese immigrants—Indians were the primary "Asian" blight on the American consciousness. Despite this fact, they were not easily or automatically included in the population called "Asian" or "Oriental," even as they were not considered part of the core American racial imaginary. Furthermore, even as "Asian Indians" were neither unqualifiedly Asian nor the original Aryans, they were neither unqualifiedly Indian. Frequently referred to as "Hindus," this particular group was likely to be Sikh, or less frequently, Muslim. They were British subjects who had colonial protections neither in their original "home" nor in British dominions. In the United States, the home of their making—in the country in which they sought refuge, as had thousands of others—they were subject to charges of sedition for their political resistance to the British in their "motherland."

    To compound matters, they were subject to the same gamut of anti-immigrant and racist legislation that had been directed toward the

147

Chinese, Japanese, and Koreans, and in some cases, against free Blacks as well. Like them, Punjabis were gradually rendered vulnerable through a range of bills passed prior to their presence in the U.S. The range of aforementioned laws, from the several Naturalization Acts, the 1910 and 1913 Alien Land Laws, miscegenation legislation, and other anti-naturalization laws contributed to the ostracization of Indians as a group unfit to own most farmland or property, too inferior to marry White women, and not Caucasian enough to be eligible for citizenship. Simultaneously, they are not accorded the respect of being political dissidents, and instead targeted and harassed as colonized upstarts. What might have contemporary postcolonial theory and American theoretical and historical discourses on race looked like had these literatures registered the presence of this population?

The Great "Hindu" Migration

Figures vary according to the source, but in 1900–1920, California saw the immigration of somewhere between fifty-five hundred and seven thousand East Indians, the majority of them arriving after the turn of the century.[1] In light of the fact that there were 14,000,000 immigrants[2] who arrived in the United States during this period, perhaps the number of Indians is miniscule; yet theirs was a significant enough presence that eventually a range of state and federal legislation would be directed at them uniquely but also in conjunction with their Asian counterparts. Initially, they arrived via Vancouver, amid much violence and controversy, to replace Chinese and Japanese workers who had already been the targets of exclusion laws.[3] Although this is a rarely known history, Asian Indians, like Chinese and Japanese immigrants before them, were subject to a range of hostile actions and legislation, which managed to regulate, discipline, and ultimately turn them out of the United States altogether.[4]

Like their Chinese counterparts, Indian, mostly Punjabi Sikh, men migrated down to California from Vancouver and Bellingham, WA, where they had been gradually disfranchised after working on railroads and in lumber. They worked throughout California, doing mostly agricultural work. Their presence had been initially welcomed as a check to the higher wages and inconsistent labor of other groups.[5] Over that thirty-year period, Indians managed to secure property, businesses, and farms throughout California. As their presence grew, they were perceived controversially as yet another wave of dark people, this time as Hindoos,[6] "coolies," "rag-heads,"[7] who had invaded the White provinces of North America. As Sen. Frank Flint said in 1907: "We don't want these Hindus and they should be barred out just as the Chinese are excluded.

When Congress meets I expect to take the matter up, and will do my best to protect the Pacific coast from the brown horde . . . There is plenty of room for citizens, but there is no room at all for *fakirs* and *mendicants*."[8] Between 1906–1908, they were subject to frequent mob actions up and down the Pacific Northwest. The first such action took place in Vancouver,[9] where among other transgressions, Indians were seen as threatening the jobs and wages of White laborers. Driven out of Canada, despite their claims to full rights as British subjects, they were subject to similar mobs in Washington and Alaska. In Bellingham, a group led by the local union waged a full-scale assault. Indians were attacked, their housing was burned, they were penned in the Bellingham City Hall by a civilian mob with the full approval of the local police chief, the city council, and the mayor.[10] They suffered similar riots in the towns of Everett and Danville, Washington and in Wrangell, Alaska, and elsewhere, by White laborers who sent them packing from farm to farm.

Eventually arriving in northern California, they were met by hostility again. In 1908, Indians in Marysville, CA, were subject to a mob composed by townspeople, who were troubled by the men's inability to dress "properly" and refusal to "observe the laws of decency," and by their alleged "indecent exposure to women and children."[11] Rounded up, threatened with weapons, robbed of two thousand dollars, they were driven out of town. Under investigation, the Marysville mob had plenty of witnesses who swore that no money had been stolen. The judge in the case, like those in other riots, blamed not the mob but the victims themselves.[12] Indians were also perceived hostilely by other ethnic groups: for example, by Japanese laborers, who considered them "English slaves," and mocked their short physical stature.[13] They were threatened by their Mexican neighbors for dating and marrying Mexican women after having been denied the ability to bring their wives from India, and having been prevented from marrying White women informally and formally.[14] Between 1908 and 1910, Indians were targeted by the San Francisco–based Asiatic Exclusion League, originally the "Japanese and Korean Exclusion League," but which had changed its name so as to be more inclusive of Indians(!) among its targets.[15]

In many ways, the plight and social and legal relationships between Asian Indians and the United States replicated the experiences of Chinese, Japanese, and Korean immigrants. They were hired by White land and factory owners, because their presence enabled employers to undercut the wages paid to competing groups of laborers. They were initially praised as more hardworking, and having more stamina to work longer hours in burning heat than their other Asian or White counterparts. And, like their Chinese, Japanese, and Korean predecessors, they were gradually harassed, vilified, and targeted violently, informally, and finally—legally. By other counts, Asian Indians fared somewhat better than these other groups. They were not brought over as indentured servants, as were the Chinese. They managed to invest in land quickly, through widespread networks, so that their ties to the United States were much more difficult to cut by the American government than were the ties of other immigrant groups. As a result, although they were targeted for harassment, theirs took a form rather different than that for other Asian groups.

This is because in certain ways they were a fundamentally distinct population: They were British subjects who technically had permission to enter the British dominion of Canada, and thus, technically, were supposed to be provided umbrage from harm by their colonial masters.[16] As colonial subjects, they were involved in resisting British colonialism in India internationally; their traces can be found in France, Germany, Canada, and the United States, among other places. In the United States, these campaigns overlapped with those claiming full citizenship and political rights for Indians, and for Asians generally. At least in the United States and in Canada, the political activities of Indians managed to land them in multiple troubles: they were the targets of British and American collusion to disenfranchise them politically and legally. Eventually, Asian Indians became the objects of anti-sedition and insurgency hunts, conspiracy trials, property-disenfranchisement laws, anti-miscegenation laws, denaturalization trends, government-led deportation drives, and finally legislative exclusion from the United States altogether.[17] In what follows I will give some details of this period to illustrate that the presence of this population was more than an incidental blip in the American self-consciousness of the time.

Political Resistance or Insurgency?

Between 1906 and 1925 several trends concerned British administrators. Diasporic Indians around the world were forming international networks that were part of several nationalist, anti-colonialist campaigns against the British; Indians in the U.S. had founded several political organizations that were agitating for home rule in India and canvassing for support among Americans. These included the *Ghadar* Party, a political resistance group whose membership included notable figures such as Taraknath Das and Har Dayal. The *Ghadar* Party had its own publication, in which it published photos of atrocities committed by the British against their subjects in India. As World War I began in 1914, an estimated 2,000 of some 10,000 Indians who were recorded as residing in the U.S. began returning to India. Finally, due to American and British surveillance, there appeared to be evidence that the Germans were aiding Indians in shipping arms to India. Even prior to this point, the British were becoming increasingly anxious about the collaboration between the Germans and certain political revolutionary parties to overthrow the British empire in India. As a result, through the British Ambassador to the United States, Sir Cecil Spring-Rice, they began to pressure the United States government to quash, or at the very least, to regulate the activities of Indians in the United States—which became popularly known as the "Hindu Conspiracy." The U.S. Attorney General's office looked at various American laws that Indians might have breached. It was not illegal for aliens to leave the U.S., except under certain conditions such as a violation of the Military Expedition Law or the Recruitment Law.[18] Nor were the photographs published by the *Ghadar* press illegal or particularly incendiary; they were judged to be appropriate criticisms of British actions in India.[19] There were four laws that Indians could be found to be in violation of, if the American government could find sufficient evidence: one was a 1903 Anarchy and Lynch Law, passed after President McKinley's assassination by a self-described anarchist.[20] This law became famous for its use in persecuting Eastern European and Russian anarchists, such as Emma Goldman. Two others were neutrality laws: one prohibited the recruitment of men to fight in a foreign army at war with a nation with whom the United States was at peace (known as the "Recruitment law"); the second prohibited the organization of a military expedition against such a nation for the same purpose (the Military Expedition Law).[21] But since they could find no evidence of these laws being broken, their next best option was to resort finally to a fourth law, namely the Conspiracy Statute of 1908. Convicting someone of violating the conspiracy statute required evidence only that one individual had discussed his potentially illegal activities with another. As Joan Jensen points out, there had been a long tradition of using this statute, dating back to thirteenth-century England. In the U.S., this statute had been unsuccessfully deployed to prevent individuals from organizing workers. There had also been a long tradition of attempting to expand the conspiracy statute to apply even in cases of politically revolutionary activities, but American courts—in keeping with the tradition that the U.S. was a political refuge—were reluctant to convict individuals of this crime in the case of revolutionary activities.[22]

However, the British had enacted a law in India, the "Ingress into India" law, with which they tried and convicted more than 50 men in Lahore, India, for conspiracy against the Imperial government in 1915.[23] Borrowing dubious testimony from that trial that more than 6,000 Indians had gathered in Sacramento to conspire against the British in India, Spring-Rice pressured the American government to arrest Indians on the grounds that they were participating in various "intrigues." An irritated

American court rejected this strange claim as having no merit. Finally, in 1917, indictments were leveled—using very weak evidence that forced to them drop some of the cases—in San Francisco, Chicago, and New York. A San Francisco grand jury indicted more than 100 men for conspiracy to violate the Military Expedition law. In Chicago, four men—one Indian and three Germans—were convicted. In San Francisco, twenty-nine persons were convicted. Fourteen of those convicted were "Hindoo."[24]

In the meantime, in 1917, because of the Asia Barred Zone Act, India was among the Asian countries targeted for the wholesale restriction of immigrants altogether—a stance that was not reversed until the 1946 Luce-Sellers Act, which finally allowed a miniscule number of Indians into the United States,[25] and then the 1965 Immigration Reform Act, which lifted many of those restrictions, and put in place a quota comparable to those for immigration from other countries.

Deportations of Indian aliens soon followed in 1920, thanks to a bill that was passed quietly amid many protests by sympathetic Americans, such as the Friends for the Freedom of India and congressional political machinations.[26] Ironically, although the bill was aimed at aliens convicted of crimes during the war, none of those deported had been convicted of crimes. In fact, a number of them were Indian laborers who worked for companies such as Bethlehem Steel. Estimates vary, although it appears that between 70 and 100 Indians were deported at that time.[27] Between these various judicial, legislative, and executive actions, as well as popular anti-Indian sentiment, the position of Asian Indians in California and the United States became increasingly precarious.

These activities overlapped with attempts by Indians, and Asian populations generally, to resist various American attempts to disenfranchise them economically, politically, and socially. Among the range of laws that were directed against immigrant populations during this period were three Alien Land Laws. The 1910 Alien Land Act would work to disfranchise them, along with others of Japanese, Chinese, and Korean descent. They were in danger of losing the land that they had worked to purchase. The 1913 Alien Act soon followed, making it difficult to rent farmland for more than three years at a time. Another law followed on its heels in 1920: "The 1920 Initiative barred guardianships and trusteeships in the name of 'aliens ineligible to citizenship' who would be prohibited from owning such properties, barred all leases of agricultural land, barred corporations with a majority of shareholders who were 'aliens ineligible to citizenship' from owning agricultural land and classified sharecropping contracts as interests in land."[28]

These Land Laws were preludes to the eventual disenfranchisement and internment of Japanese immigrants.[29] However, they managed to catch Asian Indians in their dragnets as well, barring them first from owning, then leasing for longer periods, then finally from passing their property on to trusted colleagues or associates who might hold them in trust for them. These laws were devastating to the vast majority of Punjabi Indians in California, who were primarily farmers, and whose strategy of integration had been to rely on intragroup money-saving practices, and to buy plots of farmland throughout California's San Joaquin and Imperial Valleys. This strategy, argued by some to have been imported as a cultural strategy of survival from India, enabled a relatively large number of Punjabis to settle fairly quickly as land-owners.[30] The alien land laws were used to convict 64 Indians for "conspiracy to evade alien land laws."[31]

Between 1910 and 1920 there were other laws directed against Indians. Several states, including California passed anti-miscegenation laws that prohibited Blacks, "Mongolians" and mulattoes from marrying persons from different races. Though these laws were thought to apply to Asians also,[32] it was unclear whether they were relevant to Indians until 1931, when Asian Indians were explicitly forbidden from marrying White women in Arizona (1933 in California).[33] Different states and their several municipal and county clerks interpreted the law in a variety of ways, although they often prohibited Indian men—almost none of whom had been permitted to bring spouses from India—from marrying White women. Consequently, Punjabi men married Mexican women, an alliance that was generally allowed or favored for a variety of reasons.[34]

Finally, in 1923, one of the starkest condemnations of Indians as racial subjects is found in the Supreme Court ruling on *U.S. v. Bhagat Singh Thind* (1923).[35] It is one of the most famous cases to come before the U.S. Supreme Court, and it is quite possibly the most referenced in contemporary literature on Asian Indians. The case arose in response to the 1870 Naturalization Act, which allowed only "Whites or persons of African ancestry" to be eligible for citizenship.[36] Thind challenged this restriction on the grounds that as a Hindu Indian (sic), he was one of the original Aryans, and thus even more so than any White man, was entitled to American citizenship. Needless to say, the court, using a tortuous logic, agreed with the argument that Asian Indians might have had common origins with White men, but rejected the implication that Thind could ever be considered "White" in the same way according to a judgment of the common man. This case followed on the heels of several other such naturalization cases, including *Takao Ozawa v. U.S.* (1922).[37] After the ruling in *Thind,* Indians were not only denied the opportunity to apply for U.S. citizenship, others who had been naturalized several years earlier were stripped retroactively of citizenship.[38]

Racialization

It may be obvious how the story of Indian immigrants to California map onto the framework that I described in the prior chapters. Reviewing the details will aid in illustrating both this experience, and the argument of this book.

Indians first come to the notice of the state because they are perceived as a threatening or unruly population. This perception emerges from a range of sources: They are perceived as distinct from the White, North American population into whose midst they are immigrating because of their skin color, dress, and accent. They are Hindus, Sikhs, Muslims, turban-wearing, foreign-language speaking in the middle of a resurgence of White supremacy.[39] Besides their physical conspicuousness, their presence exemplifies "economic competition, the seeming impossibility of assimilation, and racial antagonism."[40]

Their economic presence threatens to unseat their White working-class counterparts. Their habits suggest the threat to the relative cultural homogeneity of the milieu in which they are living and working. And the hostilities that their initial presence seems to engender—the series of riots, mobs, fights—appear to bring their existence into high relief: the state and the larger community first notice Indians in a socially antagonistic context. Under threat by union-led mobs, they are driven out of town, and prevented from accessing economic opportunities. They have explicit aspirations as landowners and settlers in the White West. Indian women are generally absent, and so Punjabi men are perceived to be a threat to the sanctity of White women.

Furthermore, their "unruliness" is amplified through their "unusual" political subjectivity: They were Indian Nationals and British colonial subjects in midst of nationalist struggles. The deliberate decision to agitate while in the U.S. leads to their perception as insurgents and anarchists and exacerbates the concern that they may be political traitors. Finally, I should note their emergence in the midst of political movements to exclude the Chinese and the Japanese. At first, they were welcomed by employers. But as they remain conspicuous, their normative perception changes: they are said to behave badly, indecently, not to assimilate. These struggles are morphing with the raised attention that Indians are receiving in the larger polity, and giving way to a continued perception of threat.

This "unruliness" also appears to engender a corresponding political and social vulnerability; throughout the series of riots and antagonistic social encounters, which they find themselves in the midst of, the perpetrators go unpunished. If anything, Indians are punished for finding themselves the target of hostility. They are penned up in the Vancouver City Hall by a civilian mob; in Marysville, CA, they are chastised for having accused the mob of having stolen their money. Their claims for justice go unmet. This lack of punishment engenders a corresponding vulnerability.

Their vulnerability is compounded by other semi-official aggression that is leveled against them, such as the pressure from the Asiatic Exclusion League (the newly renamed Japanese and Korean Exclusion League mentioned above) upon immigration officials, judiciaries, congressman, and Presidential staff to target them. Thanks to Canadian officials, and the U.S. Commissioner of Immigration, Anthony Caminetti, on numerous occasions, they were prevented from landing on Canadian and U.S. shores (circa 1913–1914).[41] This last turn of events is ironic, given their status as British subjects, and their understanding that they were entitled to some ostensible protection from their colonial masters.

No specific legislation targets Indians qua Indians during this time; this is the irony of their situation and my point: they are rendered the subject of physical violence, economic disenfranchisement, and mobs, without any explicit reference to them in U.S. immigration legislation. As a lawyer said at the time with regard to Japanese immigrants and the 1913 Alien Land Law, *"Of course, the Japanese were not mentioned in the act. Whenever we want to do anything very drastic, we never mention the fellow we are going to hit."*[42]

Punjabis are gradually rendered increasingly vulnerable through a range of bills that are passed prior to their presence in the U.S. The 1790s Naturalization Act (and its amendment to include persons of African ancestry) creates the conditions by which immigrants will always be rendered vulnerable to outcasting and racializing. Built onto the framework distinguishing "natural citizens" and aliens is the 1910 and 1913 Alien Land Laws, which shred the basic premise of American citizenship— American personhood: property-ownership as a claim to rights, protections, and the basic recognition afforded by the state. The farmland that Indians have worked hard to purchase and cultivate is taken away—a reinforcement that their status as persons will not be recognized, that they are unfit for membership in American society, at the same time that the U.S. Constitution is trumpeted for protecting all equally.

Their racialization was compounded by the range of anti-miscegenation legislation, and other anti-naturalization laws. Finally, they were the subject of American legal efforts to target them as enemies (of the British!). Convicted of conspiracy, and sentenced, they are subjected to deportation and denaturalization as well. Punjabis were targeted as having enemy-like characteristics, and precluded from citizenship until the long, arduous legal battle of Bhagat Singh Thind,[43] whose pursuit of citizenship was granted and then overturned by the U.S. Supreme Court. In the series of laws that affect Asians, the inability to be rendered a part of the recognized populace is construed as normal. Categories such as aliens, foreigners, immigrants, enemy aliens, which recognize Indians in a singular way, in other words, as fundamentally, legally, constitutionally, exclusionary, as not part of the polity, are normalized.[44] Today, we are familiar with their contemporary counterparts: enemy combatants, illegal immigrants, guest workers, etc. There are also additional terms that cast an absence of recognition: citizen, Caucasian, persons of African descent. Through repeated applications, these terms have become embedded in the popular and political vocabulary of the twentieth century, such that they appear to be intrinsic features of the juridical framework. Thus, already racialized upon their entrance as Indians and British subjects immigrating to North America, they are "racialized" anew as an unwanted population, to be persecuted, ostracized, and finally driven out of North America altogether. There is also the juridico-political avenue by which their unruliness and vulnerability together form a basis by which they are specifically unrecognized or misrecognized, and ultimately, dehumanized and rendered unworthy of protection.

Finally, Asian Indians at this point are sculpted in between at least two other populations. The legal terms of recognition (or unrecognition) do not gain a certain resonance except in relation/contrast to other segments of the polity that appear to have fundamentally different statuses: Whites, citizens, African-American citizens,[45] Japanese aliens, Mexican immigrants. These terms are used in juxtaposition to show how "intrinsically" unnatural the targeted population is, and thus, how integrally unable to fit in it is. These terms have a certain historical resonance as well, which ends up being ossified and shed as the moment of abandonment or violence passes. Thus, the term "Asian Indian" appears to be a neutral, ethnic category, and the political battles in which this term emerges are left behind, forgotten, and only its shell remains, to be reinformed and reinfused with new content by new generations with no memory of its history or content.

I have tried to argue that the purpose of lawmaking, the kind exhibited through the state, is a case of power rather than justice. As I state in chapter 2, the violence of which I speak emerges from the fear of being put outside the gates of the city or outside the jurisdiction of the law's protection; this is the fear that drives the collaboration of different populations with state authorities in creating outcastes.[46] But, as conspicuous as I have hoped to render it, this abandonment of unruly populations—populations that are rendered vulnerable through a seemingly inconspicuous series of legal events—is rarely so conspicuous. Rather, it hides behind the "rule of law," and is concealed in the technicalities and technologies of law, which masquerade as democratic procedure and the protection of subjects. In any case, I would suggest that the framework that I have laid out above is a more accurate gauge for law to decide who will be abandoned . . . who will become the subject of violence.

Invisibility

Asian Indians appear to have a "Forrest Gump"-like quality. They are barely recognized in the postcolonial literature or in American philosophies of race despite their core presence in a once crucial range of immigration and race battles, and their several efforts at political resistance to the British in India, while in Canada and the United States. Clearly, such large-scale targeting, conspiracy convictions, exclusion, denaturalization, and deportations of Indian aliens did not go unnoticed by American intellectuals or political activists.[47] What accounts for this eclipse in the American political imaginary? For W.E.B. Du Bois, as for other scholars in the American race framework, there appears to be an acceptance of the set of strictures and dichotomies that have framed discussions of the racial subject in the American context.

For example, the political, legal, and social recognition of African Americans is grounded in the conditions of their entrance and subsequent presence in the U.S, namely as slaves, and thus as beings without formal enfranchisement until 1865. Their political recognition, needless to add, is intimately linked to the political status of propertied Anglo-Americans since the passage of the U.S. Constitution, namely as the only political subjects who were both free and recognized as having rights. African Americans, following suit, gain a certain political status as citizens after the end of the Civil War. The initial, yet lasting, story of race in the United States is about citizenship and political rights; but as such, the story of citizenship and political rights becomes the story of *persons as property*, slaves, unfree labor, versus free White men who are landowners, slaveholders, and alone recognized as persons by the Constitution.

Property—as land, and a metonymical proof of membership—along with labor protections, wage protections, discrimination, political activities, political resistance, social integration—these too matter to immigrants, but they do not register through the exclusive theoretical narrative of race as about Black and White. Moreover, this eclipse is compounded by the bifurcated discussion of immigrants within the context of American legal history.[48] There have been several augmentations, as updated accounts of the history of the Americas have been formulated, regarding

American Indians, Mexican rancheros, and East Asian (Chinese and Japanese) immigrants. These accounts tend to be narratives that are augmented to the standard binary discourse on race, rather than a restructuring of this conversation.

It becomes easier then to see why Asians—Chinese, Japanese, Koreans, or finally—Indians, do not register in the discourse of race until they become second generation "Americans." Without an intrinsic tie to the dialectical framework of citizenship versus slaves/ex-slaves, immigrants, aliens, noncitizens, are cast as "foreigners," "outsiders," or "Other" subjects of "Other" nations. To paraphrase from Jacqui Alexander and Chandra Mohanty—in a different context to be sure, although I think it is an appropriate criticism in this one: "As 'immigrant[s]' . . . [they] were neither the 'right' color, gender, or nationality in term of the self-definition of the U.S. . . . The citizenship machinery deployed by the state . . . positioned [them] as resident aliens ('deviant' non-citizen; 'legal' immigrants) . . . It codifies an outsider status which is different from the outsider status of [persons] of color born in the United States."[49]

The conceptual place of immigrants outside the racial topography of the United States can be found in the history of plenary power doctrine that shaped and located immigrants as standing outside the gates of the Constitution, as I have discussed extensively in chapter 5. These two explanations might enable us to understand the fraught century from 1865–1965, which marks the struggle for civil rights for a range of "minority" populations who were citizens, while there is a simultaneously thwarting of claims of "non-Americans" for civil, due process, and other Fourteenth Amendment rights. This period saw the political enfranchisement of African Americans and women, claims for increasing labor protections—minimum wages and maximum hours for White working class men and women;[50] struggles against Jim Crow, lynching and segregated education,[51] claims for equal rights for women,[52] access to postsecondary education and equal treatment for minority populations in the workplace.[53] Many of these battles are associated not only with civil rights but with the fight for racial equality. They frame the racial discourse of the latter half of the nineteenth century and most of the twentieth century, reinforcing Du Bois's general argument that the racial battle in America pertained to Blacks and Whites. Michael Scaperlanda describes this period as one in which the constitutional culture emphasized the rights of the individual over other considerations.[54] His description heightens the irony since, as I have shown, there were many other populations who could have—should have—been recorded as an integral part of the race struggle of this same period.

The disfranchisement of Asians generally during the first half of the twentieth century seriously challenges the mode in which the Fourteenth

Amendment and its attendant clauses have been framed: as protecting due process, freedom of contract, and the citizenship rights of all persons within the polity. The Fourteenth Amendment has been identified as being an important formal protection[55] of the citizenship and property rights of Black Americans. It is certainly correct to suggest that the mere existence of the Fourteenth Amendment did not guarantee that many protections for ex-slaves—at least not consistently. However, since this amendment was passed as a way to redress the voting grievances that emerged after the passage of the Thirteenth Amendment; minimally, we know that it is intended to—formally—recognize the rights of African Americans. What is lost in that conversation is the tenuous meaning of "person," and whether "person" refers only to citizens, or to noncitizens also.[56] In the midst of a discourse over the expansion of political rights for Black Americans, an important population of the United States— its immigrants—and the effects of this law for that population, *is ignored entirely*. And the precedents set during that period still resonate in contemporary controversies.[57]

There is an important lesson to be learned from the bifurcation between citizens/slaves and immigrants/outsiders, namely the implicit criteria that enable the recognition of "racialized" subjects. If the American race discourse is framed in terms of a Black-White binary, which characteristics can we expect racial subjects to have who belong to either side of this divide? One's legal and politico-racial recognition depends upon eligibility for citizenship.[58] Moreover, in the long political-economic tradition of land, labor, and markets, the ability to be recognized as a politico-racial subject was also tied to one's subsequent rights to property. Thus, one's ability to claim formal rights, in the tradition of the Fourteenth Amendment and due process, depended on one's already existent standing as a member of the American polity.[59]

One might argue in response that the framing conversation for the United States at that time was about which population gets to be constituted as members of the polity, that is, qua citizens. But in the midst of that conversation, why is there so little discussion of the status of "immigrants" in relation to the "person" clause of the Fourteenth Amendment, and a corresponding set of rights? Imagine a post–Civil War race discourse that had to contend with the status of immigrants during that time, especially in relation to due process, property and contract rights? The importance of the absence of such a discussion cannot be overemphasized. First of all, the discussion of race and citizenship during the Reconstruction Era was heavily embedded in the context of labor, property, and due process. Remember that this period and continuing into the early twentieth century, is also characterized by a deepening political power

that is being accorded to labor unions and feminist organizations in order
to advocate for labor legislation and a broader suffrage—deeply important economic and political rights for a White working-class population.
And yet, even a casual perusal of the discourse of this time immediately reveals that rights of this population are being advanced in opposition to
immigrant labor rights, indeed at times—by leveraging the rights of immigrants.[60] Moreover, the eligibility for property and economic rights is
conditioned upon the eligibility for citizenship, which has been registered
through a rewriting of the 1790 Naturalization Act as pertaining to Whites
and those of *African ancestry*—thus again limiting the registering of race
on anything other than a binary (Black-White) scale.

How might the terrain have looked had their presence been recognized and digested in the race literature? First, the color line that DuBois
discusses might very well have been rearticulated in different terms. The
history of race literature has understood "Race" to take the form of a dynamic between a dominant (White) population and an enslaved or pow-
erless (Black) population. As we have seen through the emergence of
recent voices in Latino studies and Asian-American studies, the determined creation of a space that registers the presence of other populations and immigrant groups has surprisingly left the general binary
dynamic of the race framework theoretically/structurally unchanged.
The addition of historical records for other populations merely occurs as
an augmentation to the binary structure as it has been understood for
more than one hundred years. It is true that the registered presence of
Chinese-, Japanese-, and Korean- immigrants during the turn of the century enables a fundamental acceptance that these groups were indeed
construed as "races" in addition to "The White Race," and "The Black
Race."[61] However, that they are races does not shift the still dominant
Black-White narrative of American race consciousness to be a complicated racial structure that is composed of multiple races; rather, the additions of these populations are still considered afterthoughts or
incidental or periodic augmentations to the prevailing Black-White narrative of American race consciousness.[62] And the presence of Asian Indians is not registered into a dominant popular consciousness until 1965.
As such, Asian Indians are relegated to the category of "ethnic populations" that emigrated from post-Independence India.

In this regard, Asian Indians are not only eclipsed from the race discourse as "racial subjects," but within a contemporary postcolonial literature, they are exclusively located as an ethno-political diasporic
population whose coherence emerges post-Independent India, and in
consequence of having been colonized by the British during the course
of their expansive Imperialist project.[63] This is a perfectly appropriate

reading of much of the contemporary South Asian diasporic population. However, this reading, like that of the binary color line with the philosophical race discourse, eclipses some important dimensions of this population's history, which are important for both the frameworks of the race literature and the postcolonial studies literature. Postcolonial theory reflects a model of diasporic citizenship that can be seen especially vividly during the post-1965 immigration to the United States. Postcolonial literature reflects the concerns of "Third World" diasporic subjects, many of whom were academics and of professional status. They ruminate about power, law, dynamics between the colonial and the colonized, approaches that consider the status and significance of the diasporic community in history and contemporary politics, whether through literature, theory, or more recently social science written in or about the homeland, or the land of the colonizers, or in the diaspora.

Postcolonial literature in the United States has only very recently begun to reflect on what it might mean to have a "Nisei" subjectivity, in other words, that of the children of the first generation of diasporic immigrants who have grown up and begun to question their status.[64] This literature, understandably, refers to the cultural and political status of subjects in the postcolonial context, subjects who traverse back and forth between nations, borders, geographic locations. Who they are at any given time depends in part on how they are understood and interpellated. As Jacqui Alexander and Chandra Mohanty note of their existence in the United States, "We were not born women of color, but became women of color here [in the United States]."[65] But it also depends in part on what the conditions of recognition are. Postcolonial theory recognizes for example that "White men are saving brown women from brown men."[66] And often, the tendency of postcolonial theory is to challenge and resist it by "letting" the "subaltern" speak.[67]

Subaltern studies, taking its lead from this point, attempts to give voice to the subaltern, to attend to the relationship of power from the ground up, as it were. Thus, as a discourse, it attempts to find clues to the consciousness of the subaltern in the instances of rebellion, of insurgency, of violence as this group rises up against colonial power. As problematic as this construction is, it is functional insofar as the subaltern in question is recognized or at least goes through some machinations in order to be recognized. But what if the subject in question is not recognizable through the filters of this framework?

To return to Alexander and Mohanty, "From African American and U.S. women of color, we learned the peculiar brand of U.S. North American racism and its constricted boundaries of race."[68] But this peculiar brand of racism dominates the discourse in such a way that it conceals other variants, which themselves go unrecognized. South Asian male farmers and laborers are, in early 1900s, in the United States, not post-colonial subjects. And although they are colonial subjects, expatriates, they are not—could not be—recognized as such in the framework of post-colonial theory, because their struggles are conducted in the shadows of law, as immigrants, fakirs, and coolies—these are not the standard categories of postcolonial studies. And although they are fundamentally raced subjects—because they are immigrants, noncitizens, aliens and because they are neither Black nor White, they are not interpellated as such within American racial discourse—except within the moment—as "Hindu" or "brown" or even occasionally, as "White."

The "brown" people—such as I am speaking of—are difficult to theorize in the extensive frameworks of postcolonial theory, never mind American race theory and subaltern studies, because these grand narratives can only reflect they have been primed to catch. They cannot see what they are prepared to filter. Ranajit Guha simultaneously points to and reinscribes one element of the problem of representation exquisitely in what Spivak refers to as the "The problem of subaltern consciousness." "Once a peasant rebellion has been assimilated to the career of the Raj, the Nation or the people [the hegemonic narratives], it becomes easy for the historian to abdicate the responsibility he has of exploring and de-scribing the consciousness specific to that rebellion and be content to as-cribe to it a transcendental consciousness . . . representing them merely as instruments of some other will."[69]

The problem that Guha represents well is how to capture the specific consciousness of an event. But what converges with the consciousness of an event is the consciousness of the subjects who participate in the event itself. Where and how is that to be represented? Furthermore, what if the "event" is hardly that momentous as well? What if there is no rebellion? Does that preclude the recognition of a group, of different subjectivities within that group from being recognized? The eclipse of South Asian la-borers and activists, of Mexican-Hindu families, from the last framework is indeed an irony, since this framework was designed to understand the perspective of insurgent or rebellious moments from the perspective of peasants, that is, from the "ground up."

Can their consciousness be captured through some of the central features of postcolonial theory? I am thinking, for example, of the status of the preconstituted diasporic cosmopolitan subject. The men in ques-tion could be described as "cosmopolitan" in that they have certain traits that are associated with "cosmopolitanism." Often these men, once they have left India, lived and worked in several countries—from China, Hong Kong, Canada, and finally the United States. They speak several languages—Punjabi, Mandarin, Spanish, and English—learned in the course of their travels and experiences. But they have very little in common with the cosmopolitan subjects of the post-1965 Indian diaspora. They often give up their ties to their motherland entirely—from their religious practices, to their garb, their kinship ties. They have no citizenship, no claims to land in the country where they have settled, and often very tenuous ties to the partners whom they marry. Their "cosmopolitanism" results not from a surplus of property, confidence, and definitive ties to other lands or ascending populations, but from a lack of access to all of these; so I'll refer to them as "subaltern cosmopolitans."[70]

As Ann duCille points out: "The alterity of the Indian as postcolonial is generic, categorical, locational, but, interestingly enough, not racial or at least not racially specific. Race, it seems, is the proper attribute of black or African people."[71] She continues, "In the United States, the racial status of Indians and several other minorities has varied with the political and social agenda of the historical moment."[72] Could this be why South Asians are inconspicuously missing from the picture of race and history in the early twentieth century?

Subaltern cosmopolitanism, combined with the absence of the recognition of race, might begin to account why Asian Indians in this context are ignored by both postcolonial and American race literatures. How can we begin to account for the—multiple—consciousness and subjectivities of this group, during this period? I think there are several things that might be done on the part of postcolonial theory, subaltern studies, and American race discourse frameworks that might dilute the myopia of attending to this group.

Postcolonial frameworks might need to have their ideological and temporal scopes expanded such that the postcolonial begins not with the post-1947 diasporic community, but rather with migration within the very heart of the colonial period. Subaltern studies can account for this population by attending not only to moments of insurgency and rebellion of peasants—the consciousness of peasant populations occurs not only during the explosive events, or in the ruptures of history, but even in the continuity of historical quiet. And American race discourse can take into account this population by attending to how this group becomes a race—even though it does not lie within the heart of the Black-White binary, the citizen-immigrant dichotomy, the slave-citizen antinomy.

The postcolonial studies literature, had it registered the presence of this group in North America at the turn of the century, might have found it necessary to deal with the racial positioning of this population, rather than understanding Indians primarily as an ethnic group. Alternatively, the race literature might have been required to shift its analysis of race as a binary structure if it could have recognized the presence of Asian Indians and the impact that various laws pertaining to property, contracts, interracial marriage had on this group—while this population was *simultaneously* waging struggles on imperialist fronts—struggles pertaining to the privation of their rights as British subjects, conflicts over independence (analogous to the struggle for abolition and full citizenship rights for Black Americans), and as such, subject to an overwhelming collusion between the British and U.S. governments to squelch this group in North America through a state-sponsored hunt for insurgents, anarchists, radicals, seditious agents—all in an effort to disenfranchise, disempower the defiant (and nondefiant) members of this population. The form that this collusion took was to put Asian Indians on trial for insurgency, treason, anarchism; there was also the successful attempt to denaturalize already naturalized Asian Indian–American citizens, and finally, the deportation and exclusion of all Asian Indians until the 1946 Luce-Sellers Act, which finally allowed a small quota of Asian Indians to immigrate to the United States again.[73]

Now, I want to consider how the theoretical racial framework in the United States might have changed had Asian Indians been registered. First, I want to point out that in certain fundamental ways, the inclusion of Asian Indians—alongside the recognition of other early Asian, Mexican, Puerto Rican and Filipino immigrants—should signal to those who work on critical race theory that a binary racial dynamic is a fundamentally myopic structure: it does not capture the crucial structural role that visibly conspicuous immigrants play in helping to reposition the power dynamics between a dominant racial population (e.g., Anglo Americans) and a subordinate population (e.g., African Americans). If we take *any one* of the above mentioned populations into account when considering the structure of race relations in the United States context, then it should become clear that race is not a binary—but a tripartite—dynamic. How a dominant group and a subordinate group understand themselves in relation to each other requires them to take into account how they see themselves and the other population in relation to a third group. This group could take the position of an intermediary (a "Border")-population, which mediates between the two; or it could be positioned as a new "outsider," which enables a formerly subordinate group to—provisionally, momentarily—to appear to be allied with a dominant population.[74]

Another primary change that might have been registered with the presence of the Asian Indian population is the reconsideration of how domestic racial, criminal, and immigration policy is influenced by a national government's alliance with another nation, or by international political treaties, wars, or other events. In this regard, the treatment of Asian

Indian political activists resembles the treatment of Muslim, Afghani, Saudi Arabian, and other Muslim, Middle Eastern, and South Asian detainees under the U.S. government since September 11, 2001. The state's policies are also intrinsically linked to the widespread racial recognition and repositioning of multiple racial groups in relation to each other and to a dominant racial population. Finally, the recognition of the Asian Indian population earlier on, might have enabled an earlier initiation of a conversation about the intersections of phenotype, ethnicity, and the domestic and international disarticulation of various "Asian" populations, such that "East Asians, "South Asians, and "Southeast Asians" might have had a clearer, more accurate, perception in the wider American society as well as in the history of race literature. In particular, I wonder whether the term "Asian," like the terms "Latino" and "Hispanic" stand in for a "semi-generic" group that is neither Black nor White. If so, then it seems that registering the crucial presence of other groups by scholars in the race literature might have enabled a richer articulation of the racial, ethnic, political, cultural and social status of these groups in the American racial imaginary earlier than the late twentiety century.

Finally, the relationship between race, citizenship, and immigration is crucial, since it can address the links between color, race, ethnicity, and the widespread public racial perception of immigrants in relation to "homegrown" racial populations—whether these are populations who have been here for generations or are only second-generation. And so, I would suggest, it is one that needs to be incorporated fundamentally into the American literature on race and postcolonial frameworks.

Conclusion

Asian Indian immigration at the turn of the century, though small in number, had a significant impact on the American political and cultural imaginary. It constituted an important element of "Asian" immigration, as well as of the American race discourse, in that Asian Indians were the target of racial and immigration laws. Indeed, Asian Indian immigrants were a "racialized" population whose presence should have been registered both by the early American intellectuals who initiated the American philosophy of race tradition as well as by scholars in the contemporary postcolonial tradition. Asian Indians were harassed and persecuted by the Canadian and, under pressure from the British empire, by the United States government as well: they were disenfranchised, punished for their political activities regarding the British empire in India, subject to sedition, treason, and anarchy suspicions, and ultimately convicted of conspiracies to engage in the violation of various American laws regarding military expeditions and foreign army recruitment. Moreover, Asian Indian laborers were subject to deportation, while others were stripped of their citizenship, prevented from bringing spouses, marrying freely, and keeping the land that they had bought and held the titles for, and developed agriculturally. In short, Asian Indians were an important element of political and legal narratives pertaining to immigration, race, and citizenship at the turn of the century— and they were a targeted focus of the American government.

It is ironic and disappointing that this persecuted community was recognized neither by American scholars in the early race literature nor by contemporary postcolonial scholars. One reason can be attributed to their recorded presence in the American and postcolonial imagination as "immigrants," and "postcolonial subjects." Both of these categories must be interrogated for the assumptions upon which they are founded. In the American philosophy of race tradition, immigrants are squarely pitted against "citizens," "persons," with only the latter categories entitled to the legal and political protections of the U.S. constitution. Second, the antagonisms between citizens and slaves, and again between "(White) Americans and "(Black) ex-slaves" creates the foundation of an American discourse on race, which appears to neatly preclude the possibility of changing or shifting the conceptual terrain through which the notion of race can be opened up and broadened to include the stories of other (non-Black) racialized populations who entered the United States early in its history. Finally, there are nearly seamless links between territory—sovereignty—borders and citizens, and the corresponding understanding of protecting the rights and property-entitlements of those persons. By contrast, the opposing paradigm of immigration laws precluded non-Americans from enfranchisement and from possessing property—deeply cherished institutions that facilitate and enhance the pathway to becoming an "American," that is, a core member of the American polity. The bifurcation between immigrant and citizen further obscures the potential opportunity to understand how "Non-Americans" need to—and should be—seen as integral to the American philosophy of race and postcolonial literatures.

Conclusion

Toward a Political Philosophy of Race

In this book I have attempted to contribute to the rich literature concerning race in philosophy, cultural studies, postcolonial studies, and legal theory by giving an account of some of the fundamental dynamics that occur repeatedly to racialize populations within a given society. It is a conceptual account of how race works: driven by sovereign power, channeled through laws and juridical institutions, concealed through certain mythologies, and operating through the dividing of populations—some more vulnerable than others—against each other. Despite the important warnings that scholars in other fields give against the blindness and oppressiveness of "universal" theories, or overgeneralizing to the point of losing all salience, it is crucial to find a political-theoretic framework by which the building blocks of racialization can be at least provisionally identified. I have offered this account in this way because I am concerned that contemporary political philosophy and contemporary race theory and historical narratives of race have lost sight of several important lenses.

Contemporary political philosophy—whether it deals with accounts of sovereign power or with liberal political frameworks—appears to have forgotten about fundamental, insurmountable, disparities of power. And the history of political philosophy, with the primary exception of Michel Foucault's work, has overlooked the significance of race—believing it to be a transient or trivial category, or one best supplanted by accounts of class. Ultimately, these two categories—race and disparities of power—need to be the grounds of any political framework, because they are intimately linked.

It is surprising that even accounts of the structure of sovereignty such as Giorgio Agamben's, render all subject-populations to be simultaneously and equally vulnerable to the dictates—the potential abandonment by

167

sovereign authority. We know that sovereign power cannot effectively render all populations vulnerable; there must be some group whose status is secure—and most likely that security comes at the expense of another group's security. We also know—from recent experience, if not from centuries of political history—that sovereign power rarely represents the will of its subjects adequately. This has been the pressing question of modern political theory: how to account for the interests of a wider cross-section of a population. More often than not, sovereignty even—especially—in democratic frameworks represents an elite group whose interests and dictates drive the political and legal agenda. So why has this representation not been theorized more commonly in contemporary political philosophy?

In my attempts to consider race and disparities of power together, I have turned to Foucault, as one of the few recent philosophers who acknowledges this trend. In the way that I am considering race, I draw on Foucault's understanding that race is a strategy that is used to divide populations. Many scholars have argued that the racialization of populations is a much longer historical process than just the last two hundred years. In light of these arguments, it is even more puzzling that we do not have more theoretical frameworks that show how race is deployed to divide a society. Foucault's understanding of race is dazzling in what it allows us to see: how race is deployed through different forms of disciplinary and regulatory power. His arguments about bio-power illustrate the covert ways in which the racialization of populations is expressed through the medicalization of various phenomena, such as madness, the abnormal, sexuality. As profoundly insightful are his arguments that the power is disseminated through institutions, and often works reflexively through multiple nodes.

But Foucault's position that the sovereign authority of Hobbesian fame is displaced and disseminated in contemporary society, such that sovereignty is no longer of interest to him, is disappointing, because it seems that the potential of understanding sovereign power—as a centralized sovereign authority—in contemporary society—is considerable.[1] Also of great potential is understanding the consequences of disparities between sovereign authority and subject populations. The urge of sovereign power to control the threat of death and life are accurate; but there are other levels over which sovereign power also wishes to have control: control over its own regime; control over its own self-preservation; control over which populations shall be allowed to live and die. And in this regard, understanding *the differential of power amongst and between* subject populations—understood as racial divisions—can also be deeply illuminating.

There is also another dimension in accounts of race and political theory that seems to be neglected: how to account for those disparities of power between different populations? How to understand why one population will be subject to the state's wrath, while another will not, in any given context? Why are Muslim women targeted for wearing the hijab or full purdah, for example, but not Nigerian women, or Baha'i women, or Orthodox Jewish women? Certainly, in Foucault's account of biopolitics, a population is determined by its perceived threat to life. But not all threats work on the level of the biopolitical.

The biopolitical is Foucault's way of accounting for racial division, but it seems to me that racial divisions function on another level as well, especially if we bring several important themes back into the picture: First, we must account for the threats that drive sovereign authority to divide a population; that is to say, what accounts for the decision to racialize one population against another? Generally, it is the case that a population is perceived as posing a threat, but I would caution that it is a threat to a political regime (threats on the level of politics rather than life). Second, we must explicitly recognize what Carl Schmitt intimates, namely that power can create categories by which to divide and ostracize as needed on any level—and not just the biopolitical. Third, we must acknowledge that even in a world that is understood as post-monarchical, as "democratic" or "liberal," sovereign authority stands in a distinct disparity from subject populations. The ideal and equal distribution of power as understood in liberal theory is just that: ideal, not an empirical, reality. The narrative of sovereign power in classical liberal theory purports to represent its subjects' wills. But, empirically, we have far more instances of sovereign power representing the wills of an elite group—be they understood as the wealthy or those who are actually in power. Why is it so difficult for political philosophers to make this clarification?

Fourth, political philosophy must acknowledge that not all populations are equally vulnerable to being marginalized, outcasted, or racialized. Some are closer to sovereign power, while others are further away, and still others are representatives not of "the people," but of sovereign power itself. At least the first and third population are more vulnerable to being racialized than is the second group. Giorgio Agamben's account of the originary structure of sovereign power is insightful, but he also appears to have moved away from the recognition of class- or caste- divisions as fundamental to the coherence and management of society. Moreover, whereas Foucault offers an argument for why sovereign power has been displaced in contemporary society, Agamben asserts the ontological structure of sovereign power, thresholds, and the normalized state of exception without illustrating why it is the case that everyone is always on the threshold. And clearly, as we can observe, not everyone is always on the threshold—at least not simultaneously.

In this book the framework I have laid out has been an effort to understand race on the level of *onto-politics* and *onto-power*, of which bio-power is a subset. By onto-power, I want to suggest that race gets its force through the ontological status of categories that are assigned to populations under the auspices of a sovereign authority that wields enough power to influence a widespread social discourse. Such categories identify the racial status of a group through any number of phenomena— social, phenotypical, cultural, political—at any given time. The salience of these categories, as I have tried to describe in different chapters, emerges not from the particular "objective" basis of the term as it is deployed to represent a certain population—for example, that Muslims are terrorists, or that Asians are not Caucasian and therefore not eligible to be American citizens, or that Black Americans are violent and sexually uncontrolled—but from the operating assumption that these categories indicate a fundamental essence of a group, an essence that can be understood to isolate a group from the populace at large.

Those ontological categories work dynamically in conjunction with— emerge from—some perceived "unruly" threat on the part of a person or population. As I have referred to it throughout, the nature of the threat is that it is untamed, wild, in danger of challenging, even overturning, the prevailing political or onto-cultural regime. The nature of this threat is different from the threat that Foucault describes as the basis of biopolitics, which is a threat to the sovereign's ability to manage and control who lives and dies. The unruly threat might work in conjunction with the biopolitical threat, but it is mainly perceived at the level of the political and cultural. This threat becomes the lightning rod, against which a widespread hostility can be organized by sovereign authority and its collaborators. The dynamic tension between the ruly and the sovereign hostility is what is transformed into the racialization of a group. I call this phenomenon onto-politics, because the exercise of categorizing the threat is itself not grounded on physical, medical, scientific, or other necessarily objective data, but rather on the perceived transgression that its existence presents to those in power.

Race itself is the product of technologies of sovereign power, which deploys whatever resources it has at its disposal to identify a population that is threatening to its own self-preservation. But it does so through the "neutralizing rhetoric" of classifications, procedures, rule of law, judging and regulating those "threats" to the safety of the population under its care. In this regard sovereign power can function "procedurally," as the narrative of democracy and liberalism urge, and safely lulling its subjects to feel cared for and protected. Sovereign power can, through these methods, divide populations against themselves in order to seek support in identifying, isolating, and outcasting a certain population, all the while concealing its violence under the rubric of protecting the polity.

In this regard, the structure of race is rarely binary, but tripartite. Racial divisions depend upon a dominant group, a nearly outcasted group, and a group that has received fresh attention because of its unruly potential. The second group, a Border-population—is very useful in helping to marginalize a new group so that its own self-preservation might be more intact. I think this is why the creation of exceptions, or enemy populations, or racial outcastes requires the coherence of a state or a sovereign power, which can constitute a "we" that can then be posed against a "them." And so, unlike Foucault, I'm not sure it is accurate to understand racialization through a framework of biopolitics in which the sovereign is "displaced." It is not the sovereign but rather our attention, which is displaced in locating the systemic workings of disciplinary and regulatory power.

All of this is to say that power—more importantly—disparities in power, and the ability to construct categories through a centralized power, are integral to the racialization of populations in society. The power of race lies in the weight of ontological categories to hold sway, to instill fear and hostility, to incite hatred and justify state-sponsored—or at the very least, state-approved—violence. It is a systemic part of any polity, and it can pertain to any group whatsoever, given the right conditions. Can gender be a form of racial division? In a historicized context, yes. Can sexuality be a racial description? Yes. Can different racial dynamics work simultaneously? Yes. Can one group be racialized in one light and not in another? Yes. This is not to say that race has no salience. Rather, it means that race is a metaphysical mode of dividing populations. But those divisions are concealed in everyday life through other categories, which are the residue of earlier processes of racialization. Terms like South Asian, African American, Mexican, are ontic—everyday—labels that do not tell the full story of racialization. They "paper over," like gift-wrap, those narratives so that other more "powerful" narratives can be deployed to tell a different story: about terrorism, about dangerous and "criminal" populations, about the danger of immigrant labor to the cohesion of a polity. And these labels can then be deployed to engage in atrocities that seem necessary at the time, and accidental in hindsight. They effectively conceal the systemic character of racial divisions, of outcasting and marginalizing a population as an integral part of cohering polities.

This brings me to my other concern: the omission of wider theoretical apparatus that can help historical narratives of race and race theory illustrate how the particular racialization of a population has a wider resonance. I am noticing with alarming frequency that new stories about previously unconsidered populations remain just that: anecdotal histories that are unconnected to a larger political and theoretical understanding of how race and power work similarly across historical epochs, across political specifics, across populations. Certainly, one of the lessons that post-Enlightenment discourses have taught us is that universal theories are deceptive. Ad nauseum, we understand that there is no such thing as a universal truth. But does this mean that theory cannot inform us about generalities? About how power works generally? About the conditions by which a population can be marginalized? One of the implications of such a position, it seems to me, is that we reinvent the racial wheel over and over again, forgetting that racialization of groups is historically specific in any given case, but that the fact of racialization is historically pervasive. Short of offering a theoretical account of the common underpinnings of race-creation across different groups, it becomes too easy—and deceptive—to understand the story of racialization as being new, and pertaining only to some groups and not others.

In that vein, race discourse, as it has been predominantly framed in the United States must make room to discuss how new populations who enter the "gates," are racialized in old and new ways. Phenotype, skin color, and physiognomy are standard elements of racialization, but racialization of immigrants occurs on other levels as well. One tactic in expanding the race discourse is to chronicle these different levels as they occur in any specific population. And as we see through the range of histories that have been told over the last decade, the elements that are picked up as the basis of racialization vary in any given case.

This tactic is important; and in accumulating the specific histories of how different groups are seen racially, what we find is that physical characteristics are but one part of the process of racialization for any group. There are also political, legal, cultural dynamics that vary in their specificity, but must always be augmented to the story. But at the level of juridical institutions, legal regulations, and political and cultural discourse, it seems that we can abstract generally some of the dynamics that drive the racialization of any number of groups. That is the level where I think understanding the process of racialization at a more general level is useful. The nexus between vulnerable groups, the self-interest of sovereign power in maintaining its authority, and the eagerness of any given group to escape the hostile attention of the state, can be discussed in general and fruitful terms. And so what I have found, and attempted to argue, is that race is a long-standing phenomenon, and the political and legal process by which populations become racialized can be accounted for at the theoretical level by attending to the hidden machinations of the rhetorical ideologies of "rule of law," "rights," and power relationships between sovereign authorities and subject populations.

However, the picture that I have drawn—in light of this goal—appears to be much more bleak when institutions and groups are seen in a long-standing historical trajectory. Enemy groups are a constant within any society. Some populations—given the historical and political context—will be more vulnerable to the dictates of sovereign power than others. Other populations, once more vulnerable populations, will be eager to escape the wrath of law by allowing other populations to be targeted. Racialization does not necessarily happen solely at the level of skin color and phenotype. Other gestures also—clothes, modes of dress, religious customs, strange practices, lack of "proper deference" to law and culture norms—will become the lightning rods by which a group will be noticed and held for scapegoating.

That is not to say that the account that I am presenting must necessarily be seen, as some have suggested, as "nihilist" in orientation. In order for that accusation to be true, one has not only to describe law and sovereign power as destructive in its orientation, as I have done, but also to endorse this framework of law as the only proper one to abide by. I do not believe that I have engaged in the latter; to present an analysis of how I think law works, does not imply that I approve of how law works to racialize groups. Rather, my hope is that by presenting this framework, if it is accurate, that we might be able to find ways to address such instances of racialization in the future. I hope my outrage is in evidence throughout these chapters, not only with regard to the brutalities that have been engaged in the name of law over and over again, but also with regard to those who see the same series of events that I do, and insist that there is no evidence that these events are anything but accidental or unfortunate. I would suggest that the "liberal idealists" are "nihilistic" because they refuse to allow for the possibility of a preemptive approach to these atrocities, and willingly allow themselves to be deceived by believing that the fairy tale of liberalism can accommodate all equally without acknowledging deep and pervasive structures of power. The possibility of equality can not exist until we can acknowledge that law is dominated by those in power for the interests of those in power; moreover those who are in power must acknowledge their status. Even well-intentioned liberals, as cultural and ethnic studies scholars and sociologists have pointed out, find it very difficult to acknowledge their privilege despite being faced with the prospect of a solution to inequality.

Let me suggest, then, a solution to the bleak picture I have painted over the last few pages. While it is certainly the case that the law works in collaboration with those in power to disenfranchise other threatening and vulnerable populations, it is important to hold this phenomenon in balance with the aspirations of liberalism—as aspirations—and certainly by no means a reality. This is a dialectical approach, which can be seen in Hegel, Marx, and even at certain points in Heidegger's work. Marx popularizes this approach when he challenges the positivist economics method, which takes the value of a commodity at face value. In his famous chapter on surplus value, he argues that the value of a commodity is determined in the social relations of production, which are hidden, or at least not visible to the eye. Dialectically, Marx's insight is that by taking the commodity at face value, one misses out on the political, economic, legal, and social structures that have led to the production of that good. In the same way, by committing oneself to the liberal story that the framework of politics and law is about arriving at fair procedures, fair and equal treatment of all—by committing oneself to this story as an empirical description of how law and power works, rather than as an ideal, one continues to feed a dominant mentality that injustices are infrequent, accidental, and random. By extension, those who are vociferous in their complaints of unjust treatment are considered to be overly sensitive or just 'whining." This view illuminates the fundamental incapacity of those who are not in vulnerable positions to imagine the "Other" in a generous and sympathetic way, and not incidentally, continuing to reproduce a certain disregard for the "Other," which is endemic to Enlightenment continental philosophy.

My approach to thinking of sovereign power and race is meant to parallel the dialectical approach described above—in an effort not to endorse a "violent" framework of law, but to try to illuminate another perspective, which might describe the patterns of how populations become marginalized and vulnerable. I think it is crucial to see the series of brutalities that mark the last few centuries of modernity as patterns, rather than as accidental events, because this may allow for a more effective solution, one that reaches the heart of the problem, rather than one that attempts to affix solutions post-facto, after the tragedy has occurred. I think an appropriate analogy here might be a case of domestic violence, where a person beats his partner with some frequency, say for example, once every two weeks. During the other thirteen days, he is a functional and even conscientious citizen: he attends church, he is considered an exemplary employee, an engaged parent, and even an affectionate and loving spouse. He is cooperative in his interactions with his partner—for the thirteen out of fourteen days. But on the fourteenth day, he invariably becomes inebriated, and he is not in control of his temper, which is managed rather well the rest of the time. There are two ways to address this situation: One is to assess the violence with a view to the person's everyday behavior and conclude that he is a good parent, good worker, and good partner who occasionally loses his temper. It is a shame, but each instance is considered to be accidental, and we, as his community of family and friends hope that he will manage his anger more successfully in the future. In the meantime, we consider it an appropriate response to help his partner heal and ensure that their children have good care of until the abused spouse recovers and can undertake his/her part of the division of labor again. Such an approach might be "functional," in the sense that eventually, everyone will play their parts again but the crisis will not be resolved in any permanent way. For many of us, in reality, this would be considered an absolutely inadequate response.

Another approach to the same problem would be to focus directly on the violence, and insist that it is unacceptable, regardless of how good of a parent and partner the abuser is during the other thirteen days. In the latter approach, the solution must focus on the source of the violence directly, that is, what does it take to stop the violence immediately and conclusively? If the source of violence is his unmanageable temper, then it seems imperative—as a preemptive strategy—to address his temper immediately through alcoholic recovery groups, therapy, etc., among other additional steps. But to take the second approach requires us to see the occasions that he beats his spouse as a systemic series of events—a pattern—and not, as the first approach does, as an accident that occurs every fourteen days.

Similarly, I would suggest that it is important to see the racialization of a group as a part of a pattern that is endemic to political frameworks and sovereign power. It is important in order to understand these in their historical context, and in terms of certain power-relationships that undergird sovereign power. These are often discussed in other disciplines and in popular discourses about politics and race. For example in critical legal studies, it is commonplace to say that law is not about justice but about power. Moreover, other areas of legal studies point to the importance of reifying certain dynamic discourses about identity through legal stamps of approval—laws, bills, statutes, constitutional modifications. It is not such a far step to understand these as a part of a philosophical framework about law engenders race and racial identity.

By attending to the dialectical relationship between the violence of law framework and the story of liberalism as an ideal, constructive solutions in the vein of using law against itself—to counteract the violence of law—are possible. For example, the system of parliamentary democracy banks on a fundamentally different system of politics than does American liberalism: on power rather than procedure. Thus, the key to passing certain kinds of laws or using laws to protect certain populations are no longer engaged in the name of "rule of law," or procedure, but rather as an expression of a certain political group. This is hardly a new solution. It is also consistent with a tradition of social, political, and ethnic alliances that immigrant groups in this country have long utilized as a form of protection.[2]

How does one resist what appear to be endemic, intrinsic impulses to crush outsiders within liberal-juridical frameworks? Tina Chanter, in a recent article, discusses the possibilities of resistance from a position of the abject. The abject—that stage of complete loss and melancholy—like the framework that I have laid out in this book, appears to be all-encompassing, without possibilities for fighting back. Chanter, through her moving analysis of several films, argues that resistance does not have to take an overarching form; rather, it can be expressed through small steps, and its form can change in response to the situation. Chanter discusses "Margaret's Museum," in which a woman in a coal-mining town who has lost her husband, father, and brother, pickles their various body parts in order to display them to an "unknowing and uncaring public to witness . . . the horror of their death, she is asking the public not to forget, but inciting action."[3] More monumentally, as Chanter points out, the "abjection can be a response to the failure of politics, but it can also reinstigate the political."[4] In the particular instance of "Margaret," her mode of resistance is through the aesthetic representations of the horror that surrounds the lives of those in her coal-mining town.

We can borrow several lessons from Chanter's argument to think about the system of juridical racialization of outcaste groups. One lesson is that resistance can be expressed through small, even "minor" or unnoticeable actions, beginning with reflection. The argument in this book is one attempt to engage in that lesson. I want to note two things that seem appropriate here: First, in light of my argument that racialization in liberal societies occurs behind the veneer of the rhetoric of equal rights, it is important to sand off the veneer and confront our legal practices and ourselves in our ugliest mode. The condition of resolving the practice of racializing new populations is coming to terms with the fact that the ideal of liberalism is not in fact its "real" mode of practice. Second, since the form that racialization takes will constantly change, the form that resistance must take to such an invidious, intrinsic, practice must also constantly change.

Another concrete lesson is the use of the aesthetic to illuminate, raise moral outrage about the political. As I finished writing the first draft of this conclusion several months ago, Fernando Botero, a world-famous painter, was exhibiting his *Abu Ghraib* collection at Doe Library on UC Berkeley's campus. Botero painted these as an outraged response to the news of the torture of Iraqis at the hands of the American Military. Although he is exhibiting his collection in museums around the world, he will not show his paintings in any U.S. museums unless they specifically request to exhibit them. The sheer tragic beauty and pain expressed in his work, along with the publicity generated by his work and mode of exhibition, are but an instance of the kind of resistance that can be exhibited even in the face of something intrinsically destructive, dehumanizing, or abject.

The aesthetic, then, is a mode of resistance, but perhaps here is the place to explore other modes of resistance—most notably juridical or political modes. The most consistent lesson that I have learned from the exploration of how law produces racial divisions is that the rhetoric of the rule of law tends to conceal power and supercede even the most efficacious attempts to outwit the problem of "exceptions." The discourse of human rights, as exemplified through the 1948 Universal Declaration of Human Rights is an excellent example of the failure to preempt or eliminate atrocities, rapes, massacres that occur in the name of "racial" or "ethnic" divisions. The language of human rights, as I argue in chapter 3, is circumvented through the discourse of madness, which has both science and a marked "distance" from racism on its side.

How then, do we address the issue of racialization and rights in this seemingly abject context? As I discuss in chapter 5, the large-scale acceptance of the seemingly deep divide between immigrants and citizens, between "aliens" and members allows us to perpetuate a racist discourse without having to come to terms with that fact. Furthermore, this divide, as I suggest in chapter 7, closes off the possibility of theorizing how immigrants become racialized, since they are not only rendered outside the parameters of the protection of law itself—outside the gates of the city—but conceptually they are rendered outside the parameters of scholarly and popular race discourse as well. One solution is to remove the barrier between immigration and Constitutional law, which undergirds the process of racialization in the United States. By eradicating this divide through the insistence that immigration law be integrated with Constitutional law, that immigrants be guaranteed Constitutional protections, we have one—momentary, provisional—mode of attending to the current predominant form of racism in our midst.

Another possible response might be to remain skeptical of the labels ascribed to different groups in the identity frameworks. Contrary to Wendy Brown's claims in *States of Injury*, I am not sure that attempting to repossess an identity in order to revalue it is a form of resistance. Rather, in the framework that I have laid out, the act of repossession is an act of acquiescence to the state's attempts to domestic the unruly; conversely, when such an act is successful, it is likely that the state no longer considers the group in question a threat, and so the act of "claiming" an outlawed identity is in fact a descriptive rather than a rebellious act.

Moreover, identities, as we know, are fluid—capable of stretching and shrinking depending on the agenda of the shrinkers/stretchers in question. Instead, perhaps a better approach to racial identity might be to understand at which level an identity is operating: at the level of census data collection; for the purposes of medical research; for historical comparisons; etc. Once the level of racial identity is discerned then we are in a better position to decide how and in which direction an identity needs to be deployed. For example, as Richard T. Ford (2004) points out, certain cultural traits that are supposed to be representative of a certain population often have the effect of constraining/reinscribing one's ability to participate or be excluded from an identity. So, for example, we could say that the veil represents a certain kind of Muslim womanhood. Certainly, this kind of definition/ascription seems to be unduly problematic when it comes to defining membership in a population of Muslim women. But here the question is for what purpose is identification in the Muslim female community being deployed? Can we separate this purpose from a discussion of the political treatment that women receive at the doors of political and legal bureaucracies once they are determined to be Muslim? And how is the treatment that Muslim women receive, whether they wear the hijab or not, similar or distinct from the treatment that other "unruly" women have received in other political contexts? We know that this problem is not relevant to Muslim women alone. Women from every background have been racialized as a group under the system of patriarchy for wanting things that those in power were unwilling to recognize. The same goes for gays, lesbians, and transgendered populations, Black Africans and their descendants in various contexts, and many other groups who were unwilling or unable to assimilate, conform, acquiesce to the norms of those in power.

It seems to me that the question of resistance is predicated on finding patterns in the treatment that various populations have received across different contexts. Without seeing, let alone understanding, the systemic similarities, we have no way to formulate an analysis that would allow us to develop strategies for resistance that can be of use to more than one group at any given point. It is my hope that this book can be of assistance towards that goal.

NOTES

Introduction

1. After completing coursework, I moved away while I worked toward my degree; I did not have the opportunity of attending Emmanuel Eze's or Robert Bernasconi's seminars when they visited the New School. My discoveries of their writings and edited collections on race, and the works of other contemporary scholars who do philosophy of race, needless to say, changed my intellectual world.

2. Michael Foucault's and Hannah Arendt's writings are important exceptions; although I did not encounter Foucault's writings on race until after graduate school.

3. Due to a lack of adequate vocabulary, I use this unfortunate term as a modifier for those who live in the United States; I am fully aware that it does not represent the entirety of denizens of the Americas.

4. See Almaguer (1994), chapter 2. He uses this term to distinguish wealthy, landowning Mexicans from Anglos shortly after the acquisition of California by the United States.

5. Foucault (1977), p. 222.

6. See Ignatiev (1995); Wong (2005); Pfaelzer (2007) for a few examples of such dynamics.

7. I should make clear that not all postcolonial literature avoids a discussion of race, particularly in the case of writers emerging from Uganda, Kenya, and elsewhere in the East African context. I am discussing postcolonial literature that has emerged in the North American context, specifically the United States. I discuss some of the limitations of postcolonial literature in chapter 7.

8. There is, of course, a recent burgeoning Latino/Latino American philosophical discourse that is grappling with race, including works by the following authors: Linda Martín Alcoff (2000), (2006); Jorge Gracia (2000); Gracia and De Greiff(2000); Nelson Maldonado-Torres (2004); Eduardo Mendieta (1999), (2003); Mariana Ortega (2001), (2006); and Ofelia Schutte (2000), (2001); among other notable scholars. There is also an emerging, though even smaller literature on race, culture, and Asian American philosophy, which includes scholars such as Yoko Arisaka (1997), Namita Goswami (2006); Goswami and Court-wright (2008); David Kim (2002), (2003), (2004), (2007); and still an even smaller—but existent—literatures in Arab and Arab American philosophies, which includes Alia Al-Saji (2004), (2008), and Elizabeth Kassab (2005), and Native American writings on race and philosophy, which include Anne Waters (2004) and V.F. Cordova (2001). The above list is a sampling of works in these respective fields and is not meant to be exhaustive.

9. Heiddegger (1950); Foucault (1979), (2003a); Benjamin (1978).

10. Derrida (1990), pp. 943ff.

11. Schmitt (1996), pp. 30–31.

12. See chapter 6.

13. Fichte (1979), p. 22.

14. I offer another explanation in chapter 4.

15. Conner (1978), p. 322.

16. Although not necessary "minimal" interference. This might be one version of liberalism, for example, libertarianism. See Nozick (1974) for an account of libertarianism as a strain of liberalism.

17. See Waldron (1998), who describes some similar principles.

18. Mehta (1992), (1999); Metcalf (1995); Brantlinger (2003); to name just a few in this tradition.

19. Mills (2006), p. 228.

20. Berlin (1969).

21. This is hardly a radical position; this point is shared by the legal positivist tradition.

22. As Chantal Mouffe describes, using John Rawls's work as an example. See Mouffe (1993), chapter 3, esp. pp. 48ff.

23. 338 U.S. 537, 544. As quoted in Scaperlanda (1993), p. 968.

Chapter 1

1. From Heidegger (1950). I have substituted the terms "race" or "racial" for Heidegger's original use of the terms "technology" or "technological," respectively.

2. Michel Foucault argues that sovereign power has a similar function of managing populations, although not necessarily for the same reasons. See Foucault (2003a), March 17 lecture.

3. Or discipline, to draw on a Foucaultian perspective.

4. I will sketch this concept only briefly in this chapter. In chapter 3, I will develop it further.

5. Examples of "naturalized" criteria include physical identity (blackness), ethnicity (Indian), and culture ('Oriental' or 'Asiatic'), religion (Islam), sexuality (gay/lesbian), as well as legal/political categories (terrorist, immigrant, undocumented alien). I will discuss some of these examples in later chapters.

6. Heidegger (1950), p. 314.

7. See Introduction, where I describe my working definition of liberalism.

8. By violence, I mean not necessarily overt, but covert, destruction, in the senses discussed by Walter Benjamin and Michel Foucault. See Benjamin (1978). For Foucault, this sense of violence is expressed through his discussions of race, division, sovereign power, and the "mechanics of discipline." See Foucault (2003a), p. 254; p. 37. See also Foucault (1979), where violence in this sense is famously expressed as disciplinary power. I will return to a discussion of the covert sense of violence in the section subtitled "Dividing Populations" (p. 29) of this chapter.

9. Here I draw on Agamben's notion of the "ban," whereby one is subject to obey the law while always in danger of being thrust outside the juridical order and thus vulnerable to being harmed. See Agamben (1998), §§ 6.

10. I am aware that *Gestell* is concept with multiple complex dimensions; for relevance to this analysis, I wish to draw on a much narrower facet of this concept.

11. For an explication of this tension, see chapter 5.

12. Foucault (1979), pp. 137–138.

13. Sawicki (2003), p. 62.

14. Foucault makes clear that he is not interested in discussing the intentions or decisions of human beings Foucault (2003a), p. 28. Nor does he ascribe to a concept of power whereby populations are collectively deployed against each other (Foucault (2003a), p. 27; p. 29). This is one place where I depart from his understanding of power; I am interested in how populations are managed collectively against each other through sovereign power, although as I hope will become obvious, I agree with him that "[individuals] are in a position to both submit to and exercise this power." Foucault (2003a).

15. By "racialized" classifications, by which I refer to terms whose grounds are not biological but political or moral, for example, aliens, enemy combatants, terrorists. Also cf. n. 5 above.

16. Hubert Dreyfus points out the major difference between the ontologies of Heidegger and Foucault as follows: "For Heidegger, the basic way the background practices work is by appropriation, gathering so as to bring things into their own . . . For Foucault, on the contrary, the background practices reveal . . . a constantly shifting struggle." Dreyfus (2003). I hope it is clear that my discussion of the third dimension of technology reflects the influence of both thinkers: that technology of race as it conceals the relationship of violence between sovereign power and subject, is both an example of how "background practices gather to disclose new worlds," (Ibid.) as well as an example of how sovereign power constantly shifts the terrain by which populations are divided so as to hide and "normalize" the technological racism of the state.

17. Foucault (2003a), p. 249.

18. Foucault (2003a), p. 37.

19. See n. 32, where I suggest that the "unruly" is neither necessarily biological nor physical nor part of the psychoanalytic imaginary, but rather something "ambiguously real." I develop the concept of the unruly in chapter 3.

20. Foucault (2003a), p. 37. In this sense, my understanding of where race emerges is distinct from Foucault's.

21. In any of its numerous expressions: legal decisions, statutes, enforcement, etc. The other element that appears to be concealed in the prior tendency is that of subjects/populations that tend to become collectively reconstituted as "good subjects"/"bad subjects." See Engle (2004) and Mamdani (2004). I argue that this tendency manifests itself

in liberal polities through "Border-populations," that is, populations who can stand as a "third term," which distinguishes good citizens/insiders from bad citizens/outsiders. See chapter 6.

22. There are numerous literatures, in various disciplines, on this topic. In philosophy, in which this discourse has had a fierce reemergence, the debate is best represented through some of the following literature: Zack (1993), Appiah (1996), Kitcher (1999); Andreasen (2000); Hardimon (2003); Glasgow (2003).

23. For some representative examples of PO, see Said (1978); Camus (1946); Chatterjee (1986); Cohn (1996); Gandhi (1998); Chakrabarty (2000). The writings of Frantz Fanon, W.E.B. Du Bois, and Etienne Balibar represent some of the more notable exceptions that presciently bridge the divide between BR and PO. There are also some more recent works that do the same admirably. These include San Juan (2002); Loomba (2005); Clarke and Thomas (2006); and Stoler (2006).

24. Such as the centuries-old Hindu-Muslim and upper-caste/lower-caste conflicts in India (cf. Cohn 1996), the Palestine-Israel conflict, the massacre of Tutsis by Hutus in Rwanda (cf. Ch. 2), and the genocide of Bosnians by Serbians in the early 1990s. More recently, similar "intra-group" racial conflicts have been in evidence in the conflicts between the Bantu and "ethnic Somalis," and the Janjaweed, and Arab- and non-Arab-identifying Muslims in the Darfur region of Sudan.

25. By Blumenbach, Buffon, Kant, LeClerc, Linnaeus, Voltaire, and others. See O'Flaherty and Shapiro for an extensive and clear overview of how these writers shaped and informed the scientific discussion of race over a 200-year period. O'Flaherty and Shapiro (2004). Also see Bernasconi and Lott (2000) and Eze (1999) for a range of primary writings from the seventeenth and eighteenth centuries in the vein of classifying race "scientifically."

26. See Milchman and Rosenberg (2003), for a collection of essays that address the relationship between Foucault and Heidegger.

27. However, I return to his discussion in chapter 2.

28. See n. 25. Or, as in Robin Andreasen's argument, to 200,000-year-old racial groupings. Andreasen (2000), pp. S660–S661.

29. See n. 22.

30. As Foucault's discussion of biopower exemplifies. See Foucault (2003a), especially the March 17 lecture.

31. I am aware that my demarcation of the "real" is ambiguous. By referring to the "real" as the dimension in which the unruly is found, I wish to elide the insistence that what marks race is material/biological/physical/phenotypical—and to circumvent a commitment to the psychoanalytic ground of the "symbolic imaginary." Thus the real is neither a Lacanian/Zizekian category, nor does it aptly connect to Husserl's distinction between "real" and "reell." I believe my use of the "real" does pertain to Heidegger's discussion of "signs" and "references" in connection to his discussion of worldhood in *Being and Time*. See Heidegger (1996), sections 17 and 18.

32. My use of "unruly" is, at most, only slightly related to Nancy Fraser's use of the same term in her book. See Fraser (1989). There, she uses the term to illustrate the politics of "need interpretation," in contrast to traditional liberalisms' approach to calculating needs objectively. My use of the term does owe its inspiration to Michel Foucault's deft illuminations of the relations of subjects to sovereign or juridical institutions, that is, as about disciplinary and regulatory power. But the resemblance, I believe, ends there.

33. After all, this is what the "unruly" signals even in conventional discourses.

34. See Cohn (1996), for an excellent discussions of how caste-demarcations played out via regulations on clothing.

35. As Daniel Chandler paraphrases Robert Goldman and Stephen Papson, "an 'empty' or 'floating signifier' is variously defined as a signifier with a vague, highly variable, unspecifiable or non-existent signified. Such signifiers mean different things to different people: they may stand for many or even *any* signifieds; they may mean whatever their interpreters want them to mean. In such a state of radical disconnection between signifier and signified, 'a sign only means that it means." (Robert Goldman and Stephen Papson, 'Advertising in the Age of Hypersignification', *Theory, Culture & Society* 11 (August), 23–54. 1994, 50, as paraphrased by Chandler (2002) in his book, *Semiotics: The Basics*. Routledge. London./onlineversion: www.aber.ac.uk/media/Documents/S4B/the_book.html. Ch. 3: modality and representation.) Cf. also Derrida (1976) p. 20; Derrida , p. 25.

36. See Davis (1991), for an excellent, engaging, and thorough survey of the variations, causes, and implications of the one-drop rule in the United States.

37. Compare, for example, that the one-drop rule was defined as having one-eighth "Black blood" in Mississippi, Missouri, and several other

states, whereas Virginia changed its rule from one-fourth to one-eighth fraction of "Black blood." See Davis (1991), p. 9. Consider also the fact that "mulattoes" in South Carolina were designated White until 1850, and remained free to marry Whites. In *Plessy v. Ferguson* 163 U.S. 567 (1896), the Supreme Court held up Louisiana statutes that defined as "Black" those persons whose descent consists of at least "one-eighth African blood." Nearly one century later, in the same state, Susie Guillory Phipps challenged the description on her birth certificate, which designated her as "colored," and was turned down again. We know she lost the case, and lost on appeal as well. See n. 40 below.

38. We know that similar threats were presented by citizens and immigrants of Chinese, Japanese, Korean, Filipino, and Asian Indian descent between the mid-1800s and the mid-twentieth century as well. In these cases, however, the standard of measurement was not whether they were Black, but whether they could be considered "Caucasian." I will discuss this phenomenon later in this chapter and in chapter 7.

39. And implicitly creating a hierarchy between populations. I will come back to this point a bit later in this chapter.

40. The Susie Guillory Phipps case, decided in 1983, is a similar actual case. If anything, the data in her case is even more extreme. In 1970 Louisiana changed the criteria of its one-drop rule from having a "traceable" amount of "blackness" to being more than "one thirty-second" (1/32) Black. *Jane Doe v. State of Louisiana, through the Department of Health and Human Resources* (1985). See Davis (1991), pp. 9–11 for a discussion of this case and the surrounding context.

41. See David Schneider (1965), who challenges the automatic scientific ground of blood as the basis of kinship by suggesting that these are symbolically related. See also the Preface of Sylvia Yanagisako and Carol Delaney (eds.), (1995) "Culture is what makes the boundaries of domains seems natural, what gives ideologies power, and what makes hegemonies appear seamless" (p. 19). As importantly, categories and identities are understood as such by "claiming for them an autonomy from human social agency" (p. 20).

42. I would offer a similar reading of the rulings upheld in *Plessy v. Ferguson, Hudgins v. Wrights* 11 Va. 134 (1806), *U.S. v Bhagat Singh Thind* 261 U.S. 204 (1923), *Ozawa v. U.S.* 260 U.S. 178 (1922), among countless others. See Ian F. Haney Lopez, (1998), for a legal reading of the social construction of race in these and similar cases.

43. Andreasen (2000).

44. David Schneider points out that kinship can be viewed substantively (i.e., in terms of blood) or functionally (in terms of the relationships it serves to connect). There is no reason why one should be privileged over the other. See Schneider (1965), p. 85.

45. I will develop this argument in depth in chapter 2.

46. Foucault (2003a), p. 254, 256. By death, Foucault includes "indirect murder" as well, including "political death, expulsion, rejection" (p. 256).

47. Foucault (2003a), p. 255.

48. Foucault (2003a), p. 254.

49. Foucault (2003a), p. 247.

50. Foucault (2003a) pp. 49–50.

51. To be more precise, for Hobbes' Leviathan, it was the "fear of death," which was used to keep men in check.

52. Foucault (2003a), pp. 254–255.

53. Foucault (2003a), p. 37; my emphasis.

54. Biological Race. See beginning of this chapter.

55. Foucault (2003a), p. 251.

56. Foucault (2003a), p. 242.

57. For example, through "scientific" links between blood and race, as already explained.

58. Schmitt (1996), p. 42.

59. Schmitt (1996), pp. 27–28.

60. Schmitt (1996), p. 30.

61. Schmitt (1996), pp. 30–31; my emphasis.

62. I will return to this dimension of technology in chapter 2.

63. *U.S. v. Bhagat Singh Thind* 261 U.S. 204 (1923), pp. 209–210; my emphasis.

64. See the final chapter. Thus, whereas they might have been initially racialized for a different reason, say, their looks, customs, and ability to undercut other populations economically by working for lower

wages, they are now reconstituted as a race by being denied the right to citizenship. I think similar impulses are found internationally: untouchability, or caste, or religion as grounds by which to sanction political, religious, and cultural apartheid in India, for example.

65. In particular, I have in mind those conflicts that have erupted between Hindus as a unified population vis-à-vis Muslims, and which are being sanctioned through anti-terrorist statutes such as the "Prevention of Terrorism Act" (POTA), passed March 26, 2002. POTA was repealed in September 2004, following the election downfall of the Hindu extremist Bharatiya Janata Party (BJP). See Brackette F. Williams (1995) for competing positions on the debate of whether caste can be viewed in similar terms as race. Williams argues that the "facts" of caste-division, such as those among Hindus, are instantiated through rules of marriage, kinship, and community and are similar to those of race. Cox argues otherwise. See especially Cox (1987), part. 3, chapter 19.

66. There is a much longer historical and larger political context for this phenomenon. The unruly threat presented by Muslims in India is no doubt being exacerbated by more recent events, such as those of September 11, 2001. I will discuss some of the links between these events and their racialization in ensuing chapters.

67. Heidegger (1950), p. 302.

68. Heidegger (1950), p. 303.

69. Corlett (2003); and Kateri-Hernandez (1998).

70. Brown (1995), chapter 3, esp. pp. 64ff.

71. Heidegger (1950), p. 301. Heidegger is here describing Plato's understanding of *eidos*.

72. Benjamin (1978), p. 295.

73. I return to the example of Asian Indians and their racialization in the final chapter.

74. Elsewhere I trace out one example of how this works. See chapter 5, "Producing Race."

75. In relation to an existential enemy, and through the ever-present ability to declare war.

76. Heidegger (1950), p. 305.

77. Heidegger (1950), p. 306.

Chapter 2

1. Mamdani (2004), pp. 3–5.

2. See Introduction, where I describe my working definition of liberalism.

3. As Charles Mills has contended, it is quite possible to hold as simultaneous the ideal narrative of liberalism and the inherent racism of liberalism. He calls it the "symbiosis" view, and describes it as claiming that "racism is the dominant tradition, and liberal egalitarianism has been racially inflected from the start." Mills offers another view, which is less "radical," such as the "multiple traditions view," which holds that "racism and White supremacy are alternative political and ideological traditions within their own right within the political culture." Regardless of which view one prefers, Mills argues that it is important to recognize that racism as an "anomaly" is an incorrect characterization of liberalism. Mills (2006), p. 216.

4. This formulation might sound similar to Foucault's discussion of power and state racism in the SMBD lectures; however, Foucault rejected the notion of a central sovereign power in favor of a diffuse disciplinary power. Also, his notion of state racism is promulgated through "society" and "discourse," that is, not through a particular juridical or institutional source. See Foucault (2003a), January 14 and 21 lectures. In Foucault's "Governmentality" essay, he makes a claim that is similar to my formulation, although he applies it specifically to the "'art of government," and specifically *not* to sovereign power. See Foucault (1978), p. 211.

5. Here I am thinking of overt physical or psychic harm, or more subtle cases of imprisonment or privation of rights or procedures, events such as wars, deliberately induced famines, slavery, genocides, racial profiling.

6. Derrida (1990). Unless otherwise specified, all subsequent citations to this essay will be noted in the text by page number alone.

7. Brian Trainor takes issue with Derrida's formulation of the source of the law's authority as "mystical," or found simply in its existence. Trainor argues that the law's authority is found in its legitimacy, as expressed through the will of its people. His formulation appears to return us to the mythological story of liberalism with which I take issue, namely that consent to rule and the rule of law are powers accorded to the "people." Trainor (2006).

8. ". . . lawmaking pursues as its end, with violence as the means, what is to be established by law, but at the very moment of instatement, does not dismiss violence. Rather, at this very moment of lawmaking, it establishes as law not an end unalloyed by violence, but one necessarily and intimately tied to it, under the title of power. Lawmaking is power-making, and to that end, an immediate manifestation of violence." See Benjamin (1978) p. 295.

9. Benjamin (1978), p. 281.

10. Both sides of this formulation—the lack of normative grounding and the unconditional compunction to obey law—are not original. They can be seen, in less dramatic form, in the positivist tradition of philosophy of law, as well as in the tenets of the Critical Legal Studies school.

11. See the works of Marx, Althusser, Charles Mills, Heidi Hartmann, Carole Pateman, to name a few.

12. Jean-Luc Nancy describes this as the abandonment of the protection of subjects to sovereign authority, although he does not refer to this relationship as one of violence. This relationship, with its promise of annihilation, defines the ultimate vulnerability of all subject populations who may at any point become the target of the law's abandonment Nancy (1993).

13. Agamben (1998), p. 15.

14. Agamben (1998), p. 28. My emphasis.

15. Agamben (1998), p. 15.

16. Agamben (1998), p. 28–29; original emphasis.

17. Agamben develops this point in *State of Exception*, where he defines "exception" as a suspension of the juridical order (p. 4) or of the Constitution (p. 5). See Agamben (2005).

18. Precedents, ironically, are invoked in order to show how one is adhering to a common interpretation of a rule.

19. Foucault says of sovereign power, "whereas the end of sovereignty is internal to itself and possesses its own intrinsic instruments in the shape of laws, the finality of government resides in the things it manages and in the pursuit of the perfection and intensification of the processes it directs; and instruments of government, instead of being laws, now come to be a range of multiform tactics. Within the perspective of government, law is not what is important . . ." Foucault (1978), p. 211.

20. Foucault (1978), p. 213.

21. Foucault (1978), p. 215.

22. Foucault (1978), p. 218.

23. Foucault (1978), p. 219.

24. Foucault (1978), p. 219.

25. See Foucault (2003a), especially the January 14 and 21 lectures.

26. Foucault (2003a), p. 45.

27. Foucault (2003a), p. 81.

28. See Sheth (2007b). There, I explore in more detail Michel Foucault's argument on sovereign power. I argue that Foucault's framework does not account for the disparity in power between sovereign and subject, which can be accounted for by understanding that sovereign power can and does often operate directly. We need merely to look at the disparity of interests of those who are, in most Western polities, in the state legislatures and judiciaries, and the interests of those they purport to represent to show that biopolitics still needs a central authority to organize and direct it.

29. Some well-known examples include the legal division between free persons and slaves, the distinction between first and second-class citizens and those ineligible for citizenship, as these categories were informed by the 1882 Chinese Exclusion Acts, the Alien Land Acts, and the internment of Japanese during World War Two. Most recently, we have seen the creation of racial categories such as in those of enemy combatants and terrorists. I discuss the latter in later chapters.

30. See Chapter 3, where I develop this concept further.

31. See an example of the concept of the "unruly" in chapter 4.

32. This process is cyclical. These physical signifiers, along with new markers of the "unruly," will eventually become the foundations of a "new" process of racialization, the basis of the repeated and originary reinstantiation of law as it targets another population for racialization.

33. As in the struggle for abolition of slavery, or the right to naturalized citizenship, decent wages or labor protections, as were demanded by numerous immigrant groups in the history of the United States. See chapter 7 for another example of this dynamic.

34. In some ways, this discussion corresponds to Joan Jensen's description of H. Otto Dahlke's analysis of riots, even though, in my application of this framework to the case of Asian Indians (in chapter 7), I focus on the target of the riots. According to Jensen, Dalke lists the following prerequisites for the occasion of a riot: "First, the community usually must be in transition. The subordinate group . . . must have a history of being victims of violence, must be regarded as undesirable competitors, and must exhibit some trait or characteristic that can serve as a focal point for negative assessments. Established authorities usually must tacitly support violence or refuse to assume responsibility for riot control. An association devoted to propaganda or advocating violence against the minority group usually must exist, with a press that enforces the association's negative assessments. Finally, the upper and middle classes, must either stand by or encourage violence . . ." (Jensen 1988, p. 42). I came across a description of it after this section chapter and chapter 7 (originally part of this chapter) had been written. Ironically, the title of Dahlke's article is "Race and Minority Riots—A Study in the Typology of Violence" (1952). See also Pfaelzer (2007) for an excellent history that illustrates this pattern.

35. See chapter 7.

36. In the case of Asian Indians, who I will discuss in chapter 7, these can include their status as foreigners, their "odd" dress, for example, turbans, their political action in response to unfair treatment in the U.S. and British colonialism.

37. See Jensen (1988) for an exhaustive history and list of their transgressions on this front.

38. See the 1795 Naturalization Act (which supercedes the Naturalization Act of 1790); it restricts citizenship to "free White persons." In 1870 the Act was amended to include "persons of African ancestry." The U.S. Constitution of 1787 does not define membership explicitly through race, although it does identify several populations that are excluded from membership in the American polity, and assigns certain functions to citizens alone: voting, the right to run for the office of President. The jurisdiction of the Fourteenth Amendment applies to "persons," whose parameters are continually changing (see chapters 5 and 7).

39. Agamben points to the state of exception in *Homo Sacer*; however he understands it as part of the basic structure of sovereignty, instituted by the sovereign at will.

40. For example, the category of "immigrant" takes on this character in American contexts, whereby the meaning of the category loses its historical context, and instead takes on the flavors on the current political controversy. See chapter 5 for a review of the historical context of the category of "immigrant."

41. My thanks to Nelson Maldonado-Torres for an extensive conversation that is the foundation of this point.

42. In Israel, as of September 2006, the government is no longer issuing residency permits to Arabs in the West Bank. 72,000 Arabs (mostly Jordanians married to Palestinians) have been rendered illegal as a consequence. They were issuing "temporary" three-month permits, and have now begun to issue one-month permits, which for some are "final" renewals. The Israeli government, when asked, insisted that according to Human Rights Conventions, there was no obligation to issue residency permits to non-Israeli spouses of Israeli citizens. True; certainly this is an appeal to the "principle of law." But the more salient issue is the political backdrop surrounding this decision. Myre (2006).

43. Cf. *United States v. Cruikshank* (1876) 92 U.S. 542. In this case, an armed White mob in Louisiana attacked and killed a large group of African Americans during a controversial gubernatorial election in which Blacks had insisted upon the right to vote. More than 100 African Americans were killed. The Supreme Court decided that the Thirteenth and Fourteenth Amendments were federal rights, which could not supercede the state jurisdiction of Louisiana.

44. Exemplified vividly in the cases of Matthew Shepard and Brandon Teena, respectively.

45. As a poignant example of this, see the U.S. Supreme Court decision in *Oyama v. California*, which overturned one of the provisions of the 1920 Alien Land Laws as violations of the Fourteenth Amendment's equal protections clause due to the American children of Asian immigrants. This decision came 35 years after disenfranchising Asians of their property. *Oyama v. California*, 332 U.S. 633 (1948). See also Aoki (1998), p. 64.

46. Agamben (1998), p. 83.

47. This rendering of sovereign power is of Benjamin as described by Agamben (2005, p. 56).

48. Mamdani (2001), p. 16.

49. Tutsis are said to be taller, slimmer, and with lighter skin and wavy hair; Hutus are thought to be darker, more square, and "bridgeless" noses. Gourevitch (1998), p. 50.

50. See Mamdani (2001), chapters 2 and 3 for an excellent description and analysis of the Hamitic thesis in reference to Tutsis and Hutus. Cf. also Gourevitch (1998) for a more general discussion.

51. Laurent Nkongoli, vice president of the National Assembly, as quoted in Gourevitch (1998), p. 50.

52. Mamdani (2001), p. 230.

53. And to some very small extent, the Twa, who are barely mentioned in the contemporary literature on Rwanda.

54. See Aoki (1998); Daniels (1989); and Kashima (2003).

55. Kashima (2003), p. 15.

56. *Ozawa v. United States* (1922).

57. Kashima (2003), p. 15.

58. US. State Department Memorandum, as originally quoted in Bob Kuramoto, "The Search for Spies: American Counter-intelligence and the Japanese American Community 1931–1942," *Amerasia Journal* 6, no. 2 (Fall 1979), and reprinted in Kashima (2003), p. 16.

59. Kashima (2003), p. 16.

60. Saito (1997b), p. 78. Also see In re Saito, 62 F. 126 (D. Mass. 1894).

61. Saito (1997b), p. 83.

62. Issued on December 8, 1941, and based on the Alien enemies Act of 1798, this proclamation declared that all "natives, citizens, denizens, or subjects" of Japan who resided in the United States were eligible to be treated as "alien enemies" and detained. Proclamations 2526 and 2527 applied in the same way to German and Italian nationals. Kashima (2003), pp. 59, 73ff.

63. On February 19, 1942.

64. Benjamin (1978), p. 289.

65. See chapter 1, "The Technology of Race."

Chapter 3

1. Foucault (1989), Preface, p. xi.

2. Ibid., p. 89. Foucault repeats these sentiments throughout this text. Cf. pp. 94, 98, 99, 102.

3. Which stands in for complicated phenomena, as I discuss below.

4. *Oxford English Dictionary* online. http://dictionary.oed.com. Accessed June 24, 2006. Dictionary definitions for "strange" and "strangeness."

5. Note that I make a distinction between the explicit reference to "race" and the idea of race, which is manifested through other vocabulary, which can be traced back to ancient times. See Gossett (1997), p. 3 for an argument that the idea of race can be traced back at least 5,000 years, in India, China, Egypt, and elsewhere.

6. A tribe of Northern European men with enormous or long flappy ears in which they curled up to sleep. There is a tribe of Indian men with similar features, referred to as "Pandae," whose description Pliny borrows from Ctesias' *Indica* (5th BC). Pliny (2005), p. 65.

7. Described by Pliny as an Indian or African tribe (Libya) composed of dog-headed people. See "Commentary," p. 152 in Pliny (2005).

8. Pliny (2005), p. 66.

9. Referred to as Noachic or T-O maps, for their visual layout. See Velazco y Trianosky (2006). See Beazley (1900), for a discussion of the meaning of Noachic and T-O maps.

10. See chapter 1, n. 25.

11. For an extended discussion, see chapter 1, "Taming the Unruly."

12. Honig (2002/2003).

13. I refrain from using the term "passing," since this would legitimize the way the "one-drop" rule records race.

14. See chapter 1, "Dividing Populations," where I discuss this point from Schmitt.

15. Examples abound. See Metcalf (1995), which describes the rhetorical positioning of the British in India; Hochschild (1998), which describes the impetus of the Belgian conquest of the Congo in the eighteenth century; Elkins (2005), which traces the hidden history of the British government's tactics of repression against the Mau Maus in Kenya.

16. I use "culture" for the lack of a better term to signify what renders a group unique:" this would include not just its rituals, norms, and practices, but comportment, attitudes, worldviews.

17. For an excellent analysis of tolerance and its negative implications, see Goldberg (2004).

18. Rorty (1992), p. 583.

19. Butler (1992), p. 7.

20. Jacques Derrida and Giorgio Agamben, when attempting to describe a related phenomenon, refer to this institution as "Law." See Derrida (1990) and Agamben (1998).

21. Galston (2002), p. 3, emphasis mine. As a political philosopher, deputy assistant to the President for domestic policy during the first Clinton Administration and executive director of the National Commission on Civic Renewal, which was chaired by Sam Nunn and William Bennett, Galston could might be considered a quintessential representative of the tenets of Western—or more specifically—American liberalism.

22. Galston (2002) p, 5.

23. See Kymlicka (1989) and Taylor (1994) for exemplary arguments to this effect.

24. Abraham (2006), p. 66.

25. Abraham (2006), p. 66.

26. As Linda Martin Alcoff points out, who the speaker is and where s/he stands is as important as the message being delivered. Alcoff (1991–1992), especially p. 25.

27. Huntington (1993), p. 2. Pagination follows that of text as formatted online by Gale Group.

28. Huntington (1993), p. 2.

29. Rawls (1999).

30. Rawls (1999), p. 5.

31. Rawls (1999), p. 75.

32. Rawls (1999), p. 76. Bold emphasis is mine, italics are Rawls'. We could read this example as purely coincidental. However, Jeffrey Paris argues convincingly that Rawls's writings are less abstract, and more of a historical blueprint that reflects actual domestic and international politics of the latter half of the twentieth century. See Paris (2002).

33. Rawls (1999), p. 78.

34. Rawls (1999), p. 144.

35. There is some doubt as to whether Muslims are technically "irrational" in Rawls. In the text, I refer to the discursive, rather than the technical, dimension of Rawls's discussion.

36. These objections, Rawls quickly notes, fall outside the domain of public reason. Rawls (1999), p. 178, n.101.

37. Rawls (1999), p.178.

38. Mouffe (1996). Mouffe is responding to the argument of "rational consensus" of William Galston, John Rawls, Ronald Dworkin, Charles Larmore, and other liberal theorists.

39. Mouffe (1993), p. 142.

40. Mouffe (1993), p. 143.

41. And, I would suggest, inferior.

42. In reference to the latter—"religion-based" civilization, Huntington prefaces his description with a paragraph listing "ten non-Arab Muslim countries" that have formed the Economic Cooperation Organization, united by "culture and religion." The organization of this group, he suggests, was spurred by the realization that "they had no chance of admission to the European Community." The insinuation is striking: it is because they do not, or cannot, understand themselves in secular cultural, economic, and political terms. Huntington (1993), p. 3.

43. Mouffe (1993), p. 141.

44. In John Locke's *Second Treatise*, to name one such example. See Locke (1947). See also Charles Mills for an excellent review of the racial thinking embedded in the writings of liberal philosophers such as Hobbes, Locke, and Mill. Mills (2006).

45. See the frameworks of Benhabib, Dworkin, Gutmann, Habermas, Kymlicka, Rawls, among others.

46. In contrast to Carl Schmitt's thesis that the enemy is constituted by the political. Schmitt (1996).

47. Scaperlanda (1993), p. 971.

48. Foucault (2003b), pp. 316–317.

49. Foucault (2003b), p. 317.

50. The *New York Times* had an article about a children's soccer league composed of refugees from sub–Saharan Africa, which was begun in Clarkston, GA. The mayor of the town, responding to citizen complaints, banned the league from using the town park. He referred to the children as the "soccer people," even though this team was one of many others in the league. The immediate, and not inaccurate, inference is that he is referring to the fact that the team is composed of poor, Black, Africans, in other words, not Americans, citizens, wealthy, or "like us." See St. John (2007).

51. For an excellent analysis of tolerance and its negative implications, see Goldberg (2004).

52. Laclau and Mouffe's interpretation.

53. Italics mine. Butler (1992), p. 7. As cited in Mouffe (1993), p. 143.

54. Mouffe (1993), Mouffe, citing Laclau, p. 141.

55. Kymlicka (1989); Taylor (1994); Fraser (1997); Benhabib (2002); Fraser and Honneth (2003).

56. Flusser (2003). p. 16 ("On the Alien").

57. As Arendt discusses this distinction, the question of "who one is," establishes one's uniqueness, whereas the question of "what one is," serves to connect us to others like us. See Arendt (1958), p. 181ff.

58. Mouffe (1993), p. 140.

59. "[L]awmaking pursues as its end, with violence as the means, what is to be established by law, but at the very moment of instatement, does not dismiss violence. Rather, at this very moment of lawmaking, it establishes as law not an end unalloyed by violence, but one necessarily and intimately tied to it, under the title of power. Lawmaking is power making, and to that end, an immediate manifestation of violence." Benjamin (1978), p. 295.

60. Girard (1986), chapter 2.

Chapter 4

1. Honig (2002/2003).

2. All members of the North Atlantic Treaty Organization (and core representatives of the "Western" world). Thanks to Darrell Moore for pointing out the former detail. In order to reinforce this point for its conceptual implications, I will continue to modify references to these countries and others as "North Atlantic."

3. Hence, betraying the self-understanding of their inhabitants, who pride themselves on the diversity and range of their multiethnic populations.

4. I use this term to capture that dimension of any polity , whose essence consists of an intimate, irrevocable link between law or sovereign authority and a subject.

5. For a review of this concept, see chapter 1.

6. The use of this fairly nebulous term is deliberate, and I hope, reflects accurately the population under consideration as treated by the mass media and the various offices of the Bush Administration (including the FBI, Homeland Security, the Attorney General's office, BCIS). I use this term to connote the larger international trend toward the vilification of Islam; however, the term "Arab" might also be used to identify the same population. I wish to circumscribe this group in the following ways: they are generally neither natural-born nor naturalized U.S. citizens; they are often but not necessarily culturally conspicuous (e.g., through a religious commitment to Islam, dress or physical marks such as beards), and often identified as being of Middle Eastern or Arab backgrounds, but not always Muslim (I am thinking of Palestinian Christians, who have been subjected to similar treatment). These are only provisional guidelines identifying those individuals for whom this term holds. Obviously, there are significant exceptions to these guidelines; many men who have been required to register with the BCIS are of Arab background, but not Muslim. A number of detainees at Guantánamo Bay are U.S., Australian, or British citizens, and/or not of Middle Eastern background. There is also a significant population of Black American Muslims in the U.S. My argument does not address the last population.

7. BBC Web site (www.bbc.co.uk), December 19, 2002; ACLU Web site (www.aclu.org), December 19, 2003.

8. Passed January 3, 2002. The PATRIOT Act has been followed by PATRIOT II; the 2006 Military Commissions Act, and a series of other bills designed to erode the range of Constitutional protections that citizens and noncitizens alike once enjoyed.

9. Since this chapter was first drafted, the office has been renamed to United States Citizenship and Immigration Services (USCIS). Until March 1, 2003, it was known as the Immigration and Naturalization Service (INS)—and the FBI. The definition of domestic terrorism according to the PATRIOT Act is as follows: "The term 'domestic terrorism' means activities that" (A) involve acts dangerous to human life that are a violation of the criminal laws of the United States or of any State;" (B) appear to be intended—"(i) to intimidate or coerce a civilian population;" (ii) to influence the policy of a government by intimidation or coercion; or "(iii) to affect the conduct of a government by mass destruction, assassination, or kidnapping; and "(C) occur primarily within the territorial jurisdiction of the United States." (H.R. 3162, Sec. 802). Among the list of actions authorized by the PATRIOT Act was the express requirement that immigrants from twenty-five countries (twenty-four of which are predominantly Muslim) register their presences with the INS, and "voluntarily" speak with fed-

eral agents about intelligence concerning Al-Qaeda, Osama bin Laden, terrorist organizations in general, and more recently, about Iraq. As of January 16, 2003: The countries in question are as follows: Indonesia, Egypt, Bangladesh, Jordan, Kuwait, Saudi Arabia, Pakistan, Iran, Iraq, Libya, Sudan, Syria, Eritrea, Afghanistan, Algeria, Bahrain, Lebanon, Morocco, Oman, Qatar, Somalia, Tunisia, Yemen, United Arab Emirates. The sole non-Muslim country included in this list is North Korea. Since these policies have been announced, thousands of families of Arab Muslim origin, residing in the U.S., have fled to the U.S.-Canadian border to ask for asylum from the Canadian Immigration Authorities, only to be given appointments as late as two months hence. On their return from the border to wait for their appointments in the nearest American cities with Salvation Army and other immigrant and refugee service organizations, the men of these families were detained by the American Immigration Authorities for questioning and with alarming frequency held on bonds. Powell (2001); Cregan (2003).

10. The sparse coverage included several cases whereby "enemy combatants" were trying to challenge their detention in court (Denniston 2003). In 2003, the U.S. government, led by Solicitor General Theodore B. Olson, representing the case against the Guantanamo Bay Naval Base detainees, is arguing to reject the Supreme Court's jurisdiction over the status of these prisoners in Guantanamo Bay (Greenhouse 2003). For three and one-half years, the attorneys for José Padilla and several others tried to contest their incarceration without habeas corpus and other typical due process rights. Padilla, along with Adham Hassoun and Kifah Jayyousi were finally brought to trial in January 2006, and in August 2007, convicted of conspiracy to murder, kidnap and maim overseas, conspiracy to provide material support for terrorists and of material support for terrorists. As of this writing, they are still awaiting sentencing. As I discuss with regard to a similar circumstance facing South Asian political activists in early twentieth-century United States, "conspiracy" charges are substantially less difficult to "prove" than sedition (or terrorism).

11. For details on the treatment of Muslim men since September 11, 2001, see Saito (2007); Cole (2003); Danner (2004); Margulies (2006). A recent film, *The Road to Guantanamo* (directed by Michael Winterbottom) reconstructs the journey of three British Muslim men who were wrongly incarcerated in Guantanamo Bay Military Camp. For details of similar treatment of Muslims in the U.S., see Cohler-Esses (2005).

12. Cole (2003), "Introduction"; Dershowitz (2002). Dershowitz endorses torture, secret military tribunals, extensive surveillance, identity cards, detention (see Dershowitz, ch. 5) and the racial profiling, though not automatic detention, of Muslims/Arabs (pp. 192, 207–208). Racial

profiling is an unfortunate strategy taken toward this objective, argues Cole, and should be abrogated in favor of better strategies such as screening for "preattack" behaviors or community policing. Cole, pp. 183ff. By addressing their acceptance of the notion that the Bush Administration is justifiably waging a war on terror, I do not mean to equate Cole's and Dershowitz's general stance on liberalism. Cole argues in the typical liberal tradition of civil liberties and protections. Dershowitz's liberalism is more conservative; he insists that national (and citizens') security must be favored above civil liberties. However, I do list them both in the broad-ranging camp of "liberalism," because they share certain premises about the role of law, rights, and protections. Certainly, Cole's position on how far to extend certain civil rights, [not to mention his long and demonstrable moral commitment to defending many individuals, such as 13 men in secret evidence deportation cases. Saito (2007), p. 146] is much more generous than Dershowitz. My point in listing them together is to show how scholars who share very few opinions can be of similar mind on the issue of preemptive policing and the "objective" stature of law.

13. Gerges (1999) offers an excellent detailed discussion of the hostility and racist discourse surrounding Muslims and Islam from the Carter to Clinton U.S. presidential administrations. He surveys a range of areas, from American foreign policy to the literature by "experts" on Islam. Khalidi traces American foreign policy and Western colonialist policies toward the Middle East since the end of the nineteenth century.

14. Since September 11, 2001, only 10 of the 460 prisoners currently held in Guantanamo Bay have ever been charged; 287 have been released or transferred to other governments. Of those 10, none have been charged with direct involvement in the September 11 attacks (Barnes and Williams 2006). Since September 11 in the United States, more than 1,200 Muslim men had been held without charges on suspicion of terrorism. All of them, as of July 2006, have been released without being charged with terrorism or related offenses (Hays 2006).

15. And women, as I will discuss below.

16. See Gerges (1999), especially chapter 2, "The intellectual context for American Foreign Policy" for an excellent review of writers including Gilles Kepel, Bernard Lewis, Amos Perlmutter, Daniel Pipes, and others, *who assert that Islam is a culture that "produces" terrorists, and is fundamentally incompatible with liberalism and democracy.* Paul Berman traces the reaction of the events of 9-11 to the cultural appeal of Sayyid al-Qutb, an Egyptian religious scholar, member of the Muslim Brotherhood, and "the Arab world's first important theoretician of the Islamist

cause," who called for a return to the principles of Islam (Berman 2003), p. 62.

17. See Okin (1999) and Gutmann (1993), both of whom lump polygamy with purdah and veiling. I will return to Okin's analysis later in this chapter. Ayaan Hirsi Ali, a self-described "ex-Muslim," criticizes Islam as the source of women's oppression without distinguishing between schools of thought. See Ali (2006) for one such example. See also Leila Lalami's excellent, detailed review of Ali's and Irshad Manji's writings on Islam and women (Lalami 2006).

18. Jacques Derrida and Giorgio Agamben, when attempting to describe a related phenomenon, refer to this institution as "Law." See Derrida (1990) and Agamben (1998) and my discussion of their argument in chapter 2.

19. I use this term to denote a regime that has deep roots, or appears as foundational or "given," in distinction to a short-lived political order, such as New Deal liberalism.

20. For a more developed explanation of this concept, see chapters 1 and 3.

21. I use this term to capture that dimension of any polity whose essence consists of an intimate, irrevocable link between law or sovereign authority and a subject.

22. Saito (1997a); Ngai (2004); Pfaelzer (2007); Takaki (1993); Takaki (1998).

23. Cf. Mamdani's analysis of Hutus and Tutsis in Rwanda (2001); Arendt's discussion of Jews as pariahs and parvenus (1966); Sander Gilman's analyses of "Jewishness" (2003); various analyses of Chinese immigration to Mexico (Schiavone-Camacho 2006); Romero (2003); (Neri 2005); Italians (Guglielmo 2003); American Indians (Deloria and Salisbury 2004) Of course, the framework of colonialism and imperialism reverses the relationship between "immigrants" and dominant sovereign powers, as in the case of the British in India (Cohn 1996), or early settlers in California (Deloria 1994), (Almaguer 1994); but the reading of the "other" remains similar. Cf. David Theo Goldberg's masterful analysis of racialization throughout many regions of Europe across many eras (2002).

24. Honig (2001), ch. 3, esp. pp. 62–67.

25. By "facial aesthetic," I refer to beards for some Arab/Muslim men and various forms of the hijab for women. I will explore some of these later in this chapter.

26. Such as in the taxi industry in New York City. See Mathew (2006). However, I want to reiterate that while these individuals may not identify themselves as Muslim primarily or at all (perhaps because they are not), and perhaps instead by national or geopolitical identity (e.g., as Bangladeshi or South Asian), they are—especially in the context of September 11 politics—seen immediately, primarily, and often solely as Muslim.

27. See Pfaelzer (2007) regarding the treatment of Chinese immigrants in the nineteenh century and Jensen (1988) on that of South Asians in the early twentieth century. I will return to the latter example in chapter 7.

28. These inquiries were conducted by a range of academic scholars as well. Paul Berman explores the relationship between Qutb's understanding of Islam as a political ideology and its antagonism to liberalism (Berman 2003). Roxanne Euben also has a more considered treatment of the same topic, though written well before 9-11. See Euben (1999).

29. CBS, 60 Minutes.

30. Quotes are taken from Fedwa Wazwaz, *CounterPunch*, 10-10-02, "Falwell, Graham and Friedman: Inexcusable Tolerance for Religious Extremism in America."

31. Paraphrase of quote found in "Rumsfeld Praises Army General Who Ridicules Islam as 'Satan'" (2003).

32. White (2005).

33. Lelyveld (2002).

34. Lindh, a convert to Islam, was convicted on scant and dubious evidence according to a prominent terrorism scholar who is convinced that Lindh knew nothing about Al-Qaeda's plot on 9-11. See Mayer (2003), p. 52.

35. Harvey (2003), p. 34; p. 32. See n. 10.

36. Arnone (2003).

37. Temple-Raston (2007).

38. National Security Entry/Exit Registration System. Based on an old entry-exit system left from the era of the incarceration of Americans and immigrants of Japanese descent, this augmented system was put in place in December 2002, and increased monitoring procedures and registration obligations for aliens in the United States. A visit to the State Department Web site offers details about NSEERS, including "Because of regulatory ex-

emptions, rigorous registration and fingerprinting is currently required only for nationals of Iraq, Iran, Sudan, and Libya who are required to be fingerprinted and photographed at the port of entry, under 8 C.F.R. ' 264.1(f). The Attorney General has the authority to expand this list of countries through the publication of a Federal Register notice." NSEERS is explicitly designed for the purposes of catching "terrorists" who masquerade as alien immigrants in our midst. http://usinfo.state.gov/is/Archive_Index/Entry Exit_Registration_System.html. The U.S. Immigration and Customs Enforcement Web site offers more details: "[c]itizens or nationals from Afghanistan, Algeria, Bahrain, Bangladesh, Egypt, Eritrea, Indonesia, Iran, Iraq, Jordan, Kuwait, Libya, Lebanon, Morocco, North Korea, Oman, Pakistan, Qatar, Somalia, Saudi Arabia, Sudan, Syria, Tunisia, United Arab Emirates, and Yemen. However, to date, individuals from more than 150 countries have been registered in the NSEERS program." http://www.ice.gov/pi/news/factsheets/nseersFS120103.htm.

39. Woodbury (2003).

40. He was ultimately released and honorably discharged from the Army. Mitchell (2004); Simpson (2003).

41. Lewis (2006).

42. Under the now widely acknowledged policy of "extraordinary rendition." Mahar Arar, a naturalized Canadian citizen from Syria, is the most well-known target of rendition, which occurred under the auspices of the Canadian government's collaboration with the United States. See Mayer (2005).

43. See Waldman (2006), and Hasan (2007), for two examples.

44. And as of August 1, 2007, the ability to spy on U.S. residents/ citizens has been legalized by the U.S. Congress; it is known as the "Protect America Act of 2007" (Pub.L. 110–155, S. 1927), and amends the 1978 Foreign Intelligence Surveillance Act (FISA). It provides additional steps for the expanded accquisition of foreign intelligence information, as well as for other expanded domestic surveillance powers.

45. A perusal of the *San Francisco Chronicle* over the five years since this expanded permission was granted to the FBI reveals the systemic focus on mosques that were investigated, spied upon, and raided by FBI agents.

46. Khalidi (2004); see also Gerges (1999).

47. Many of which have increased since 2001, especially in France.

48. Delves Broughton (2004).

49. "Catholic Chaplains Affected by French Veil Law" (2004).

50. "Nun Identity Card Photo Sparks Veil Debate" (2004).

51. Homola (2004).

52. Kramer (2004).

53. This retreat was staged by England's Chair of the Commission on Racial Equality Trevor Phillips. He was joined by many other British leaders, including Head of House of Commons Jack Straw and Prime Minister Tony Blair.

54. Simons (2006).

55. "Note to Would-Be Immigrants: You Can't Stone Women Here: Quebec Town Adopts List of Official 'Norms'" (2007). This code of conduct was adopted by the city council in Hérouxville, Quebec in October 2006, although the ensuing controversy resulted in the removal of several clauses, including the "prohibition" against circumsion and stoning women in public. The resolution was supported by seven other neighboring towns in the region. See "Hérouxville Drops Some Rules from Controversial Code" (2007).

56. There is no "binding value" to this charter, however, as the Italian government is quick to note. See "Government Unveils 'Charter of Values'" (2007).

57. Guns were the weapon of choice in nearly 20% of domestic violence incidents in the state of Maine in the United States in 2003. Source: Maine Statistics Analysis Center, 2004 Report, "Gun Violence: How Big is the Problem in Maine."

58. In the United States, a number of these men were Sikh, although this detail makes their deaths no less egregious nor any more justified. However, it confirms a widespread public association of turbans and beards with "terrorists." Valarie Kaur has produced a documentary on the harassment of Sikh men and women, who were mistaken for Muslims/terrorists in the wake of September 11, 2001. Her documentary is entitled, *Divided We Fall: Americans in the Aftermath.* New Moon Productions. Other attacks have been recorded in Australia, Canada, England, France and the Netherlands, among other places.

59. For full details, see Bernstein (2005c).

60. Bernstein (2005a). It is difficult to discern the exact greeting.

61. Bernstein (2005b).

62. My use of the terms "West" or "Western," indicates a geographical region, that is, North American and (mostly Northern) Europe, as well as a cultural signifier of modernity and progress.

63. For an excellent analysis of tolerance and its negative implications, see Goldberg (2004).

64. In contrast to Carl Schmitt's thesis that the enemy is constituted by the political. Schmitt (1996), p. 26ff.

65. Oxford English Dictionary Online; Oxford University Press, definitions for "strange," and "strangeness."

66. Mahmood (2001); Abu-Lughod (2002).

67. Spivak (1988), p. 121.

68. See Stoler (1995), chapter 5, especially p. 152ff. See also Mehta (1992) and (1999) for excellent discussions on this topic.

69. The hijab presents a similar affront to European liberal states such as France, England, and Germany, although the form that liberalism takes there is distinct from American liberalism. See the introduction to this book, where I describe and develop my understanding of liberalism.

70. This includes a range of terms and versions of hijab: the niqab (concealing the entire face except for the eyes); the jilbab (concealing the entire body), the burqa and yashmak (concealing the entire face including the eyes), the dupatta and chunni (covering the hair).

71. See chapter 1.

72. This is something that psychologists and linguists have known for years, as the writings of Deborah Tannen and Carol Gilligan inform us.

73. The classic film by Gillo Pontecorvo, *The Battle of Algiers* (1965), underscores the usefulness of the "cloaked" Algerian woman in hiding arms and helping the Algerian resistance. Ironically, the veil has been described as liberating in its ability to shield the wearer's expressions or gestures. See Franks (2000), pp. 920–922. The title is deceptive; Franks interviews a range of women, not all of them "unambiguously White."

74. Thanks to Ronald Sundstrom for reminding me of this point.

75. In other words, one's moral or religious worldview.

76. Rawls (1999), p. 155.

77. Rawls (1971). Part 1, section 24. pp. 136–142.

78. Laborde (2005); Thomas (2006).

79. Often, these are identical.

80. The sari has function in a similar role to that of the hijab. Cf. Sheth (2008). In the late 1970s, Mary Daly wrote about how the "Hindu" practice of sati stood to oppress an entire population of women in India. Her concern was that sati, along with dowry-related harassment and violence, poor treatment of Indian widows, high mortality incidents among women, represents the religious and patriarchal obstacles to freedom that Indian women face. As Uma Narayan points out, the fact that sati was most often practiced during a very narrow time period in a small region of India, by an even smaller group of women—and barely at all when Daly's book was published—seems not to figure into Daly's analysis at all. Daly (1978); See Narayan (1997), especially chapter 2, "Restoring History and Politics and 'Third-World Traditions'" for an excellent critical analysis of Daly's position, as well as those of other Western feminists who commit similar fallacies. Narayan (chapter 2) also points out that there were many reasons why sati was practiced—not only because of religious beliefs, but because of inheritance traditions, political resistance, etc. Sati, time and time again, became a reference in the writings of (Western) feminists to the proof that Indian women were oppressed. Daly (1978); Hosken (1981), as cited in Mohanty (1991); Okin (1997).

81. Okin (1997).

82. Okin (1997).

83. Okin (1997).

84. Hosken (1981) as cited in Mohanty (1991), p. 66.

85. Hosken (1981) as cited in Mohanty (1991), p. 66.

86. See Nancy Hirschmann's excellent treatment of the misunderstandings and assumptions by Western feminists on the practice of veiling. Via writings by Leila Ahmed and other "non-Western" feminist scholars, Hirschmann also points out that prohibiting veiling was a part of the Western colonialist (and subsequently feminist) project to liberate Muslim women in the name of progress and enlightenment. See Hirschmann (1998). Faegheh Shirazi also points to the ubiquitous message sent out through Western popular media that veiling is oppressive, exploitative, and indicative of an irrational fundamentalism. Shirazi (2001), especially chapters 1 and 2.

87. See Okin (1999); Gutmann (1993); see also Cecile Laborde's article on the stance of the French government on the hijab Laborde (2005).

88. See Sajida Alvi (2003), for examples of women who have decided to wear the veil in order to negotiate different life contexts; also see Franks (2000).

89. Hoodfar (1997); Hirschmann, 1998; El Guindi (1999). Abu-Lughod (2002).

90. Mahmood (2005), chapter 1, especially p. 11ff.

91. Shirazi (2001) points to the myriad ways in which the veil is used to depict a monolithic patriarchal, and oppressive vision of Muslim women through advertising in the United States. Her larger analysis also points to the ways in which certain normative roles for Muslim women are reified through advertising in Iran and various regions in the Middle East.

92. See notes 86, 88, and 89.

93. El Guindi (1999) points to the myriad messages and signs that the veil can convey in various regions of the Middle East.

94. Fanon (1965) chapter 1.

95. Mohanty (1991), p. 67.

96. Ibid. Also see Narayan (1997), (1998); Hoodfar (1997); El Guindi (1999); Mahmood (2005).

97. Mahmood (2005), p. 22.

98. See Uma Narayan's especially insightful writings on this point (1997); (1998), among others.

99. We see ample evidence of this in the disruption of goverment services, the shutdown of commercial establishments, and public marketing of Christmas in all of the countries named above, along with the near fastidious absence of recognition of most other religious holidays—certain sporadic exceptions notwithstanding.

100. As I will explain below, I think that the primary difference between the acceptance of the former aesthetic and the nonacceptance of the latter has to do with the distinct absence of a perceived threat (at this point in time) from the "cultures" with which the former fashions are affiliated. Cf. also Sheth (2008). And so, for example, it could be the case that to wear a dashiki in the late 1960s United States, during a surge in Black Nationalist movement, would engender a much stronger hostility from the surrounding society and the state.

101. Such as France, Italy, Germany, and Canada, all of which have either passed legislation or endorsed policies that prohibit women

from wearing the hijab, chador, or full purdah in public (or in public institutions).

102. Besides the fallacy of arguing that culture "produces" terrorists and bombs, this equation also overlooks the correct history of some of these phenomena. For example, Mike Davis has written a history of the car-bomb, which has its origins in the "Middle East,"—namely in the Stern Gang's resistance to the British presence in Palestine. See Davis (2006).

103. And perhaps inferior to liberalism.

104. See pp. 91 and 98 for a list of some such alien acts.

105. There is another side to this heterogeneity: the multiplicities of Islam render it uncontainable by the dominant cultural paradigm of liberalism. Liberalism can accommodate differences that are minor, banal, varietal, so long as these are linked to a cultural foundation that is considered fundamentally similar to itself (liberalism). But when the dominant (homogenous) regime is confronted with a heterogeneity that is perceived to be fundamentally distinct, then the threat of the heterogeneous culture is intensified and so becomes uncontainable. This is the other side of the "unruly." My thanks to David T. Goldberg for clarifying this point.

106. I cannot locate original source for this quote; it was initially uttered by President Bush in defense of his administration's decision to disregard the Geneva Convention protections for prisoners of war in Guantanamo Bay Naval Base. In my search for the original source, I typed in with surrounding quotation marks, "These people are not like" and found that it has become a ubiquitous statement on blogs and numerous Web sites to describe Arabs, Muslims, and to defend Bush administration policies.

Chapter 5

1. Arendt (1966), pp. 301–302.

2. See chapter 4, first section, "Racializing and Outcasting . . ."

3. Arendt (1966), pp. 272–273. The intended function of the "Minority Treaties" was to "[safeguard] . . . the rights of those who, for reasons of territorial settlement, had been left without national states of their own."

4. Carl Schmitt discusses a notion of the "exception," but as a situation, as in "state of exception." According to George Schwab, Schmitt

intends the "exception" to refer to "any kind of severe economic or political disturbance that requires the application of extraordinary measures." Schmitt (1985), p. 5 n. 1.

5. The description of the enemy or the exception that is being ascribed to Muslims, as I discuss further on, is a status that many groups have held during previous moments in American history. Prior instances where such enemy status has been ascribed includes the Irish, Japanese-Americans, Chinese, East Indians, Jews, Italians. See Almaguer (1994); Ignatiev (1995); Aarim-Heriot (2003); Ngai (2004); Saito (2007); and ch. 7.

6. Locke (1947), Book II, par. 6. Similarly, Jean-Jacques Rousseau's Social Contract is grounded upon the General Will, the unity of which depends on the close, intimate co-operation of men who are cultivated and socialized to be good and proper citizens, as in the namesake of Rousseau's *Emile*, while Sophie's proper place is to support her husband's political responsibilities by taking up her proper duties as wife and mother in the home. Jean-Jacques Rousseau, "The Social Contract," Book II, in Rousseau (1979b); Rousseau (1979a). See especially Book V, for a description of Sophie and her responsibilities.

7. This argument has been found in different versions in recent scholarship on liberalism. Carole Pateman and Charles Mills have both argued that the "universal" right of the social contract in liberal theory intrinsically depends on a gendered or "raced" reading. Pateman argues that marriage rights are intrinsically sex-rights that men hold to women's bodies; Mills argues that the Social Contract is a trope by which it is understood that only individuals of certain races (depicted by color, class, culture, or some other set of characteristics) are understood to qualify for the ability to consent to its enactment. See Pateman (1982), and Mills (1997).

8. I will discuss this method of selective awarding of rights more fully in the next section.

9. See chapter 3 for a developed discussion of this point.

10. Schmitt (1996), p. 26.

11. Schmitt (1996), p. 27.

12. Schmitt (1996), p. 28.

13. In the text, Schmitt does not specify that the enemy is necessarily external to the polity, although he appears to imply as much when he says, "[a]n enemy exists only when, at least potentially, one fighting collectivity of people confronts a similar collectivity." Schmitt (1996)

p. 28. In subsequent pages, he discusses war as the existential negation of the enemy, but he also points out that "[e]very state provides . . . some kind of formula for the declaration of an internal enemy" (ibid., p. 46).

14. See chapter 2, "The Violence of Law," and chapter 6, "Border-Populations," for more extensive arguments about these tactics.

15. Here I am thinking of the status of Black Americans in their initial introduction to this country as slaves, as well as their treatment at the hands of various state authorities in post-emancipation United States. For a fuller treatment of Black Americans as one of the original "exception" populations, see Sheth (2003). The same understanding can be also be applied to other groups in the history of United States Immigration. For a discussion of Chinese migrant laborers in this framework, see Salyer (1995), of Mexican immigrants, see Almaguer (1994), and of Irish immigrants, see Ignatiev (1995).

16. "If the exception is the structure of sovereignty, then sovereignty is not an exclusively political concept, an exclusively juridical category, a power external to law . . . , or the supreme rule of the juridical order . . . : *it is the originary structure in which law refers to life and includes it in itself by suspending it.*" Agamben (1998), p. 28. My emphasis.

17. Agamben (1998), p. 15.

18. A pursuit that has been successful, as I will show further on in this chapter.

19. Agamben (1998), pp. 28–29.

20. Agamben (1998), p. 83.

21. Foucault (2003a), pp. 254, 256. By death, Foucault includes "indirect murder" as well, including "political death, expulsion, rejection," etc. Foucault (2003a), p. 256.

22. See Schuck (1998) See Neuman (1996), for exemplary if disparate readings of the selective reading of Constitutional rights to "foreigners," "aliens," and other kinds of "strangers."

23. See Schuck (1998), especially chapter 2, where he argues that immigration law is the vehicle by which U.S. can maintain itself as a national community, which has the right to refuse admissions to enemies or outsiders.

24. During this time Congress reassigned the power to create immigration law, from federal courts to the federal legislature and also awarded

"federal administrators the sole power to enforce immigration policy" Salyer (1995).

25. Schuck (1984); Fiss (1998); Ngai (2004); Salyer (1995).

26. Cf. Schuck (1984); Salyer (1995).

27. For example, Seyla Benhabib, drawing upon Jürgen Habermas' distinctions, distinguishes these as legal rights, or claims of membership, rather than human rights, which are grounded on fundamental moral claims. Cf. Benhabib (1999), p. 17. Benhabib credits Habermas with this distinction, although she offers no specific citation. And yet, legal scholars such as Peter Schuck insist that the goals of community must be reconciled with the universal aspirations of liberalism; the U.S. Constitution's protections are extended to "all persons," living under its jurisdiction, that is, on U.S. soil, and not merely to those who can legally claim "citizenship," suggesting that these rights are moral claims rather than the privileges of legal membership. Cf. Schuck (1984), p. 10. See also Walzer (1983), whose work seems to inaugurate the most recent round of this debate over the last two decades, in philosophy, legal theory, and political science.

28. Parker identifies the liberal "insider" narrative as shared by scholars such as Peter Schuck, Rogers Smith, and Michael Walzer. Parker suggests that a more accurate, although less congenial, narrative would locate the U.S.'s attitude toward immigrants as a "gesture of pure refusal," that is instantiated and institutionalized through a set of laws and policies set up to anticipate and preclude a "foreigner's" claim to citizenship rights. As Parker says, "[R]ather than conceiving of the relative moral urgency of individual's claims upon the community in terms of their location vis-à-vis a territorial community already organized on the basis of citizenship, as various liberal historians of American citizenship have done, one should always conceive of the state's construction of citizenship as a barrier to the individual's territorial rights as itself being a strategy for defeating the individual's claim upon the community" Parker (2001).

29. Arendt (1966), p. 300.

30. Arendt (1966), pp. 298–302.

31. Arendt (1966), p. 299.

32. See Waldron (2003), pp. 191–210. Waldron points to an instance of this when he discusses section 214 of the USA PATRIOT Act, whereby "United States persons" will remain protected from searches "conducted solely on the basis of those activities protected by the first Amendment to the Constitution." As Waldron points out, "United States

persons" refers to American citizens and legally admitted permanent residents, but not nonresident aliens living legally within the U.S. borders Waldron (2003), p. 200.

33. Most directly: ". . . [N]or shall any state deprive any person of life, liberty, or property, without due process of law; *nor deny to any person within its jurisdiction the equal protection of the laws.*" United States Constitution, Amendment XIV, Section 1; my emphasis.

34. Mills (1997), 57. He also points out that this category emerges within the context of Kantian literature on moral and natural rights, which are thought to enshrine the sanctity of individuals "whose rights must not be infringed."

35. See chapter 3 for a discussion of strangeness and heterogeneity.

36. For excellent and detailed arguments that survey the literature on immigration law and scholarship and how "aliens" and "foreigners" are conceived of and treated within the American context, see Neuman (1996) and Bosniak (1994).

37. Chin (1997), p. 1.

38. This occurred through the Immigration Reform Act of 1891. See Salyer (1995), chapter 1.

39. 130 U.S. 581 (1889). This case is commonly known as the Chinese Exclusion Case.

40. *Fong Yue Ting v. U.S.*, 149 U.S. 698 (1893). See Scaperlanda (1993) for an excellent discussion of how the plenary power doctrine works to undermine the rights of immigrants and eclipse their political status in United States jurisprudence.

41. See *Yick Wo v. Hopkins*, 118 U.S. 356 (1886) for a Supreme Court decision based on the first model. See *Fong Yue Ting v. U.S.* for a Supreme Court decision based on the second model.

42. See Scaperlanda (1993), p. 973, where he discussed the four models—affinity, territory, textual theory (what might elsewhere be called a "semantic" model), and sovereignty. With some exceptions here and there, Scaperlanda argues, the Courts have generally insisted on the sovereignty model—with its attendant characteristics of absolute power to defend the nation, and by extension, to decide the fates of immigrants.

43. *Chae Chan Ping v. United States*, 130 U.S. 581 (1889).

44. Scaperlanda (1996), p. 966.

45. This attitude is best expressed through the Court's position in a case decided over half a century later: "Whatever the procedure authorized by Congress is, it is due process as far as an alien denied entry is concerned." United States ex. rel. *Knauff v. Shaughnessy*, 338 U.S. 537, 544 (1950). As quoted in Scaperlanda (1993), p. 966.

46. Chin (1997), p. 4.

47. Quote taken from the Supreme Court's decision in *Fong Yue Ting v. United States*, 149 U.S. 698, as cited in Chin, 18–19.

48. Mills (1997), p. 56. Mills is referring to mainstream political philosophy's rendering of the Social Contract. Mills also points to the inevitable interpretation that such treatment of subpersons is contingent or accidental in order to render race marginal to the contract *rather than a central, intrinsic element.* Again, I would extend this reading to liberal polities more generally.

49. Saito (1997a), p. 344.

50. Bickel (1975), I must acknowledge Linda Bosniak's article for first alerting me to this statement. See Bosniak (1994).

51. The figure of the immigrant is not the sole version of the "exception," or the not-yet-human-like-us, or the pariah. We saw a similar phenomenon during 1920s America. During the "Red Scare," serious consideration was given to denaturalizing scores of Communists, Anarchists, and other presumed "subversives," on the grounds that they were not fulfilling their responsibilities of citizenship by turning potential insurgents— the "enemy aliens" of that era. There are also the cases of the internment of Japanese Americans, and of course, U.S. slavery.

52. The Bush Admistration is consistent in promoting this link: Droves of immigrants were rounded up for being publically critical of the Justice Department's procedures, as in the case of Yemeni-Americans in Lackawanna, NY, while the Administration emphasized its commitment to freedom and democracy. See Wypijewski (2003).

53. Viewing terrorism as truly a fact of cultural difference seems to border on racism, but at the very least, this understanding is a fallacy that need not concern us here. I am interested rather in the perception of cultural difference.

54. Arendt (1966), p. 276.

55. Arendt (1966), p. 275.

56. Arendt (1966), p. 275.

57. Arendt (1966), p. 269.

58. Indeed, a number of cases have been reported whereby Muslim immigrants are sent to countries where they believe they are in danger of harm, undue and warranted incarceration, or losing their lives, as in the case of Mahar Arar, a Canadian citizen who was sent to Syria by the United States, where he was incarcerated and tortured for 10 months.

59. We also see the rise of statelessness in an increase of deportations by the American immigration authorities since 9-11, as well as in the insistence of the Bush Administration in increasing deportation powers even further under the Domestic Security Enhancement Act, otherwise known as PATRIOT II. Under this act, citizens—naturalized and native-born alike—and immigrants who have been deemed by the Attorney General's office to be a "threat to our national defense, foreign policy, or economic interests" would be subject to deportation powers even without judicial review, without requiring the country to be open to welcoming said deportees, and finally, without requiring that the country or region have an operating government (i.e., Somalia). Cf. Cole (2002b). This act has not been officially passed by Congress, but passages have been snuck into other seemingly innocuous legislation. See Martin (2003).

60. Another dimension of statelessness, namely the reluctance of other states to consider asylum claims, has also found resonances in recent relevant actions. In particular, the newly signed Safe Third Country Agreement, which was signed in December 2002, renders the U.S.-Canadian Border effectively closed for U.S.-residing refugees asking for asylum from the Canadian authorities. This agreement requires immigrants seeking refuge in Canada to appeal to the U.S. immigration authorities first, thereby risking long-term incarceration and (most likely) eventual deportation to the country from which they were fleeing. They must then try to find a consulate in their "home" country from which to appeal for asylum. The third element, namely the inability to claim entitlement to the native country by origin or blood, is less relevant here, in that claims to American citizenship—whether by country of origin or by special laws (such as the laws of naturalization) have become much more unstable in the last twelve months, leaving citizens of Muslim background fairly defenseless in claiming the Constitutional rights normally afforded to other non-Muslim citizens, for whom as well these privileges are being starkly restricted.

61. Rightlessness stems from the inability to claim a set of rights that have been instantiated as human rights, that is, the rights of all persons

and not merely the rights of American citizens—once a popular reading of the U.S. Constitution. See Neuman (1996), chapter 1; Cole (2002a).

62. See the text of "Patriot II," a bill that was not passed, but clauses from which were quietly inserted into other bills. See n. 59.

63. Cole (2002a).

Chapter 6

1. See chapter 4.

2. (www.cnn.com, Dec. 13, 2002). For an extended summary of this controversy, see "Changing of the Guard" (2002).

3. See Agamben (1998); Girard (1986), chapter 2, argues that a scapegoat must inevitably be identified in the aftermath of a crisis, in order to restore and maintain mythologies of who is good and evil.

4. In chapter 5, I suggested that this phenomenon might be usefully understood as a long-standing mode by which certain ethnically, culturally, or racially conspicuous groups—seen as a threat to a national population that understands itself as internally united, stable, and secure, but for this group—are outcasted politically and legally.

5. Fichte (1979), p. 22.

6. By the terms "serve" and "function," I am not suggesting a voluntary or ontological status on the part of African Americans or any other group who may be understood as a Border-population. Rather, I wish to show how this group is positioned in light of competing dynamics or antagonisms on the part of different institutions and/or populations.

7. I refer interchangeably to Arabs and Muslims, and without specifying their legal status in the United States, because I wish to point to the negative stigma surrounding this population. Such a stigma, I would suggest, ignores the salient differences in religious affiliations, specific ethnic backgrounds, or legal standing in favor of a general negative perception of all "Arabs" or "Muslims." The latter term, despite its reference to a religious affiliation, is often (incorrectly) used indiscriminately in a casual American discourse to refer to person of Arab or Middle Eastern descent.

8. I use the terms "outcaste" and "outsider" interchangeably in this chapter.

9. See chapter Four.4.

10. Fichte (1979), pp. 223–224; emphasis mine.

11. For the purposes of this argument, such recognitions reflect the "official" or institutional acknowledgement of a sovereign authority that the population in question "belongs" squarely within the polity, in other words, it secures their status as insiders. The external boundaries might be of those officially demarcating a nation, state, or a similar procedural, political, or social organization.

12. This term denotes the nebulous unity behind the concept of the state, or that which underlies a "society or a community, an enterprise or a beehive or even a basic procedural order," Schmitt (1996), p. 19.

13. Schmitt (1996), p. 31.

14. Schmitt (1996), p. 31 n. 12.

15. Thus, Arendt discusses outsiders in terms of statelessness and rightlessness (1966), Fichte discusses outsiders in terms of internal and external borders, and language, among other things (Fichte 1979, ch. 4 and 13), and Balibar points to apartheid as the systematic reference by which to distinguish outsiders (2004). For a discussion of how Muslims have been made outsiders, see chapter 4.

16. See Arendt (1966).

17. In the sense of being coopted, acquiescing, or not voicing a clear, concerted, unified opposition to the sovereign authority's initiative. Obviously, ethnic and racial—unlike political or religious—groups do not typically act in concert toward a particular agenda. Thus, I am neither lobbing a moral accusation nor ascribing guilt to this group, but rather offering a description of how racial/ethnic populations are deployed by sovereign institutions in the absence of conscious and concerted opposition, as well as suggesting that these groups respond in certain ways to certain kinds of threats, fears, or vulnerabilities.

18. Border-guards and Border-populations refer to the same pariah group in slightly different lights. The latter term refers to the status of the pariah population, whereas the former term signifies a less passive, more watchful function.

19. For a revealing example of the similarities between Border-guards and the populations they are assigned to exclude, see Ralph Blumenthal (2004).

20. A parallel example in history might be that of the Irish as Border-guards in relation to Black Americans. Noel Ignatiev points out that the Irish as policemen were key to breaking up spontaneous labor demonstrations by Blacks, and as union leaders, refused admittance or membership to them, among other such dynamics. See Ignatiev (1995).

21. As we see through concrete instances of racial profiling, selectively targeted and enforced drug-prohibition laws, which routinely criminalize poor and minority populations, three-strike felony sentencing, police harassment of minority suspects, etc.

22. Agamben (1998), chapter 1: 1.17.

23. Foucault (2003a), March 17, 1976, lecture; 242–246.

24. Foucault (1979), 3.3.

25. Butler (1997), p. 2.

26. Butler (1997), p. 107; my emphasis.

27. I do not mean to suggest that the concrete characteristics of the population must remain identical, for example, as in an Anglo-Christian ruling class. The ethnic, racial, or other features of such a population will change according to changing historical, social or political tendencies; I do nevertheless peer through a radical structuralist (Marxian) lens here, one that is committed to the position that the class foundations of this ruling population will most likely remain constant independently of other changing characteristics such as ethnicity or race.

28. The sovereign authority also has good reason to collaborate with the pariah population in finding another group to marginalize, as I will discuss further on.

29. In particular, I am thinking of concrete (if not formal) political and legal disenfranchisement that American minority populations share with "foreigners," such as racial profiling, violations of due process, various forms of legal criminalization such as drug laws and being an "illegal" alien.

30. In the case of Black Americans and Muslims, such a differentiation would be manifested in the difference of systems of incarceration for each group: African Americans, while routinely subjected to criminalization, are subject to an American prison system, albeit with certain formal protections and rights, such as a periodically met standard of due process and right to trial. In the case of Muslim immigrants, for whom immigration law is distinct from Constitutional law, due process, writs of habeas

corpus, rights to trials are ad hoc privileges and, especially in the last five years, granted and withdrawn peremptorily. See Cole (2003); Schuck (1998); Salyer (1995). Also a perusal of any major newspaper, such as the *New York Times* since September 11, 2001, to the current day, will reveal treatment for Muslims (immigrants and foreigners) that is a consistent departure from the standard civil liberties afforded to American citizens. See chapter 4 for a detailed discussion of the logic and treatment behind the ostracization of Muslim immigrants in the United States after 9-11.

31. Here I am summarizing an argument that I have developed in detail elsewhere. This position is an extension, although somewhat different from Carl Schmitt's, who defines the coherence of the political through the direct and overt identification of an enemy (Schmitt 1996, 29ff). I suggest that the enemy in liberal polities must not be directly identified as such, but must be cast as an "exception" to the group of human beings who stand to receive as their due a standard set of political rights and legal protections (See chapter 5).

32. I am aware that some might object to this characterization of Black Americans as having a long-term marginal status. Indeed, while this article argues for the application of the outsider-pariah dynamic to Muslims and Black Americans, this dynamic can be repositioned between Muslims and Mexican immigrants, as suggested by the Bush Administration's recent proposal to grant illegal immigrants temporary guest worker status (*New York Times*, Editorial, January 3, 2003); or to Muslims and Sikhs in the long history of colonial and postcolonial India; or the French Quebecois and Muslim immigrants in Canada, or to contemporary Persians and African Americans in Los Angeles, among countless other examples. In earlier periods of history, we might consider a similar relationship between, for example, Black Americans and American Indians during the 1880s (as exemplified in the deployment of Black soldiers of 9th and 10th Cavalry Regiments, for the purposes of "pacification" of the Apache Indians under Geronimo), or between Chinese Americans and Japanese Americans during World War II, discussed briefly by K. Scott Wong in his book (2005).

33. Ignatiev (1995).

34. See Aarim-Heriot (2003), chapter 2.

35. For an excellent exposition of this point, see Mills (2003).

36. For an earlier, but especially enthusiastic version of this move, see D'Souza (1995). It can certainly be argued that this trajectory did not begin just with September 11, 2001, and the outcasting of Muslims;

rather, I would argue, it began decades earlier, similar to the way that the outcasting of Muslims began decades earlier, although the relationship does not play out vividly until 9-11.

37. I am aware that characterizing the entire Black population in the U.S. as being "included" or integrated into a dominant mainstream population is an abstract and not entirely accurate claim. For reasons that will become clearer as this argument develops, I wish to circumscribe the category of Black Americans in the following way: I am thinking not necessarily of the entirety of the Black population in the United States, but rather of that segment of the group seen to be an upwardly mobile, professional, class, whose socio-economic characteristics enable the state to reconceptualize this group—to a limited and provisional degree—as "transcending race," or as integrated into a "multiracial" or "nonracial" middle- or upper-class American population. I am not including Black Muslims in this population—who are an important segment of the Black population with regards to this paper, but with sufficient singularities to merit separate treatment.

38. It is also a standard practices at corporate newspaper chains such as Gannett to require its reporters to always look out for the "minority" view.

39. See footnote 1.

40. This openness was staged through such symbolic gestures such as candidate Bush's learning a few Spanish phrases in order to appeal to Latino constituents in Texas.

41. See Andrews (1999). Andrews remarks on this trend prior to these appointments; nevertheless, I think they confirm his general insight.

42. In addition to 24 states and territories, and 70 "Fortune 500" companies.

43. *New York Times,* op-ed page, Opinion, 3-30-03.

44. Cf. *UC Regents v. Bakke* 438 US 265 (1978); *Gratz v. Bollinger* 539 US 244 (2003); *Grutter v. Bollinger* 539 US 306 (2003).

45. As Arendt acknowledges were necessary for minorities during and after World War II.

46. As in the case of the Clinton Administration's formal 1997 apology for the Tuskegee Experiment.

47. Well-documented in alternative media, if not mainstream press. See also Darity and Mason (2004).

48. Ibid. See also Andrews (1999).

49. *Goodridge v. Department of Public Health* 440 Mass 309.

50. See "Black Ministers Protest Gay Marriage" (2004); Clemetson (2004). A recent Lexis-Nexis search using the search terms "Black Ministers Protest Gay Marriage," returned more than 125 different newspaper articles on the topic, including media articles that condemned African Americans who opposed marriage for same-sex couples of "shoving their own history into the closet." See the *Advocate*, April 27, 2004, and Jackson (2004). Legal theorist Kimberle Crenshaw points to the role that African Americans must play as moral guardians on such issues, "The Constitution has been re-made by the slaves, by African Americans, the mothers and fathers of the Constitutional structure that we take for granted, that's us . . . we (African Americans) are the authors of a wonderful amazing notion that there is no second class citizenship . . ." Crenshaw (2004).

51. See Owens (2001). Interestingly, this column was printed in a Detroit newspaper, a location of one of the largest Arab populations in the United States. A quick Google Internet search can find a vast range of Web sites carrying social commentaries that echo this same position. Stand-up comedians such as Sherrod Small performed routines on a similar theme (see summary of his act on www.cringehumor.net/reviews/6pack). Although I have not seen them, students from a fall 2003 critical race theory course tell me they have watched similar stand-up comedy routines on performed by African-American entertainers on Black Entertainment Television (BET).

52. In this regard, with reference to 9-11, any number of key minority figures, and not just Black Americans, can be shown to collaborate with the state to ostracize Muslims. Examples include former National Security Adviser and current Secretary of State Condoleezza Rice, Attorney General Alberto Gonzales, and John C. Yoo, a former Justice Department attorney. The latter two figures are among the chief architects of the U.S government's draconian treatment of prisoners at Guantanamo Bay. Even a perusal of mainstream newspapers such as the *New York Times* shows these individuals to be responsible for endorsing the stripping of human rights, due process, and the legitimating of torture for suspected terrorists, enemy aliens, and enemy combatants.

53. The state must have populations that are or can be marginalized, in order to enhance the value of the rights that it selectively extends

in the name of "universal and equal protection." See chapter 5 for a more detailed discussion of this logic.

54. Gramsci (1971), chapter 3, 55–60.

55. See chapter 5.

56. For example, the pariah is reminded that he/she (it) is no longer an outsider, but rather one of them—an insider—and therefore the reparative policies that it has been extended (affirmative action, reparations, apologies for past atrocities) are no longer necessary "protections" or "privileges."

57. Heidegger (1996) Cf. Introduction, Section II.7.b, and part 1, section 44, especially (c).

58. Saito (1997a) makes this argument. Saito suggests that Asians, — throughout the history of the United States, have been consistently designated the "racial other," or the foreign population who serves as the middle-term between White Americans and Black Americans.

59. For example, we might consider the positioning of Black Americans vis-à-vis established East Asian or Persian populations in Los Angeles, or the relative relationship between other groups in other locales.

Chapter 7

1. It is difficult to discern the exact number because the tables record immigrant arrivals based on country of last permanent residence and country of birth. As we know, these figures can include Anglo British subjects, Anglo Indians, or those who are not "ethnically" East Indian. See Chandrasekhar (1982), whose tables estimate approximately 5,000 Asian Indians residing in the U.S. during this period (see tables 2 and 3); Rangaswamy estimates that 7000 Indians entered the U.S. 1904–20. Rangaswamy (2000b), p. 43.

2. Figures vary. This number is drawn from Carter and Sutch (2006).

3. Specifically the Chinese Exclusion Laws (1882), and the Gentlemen's Agreement (1908). The latter was struck between the U.S. and Japan, whereby the Japanese government agreed to withhold the distribution of passports to Japanese laborers who wished to emigrate to the United States.

4. My argument in this section draws largely on Joan Jensen's excellent study of Asian Indians, although I have drawn on additional research when I have been able to find it. However, very little work on this population exists, except as archival material. Jensen (1988).

5. Jensen (1988), p. 42; 30; 36.

6. Most were Punjabi Sikhs who had converted from Hinduism under pressure in the British colonial army in India. See Jensen, p. 8. The misspelling of the term suggests its polemical tone.

7. Jensen (1988), p. 44.

8. Jensen (1988), p. 141. My emphasis.

9. See Jensen (1988), chapters 3 and 6, especially regarding the story of Komogata Maru.

10. Jensen (1988), p. 46.

11. Jensen (1988), 1988, p. 54; 61.

12. Ibid.

13. Jensen (1988), p. 40.

14. For an extensive discussion and analysis of the trend of marriages between Asian Indian men and Mexican and American women of Mexican descent, see Sheth (2007a).

15. Jensen (1988), p. 44.

16. Similar to Filipino immigrants, who arrived in the U.S. soon after Indians did. Filipinos were American subjects after the U.S. victory in the Spanish-American war until the Philippine Repatriation Act in 1935.

17. Through the 1907 riots, the 1910 Exclusion league campaign, the 1917 Barred Zone Immigration Act, the 1920 Alien Land Act, and various anti-miscegenation laws, and finally under the 1790 Naturalization Act, which barred those who were neither White nor of African nativity or descent from being eligible for U.S. citizenship. They were also tried for conspiracy, and were the subjects of attempted deportation under the 1903 Anarchy Law.

18. See below for fuller explanation.

19. Jensen (1988), p. 219.

20. Sections 2 of the act of March 3, 1903, entitled 'An Act to Regulate the Immigration of Aliens into the United States' (32 Stat. at L. 1213, chap. 1012). See Turner v. Williams 194 U.S. 279 (1904). This law is an eerie and prescient reminder of the more recent PATRIOT Act, passed in October 2001.

21. Jensen (1988), p. 214. See Dumbauld (1937) for details of these laws.

22. Jensen (1988), chapter 10, 214.ff.

23. Jensen (1988), p. 218. 24 of these men were executed, and 27 were sentenced to long prison terms. In 1916, they convicted 17 more men.

24. *San Francisco Chronicle*, April 24 and May 5, 1918, 1:1.

25. And Filipinos. Also known as the Asian Exclusion Repeal Acts. There is also another bill, the McCarran-Walters Act, passed in 1952, which abolishes the 1917 Barred Zone Act.

26. Jensen (1988), p. 242.

27. As estimated by the Friends of the Freedom of India. Cited in Jensen (1988), p. 245.

28. Aoki (1998), p. 57, and n. 58.

29. As Keith Aoki has argued. Aoki (1998).

30. See Leonard (1992).

31. Jensen (1988), p. 271.

32. In 1933, the California legislature amended the law to include a prohibition against those from the Malay race; this amendment was directed against Filipinos. Melendy (1977), pp. 52–53.

33. In *Perez v. Sharp*, the 1948 case overturning the miscegenation laws, the Court ruled they did not apply to "Hindus and Mexicans." See Melendy, 240. However, contrary to Melendy's inference, this ruling does not mean that "Hindus" were necessarily allowed to marry whomever they wished. In 1931, Arizona ruled that miscegenation laws applied to "Hindus and Malays." (See Pascoe, 1996, p. 49 n. 13.) It is unclear whether other states also implicitly intended the same prohibition to apply to Indians, although Georgia and Virginia name Asian or Asiatic Indians among other groups. See Leonard (1992), who has interviewed the children of Punjabi-Mexican couples; they tell a markedly different story of their parents'

unions than does Melendy. Aside from the legal restrictions, there were also practical reasons that influenced the decisions Indian men and Mexican women to marry. According to Karen Leonard, Mexican men found it more difficult to secure property in the United States than Punjabi laborers, who by and large formed cooperative ventures to accumulate farmland. Due to the 1910 Alien Land Act, Sikh men—like other noncitizens, were under threat of being disenfranchised from their property. Anxious to retain control over their only wealth, they married Mexican women— even though they too were technically ineligible as noncitizens to hold property, but weren't targeted explicitly for it—and transferred their wealth to their wives' names, and to their native-born progeny. In this context, Mexican women, suggests Leonard, are interested in upward mobility (I would suggest that this impulse is hardly particular to them, but is rather a common and transcultural impulse), and so they were not averse to marrying Sikh men, presumably for this reason and others notwithstanding. Both Mexican women and Sikh men introduced their friends and siblings to the friends and siblings of their spouses, and engendered a pattern of intermarriage between these groups. See Leonard (1992), Part II.

34. Leonard (1992), chapters 4–6. Also see Sheth (2007a), in which I explore the implications of these partnerships for a racialized subjectivity.

35. 261 U.S. 204. I discuss the court's opinion briefly in ch. 1.

36. This was a limited improvement upon the Naturalization Act of 1790, which restricted citizenship to Whites alone.

37. 260 U.S. 178.

38. *Akhay Kumar Mozumdar v. United States* 299 Fed. 240 (1924). Jensen reports that by December 1926, 43 Indians were denaturalized, with other cases pending. Jensen (1988), p. 264.

39. Almaguer (1994), Jensen (1988), Aarim-Heriot (2003).

40. Hess (1969), p. 60.

41. Despite their claims to all full rights as British subjects in the case of Canada, circa 1913–14. Jensen (1988), chapter 6, esp. 134ff.

42. As quoted in Jensen (1988), p. 146.

43. See n. 35.

44. See chapter 5, especially section II, where I address the theoretical underpinnings of this issue.

45. See Aarim-Heriot (2003), p. 170 and elsewhere, for a discussion of the rights of African Americans in contrast to Chinese immigrants in the late 19th century in California.

46. As I have argued with regard to the outcasting of Muslims from the Western world.

47. For example, W.E.B. Du Bois was aware of these trials and the efforts of Indians to agitate for home rule and anticolonial politics. He made several speeches endorsing the efforts of Indians to this effect in 1907. See Mullen (2003), p. 321. Du Bois' acknowledgment of the struggles of Asian Indians qua "Hindus," can be found in several essays, including *Dark Princess, Conservation of Races* and *Darkwater.* And yet, in his multiple references to Asian Indians, Du Bois does not seem to cognize the struggle of Asian Indians as "racial subjects" within the American political and racial imaginary. He appears to accept uncritically, as did many others of his day who sympathized with the plight of Indians, the equation between Asian Indians and their presence on the international scene. For a more extensive discussion of this argument, see Sheth (2007a).

48. See chapter 4 for this discussion.

49. Alexander and Mohanty (1997), xiv.

50. See *Muller v. Oregon* 208 U.S. 412 (1908); *Lochner v. New York* 198 U.S. 45 (1905), and *West Coast Hotel v. Parrish* 300 U.S. 379 (1937).

51. *Brown v. Board of Education* 347 U.S. 483 (1954).

52. *Griswold v. Conn.* 381 U.S. 479 (1965), *Roe v. Wade* 410 U.S. 113 (1973), and *Reed v. Reed* 404 U.S. 71 (1971), to name a few.

53. This period marked the introduction of Title VII and IX of the Civil Rights Act, precipitating the introduction of affirmative action policies for women, and augmenting the affirmative action bill signed into law by President Lyndon B. Johnson.

54. Scaperlanda (1993), p. 1024.

55. If not enforced consistently.

56. And indeed the reading of this term is quite selective, often interpreted against the interests of non-citizens. See Scaperlanda (1993), pp. 997–1000, with attendant footnotes 152–160 for some examples of readings that are antagonistic to noncitizens.

57. On immigration, due process, categories of legal protection for those not designated as citizens (aliens, enemy combatants, enemy aliens,

etc.). See Bosniak (1996); Akram and Johnson (2002); Saito (2003), and Cox (2001) to see a few examples of recurrent immigration issues.

58. I am distinguishing between the characterization of ethnic groups as races, as politicians and government administrators were wont to do at the turn of the century—and their recognition as part of the "American racial discourse."

59. See Scaperlanda (1996), pp. 995ff.

60. See Jensen (1988), chapters 2, 3, 5, 7. Also cf. Ngai (2004), chs. 3 and 4.

61. Asiatic or Oriental races.

62. With the exception of recent race literature such as that emerging from Ethnics Studies, such as the work of Ronald Takaki, among others.

63. The only moment of recognition of their presence prior to the 1965 wave of immigration is in the—constantly—cited *U.S. v. Thind* (1923).

64. For a more extensive analysis of the ways in which postcolonial and subaltern studies frameworks necessarily eclipse the early-twentieth-century South Asian population in the United States, see Sheth (2007a).

65. Alexander and Mohanty (1997) "Introduction," p. xiv.

66. Spivak (1985).

67. Taken from Chakrabarty (2000), p. 480, who cites it from Spivak (1985).

68. "Introduction," p. xiv. Alexander (1997).

69. Guha (1988), p. 82. Cited in Spivak (1988), p. 203.

70. Credit to Robert Prasch for coining this phrase.

71. duCille (1996), "Discourse and Dat Course," p. 131.

72. Ibid.

73. See Rangaswamy (2000a), p. 45. In 1964, the Immigration Reform Act was passed, which opened American borders to larger groups of Indian immigrants.

74. For a more extensive discussion of race as a tripartite structure, see Sheth (2005).

Conclusion

1. I do not think the sovereignty is displaced in contemporary society so much as that Foucault's focus on sovereign authority is displaced in favor of other sites of power. He does raise the issue of the intensification of sovereign power in his 1973–1974 lectures in order to talk about the family. See Foucault (2006). However, he refocuses his interest in sovereignty there in order to reconnect it to biopolitics. I discuss this further in Sheth (2008b). Thanks to Marcello Hoffman and others at the 2007 Foucault Circle Meetings for alerting me to this point.

2. As Linda Martín Alcoff has discussed. See Alcoff (2007).

3. Chanter (2006), p. 96.

4. Chanter (2006), p. 97.

WORKS CITED

Aarim-Heriot, Najia. 2003. *Chinese Immigrants, African American, and Racial Anxiety in the United States, 1848–82.* Urbana and Chicago: University of Illinois.

Abraham, Matthew. 2006. "Supreme Rhetoric: The Supreme Court, Veiled Majoritarianism and the Enforcement of the Racial Contract." In *Race and the Foundations of Knowledge.* Edited by Joseph Young and Jana Evans Braziel. Urbana and Chicago: University of Illinois Press, 2006.

Abu-Lughod, Lila. 2002. "Do Muslim Women Really Need Saving? Anthropological Reflections on Cultural Relativism and Its Others." *American Anthropologist* 104, no. 3: 783–790.

Agamben, Giorgio. 1998. *Homo Sacer: Sovereign Power and Bare Life.* Translated by Daniel Heller-Roazen. Stanford, CA: Stanford University Press.

———. 2005. *State of Exception.* Translated by Kevin Attell. Chicago: University of Chicago.

Akram, Susan M., and Kevin R. Johnson. 2002. "'Migration Regulation Goes Local: The Role of States in U.S. Immigration Policy': Race, Civil Rights, and Immigration Law after September 11, 2001: The Targeting of Arabs and Muslim." *New York University Annual Survey of American Law* 2002: 295–355.

Al-Saji, Alia. 2004. "Who Is the Muslim Woman? Towards an Intersubjective Theory. Part of a Panel Entitled 'How Race Counts: Arabs, Muslims and the Politics of Visibility in the Diaspora'." Paper presented at the Forty-Third Annual conference of the Society for Phenomenology and Existential Philosophy, University of Memphis, Memphis, TN, October.

————. 2008. "Muslim Immigrants in Post–9/11 American Politics: The 'Exception' Population as an Intrinsic Element of American Liberalism." In *The New United America? A Race and Nationalism Reader.* Edited by Linda Martin Alcoff and Mariana Ortega. Albany: State University of New York Press, 2008.

Alcoff, Linda Martín. 1991–1992. "The Problem of Speaking for Others." *Cultural Critique* 20. Winter: 5–32.

————. 2000. "Is Latina/O Identity a Racial Identity?" In *Hispanics/Latinos in the U.S.: Ethnicity, Race and Rights.* Edited by Jorge Gracia and Pablo De Greiff. New York: Routledge Press, 2000.

————. 2006. *Visible Identities: Race, Gender and the Self.* New York: Oxford University Press.

————. 2007. "Comparative Race, Comparative Racisms." In *Race for Ethnicity? On Black and Latino Identity.* Edited by Jorge. J. E. Gracia. Ithaca: Cornell University Press.

Alexander, M. Jacqui and Chandra Talpade Mohanty, (eds.) 1997. *Feminist Genealogies, Colonial Legacies, Democratic Futures.* Edited by Linda Nicholson, *Thinking Gender.* New York: Routledge.

Ali, Ayaan Hirsi. 2006. *The Trouble with Islam: An Emancipation Proclamation for Women and Islam.* New York: Free Press.

Almaguer, Tomas. 1994. *Racial Faultlines: The Historical Origins of White Supremacy in California.* Berkeley and Los Angeles: University of California Press.

Andreasen, Robin. 2000. "Race: Biological Reality or Social Construct?" *Journal of Philosophy* 67 (Proceedings Volume) pp. S653–S666.

Andrews, Marcellus. 1999. *The Political Economy of Hope and Fear.* New York: New York University Press.

Aoki, Keith. 1998. "No Right to Own?: The Early Twentieth-Century 'Alien Land Law' as a Prelude to Internment." *Boston College Law Review* 40: 37–72.

Appiah, Anthony. 1996. "Race, Culture, Identity: Misunderstood Connections." In *Color Conscious: The Political Morality of Race.* Edited by Anthony Appiah and Amy Gutmann. Princeton: Princeton University Press, 1996.

Arendt, Hannah. 1958. *The Human Condition.* Chicago and London: University of Chicago Press.

———. 1966. *Origins of Totalitarianism.* New York: Harcourt.

Arisaka, Yoko. 1997. "Beyond East and West: Nishida's Universalism and Postcolonial Critique." *The Review of Politics* 59, no. 3: 541–560.

Arnone, Michael. 2003. "Closing the Gates/Watchful Eyes: The FBI Steps up Its Work on Campuses, Spurring Fear and Anger among Many Academics." *The Chronicle of Higher Education* 49, no. 31: A14.

Balibar, Etienne. 2004. *We, the People of Europe?: Reflections on Transnational Citizenship.* Princeton: Princeton University Press.

Barnes, Julian, and Carol J. Williams. 2006. "Guantanamo's First Suicides Pressures U.S." *Los Angeles Times,* June 11.

Beazley, C. Raymond. 1900. "New Light on Some Medieval Maps." *Geographic Journal* 15, no. 4: 378–389.

Benhabib, Seyla. 1999. "Citizens, Residents, and Aliens in a Changing World: Political Membership in a Global Era." *Social Research* 66, no. 3: 709.

———. 2002. *The Claims of Culture : Equality and Diversity in the Global Era.* Princeton: Princeton University Press.

Benjamin, Walter. 1978. "The Critique of Violence." In *Reflections: Essays, Aphorisms, Autobiographical Writings.* Edited by Peter Demetz. New York and London: Harcourt Brace Jovanovich, 1978.

Berlin, Isaiah. 1969. *Four Essays on Liberty.* London, New York: Oxford University Press.

Berman, Paul. 2003. *Terror and Liberalism.* 1st ed. New York: Norton.

Bernasconi, Robert, and Tommy L. Lott, eds. 2000. *The Idea of Race.* Indianapolis: Hackett Press.

Bernstein, Nina. 2005a. "Girl Called Would-Be Bomber Was Drawn to Islam." *New York Times,* April 8.

———. 2005b. "Teachers and Classmates Express Outrage at Arrest of Girl, 16, as a Terrorist Threat." *New York Times,* April 9.

———. 2005c. "Questions, Bitterness and Exile for Queens Girl in Terror Case." *New York Times,* June 17.

Bickel, Alexander. 1975. *The Morality of Consent.* New Haven: Yale University Press.

"Black Ministers Protest Gay Marriage." 2004. *Associated Press State and Local Wire*, May 23.

Blumenthal, Ralph. 2004. "New Strains and New Rules for Agents Along the Mexican Border." *New York Times*, National Report, August 12.

Bosniak, Linda S. 1994. "Membership, Equality, and the Difference That Alienage Makes." *New York University Law Review* 69 1047–1149.

Bosniak, Linda S. 1996. "Opposing Prop. 187: Undocumented Immigrants and the National Imagination." *Connecticut Law Review* 28: 555–619.

Brantlinger, Patrick. 2003. *Dark Vanishings: Discourse on the Extinction of Primitive Races, 1800–1930*. Ithaca: Cornell University Press.

Brown, Wendy 1995. *States of Injury: Power and Freedom in Late Modernity*. Princeton: Princeton University Press.

Butler, Judith. 1992. "Contingent Foundations: Feminism and the Question of "Post-Modernism." In *Feminists Theorize the Political*. Edited by Judith Butler and Joan Scott. New York and London: Routledge, 1992.

———. 1997. *Psychic Power of Life: Theories in Subjection*. Palo Alto: Stanford University Press.

Camus, Albert. 1946. *The Stranger*. Translated by Stuart Gilbert. New York: Knopf.

Carter, Susan B., and Richard Sutch, eds. 2006. *Historical Statistics of the United States: Millenial Edition*. New York: Cambridge University Press.

"Catholic Chaplains Affected by French Veil Law." 2004. *Catholic News*, October 8.

Chakrabarty, Dipesh. 2000. *Provincializing Europe: Postcolonial Thought and Historical Difference*. Princeton: Princeton University Press.

Chandler, Daniel. "Semiotics: The Basics." London: Routledge. 2002 (accessed September 10, 2004).

Chandrasekhar, S., ed. 1982. *From India to America: A Brief History of Immigration; Problems of Discrimination, Admission and Assimiliation*. La Jolla, CA: Population Review Publications.

"Changing of the Guard." 2002. *New York Times*, Dec. 21. Editorial.

Chanter, Tina. 2006. "Abjection and the Constitutive Nature of Difference: Class Mourning in Margaret's Museum and Legitimating Myths of Innocence in Casablanca." *Hypatia* 21, no. 3: 86–106.

Chatterjee, Partha. 1986. *Nationalist Thought and Colonial World: A Derivative Discourse.* Minneapolis: University of Minnesota Press.

Chin, Gabriel J. 1997. "Segregation's Last Stronghold: Race Discrimination and the Constitutional Law of Immigration." *UCLA Law Review* 46: 1.

Clarke, Kamari Maxine, and Deborah A. Thomas. 2006. *Globalization and Race: Transformations in the Cultural Production of Blackness.* Durham, NC: Duke University Press.

Clemetson, Lynette. 2004. "Both Sides Court Black Churches in the Battle over Gay Marriage." *New York Times,* March 1.

Cohler-Esses, Larry. 2005. "Terror Suspects Allege Abuse." *New York Daily News,* February 20.

Cohn, Bernard S. 1996. "Cloth, Clothes, and Colonialism." In *Colonialism and Its Forms of Knowledge,* 106–162. Princeton: Princeton University Press, 1996.

Cole, David. 2002a. "Enemy Aliens and American Freedoms." *The Nation,* September 23.

———. 2002b. "Patriot Act's Big Brother." *The Nation,* March 17.

———. 2003. *Enemy Aliens: Double Standards and Constitutional Freedoms in the War on Terrorism.* New York: New Press.

Conner, Walker. 1978. "A Nation Is a Nation, Is an Ethnic Group Is A . . ." *Ethnic and Racial Studies* 1, no. 4: 377–400.

Cordova, V.F. 2001. "Native American Philosopher." *Newsletter on American Indians in Philosophy* 00, no. 2.

Corlett, J. Angelo 2003. "Ethnic Identity and Public Policy." In *Race, Reparations and Latino Identity.* Ithaca: Cornell University Press, 2003.

Cox, Lisa. 2001. "Comment: The Legal Limbo of Indefinite Detention: How Low Can You Go?" *American University Law Review* 50: 725–754.

Cox, Oliver. 1987. *Caste, Class and Race: A Study in Social Dynamics.* New York: Modern Reader Paperbacks.

Cregan, Dennis. 2003. Personal Interview, Salvation Army/Plattsburgh, NY, March 19.

Crenshaw, Kimberle. 2004. *Commentary:* Tavis Smiley Show, March 16.

D'Souza, Dinesh. 1995. *The End of Racism: Principles for a Multiracial Society.* New York: Free Press.

Dahlke, H. Otto. 1952. "Race and Minority Riots—A Study in the Typology of Violence." *Social Forces* 30: 419–425.

Daly, Mary. 1978. "Indian Suttee: The Ultimate Consumation of Marriage." In *Gyn/Ecology: The Metaethics of Radical Feminism.* Boston: Beacon Press, 1978.

Daniels, Roger. 1989 (orig. 1971). *Concentration Camps-North America: Japanese in the United States and Canada During World War II.* Malabar, FL: Krieger Publishing Company.

Danner, Mark. 2004. *Torture and Truth: America, Abu Ghraib, and the War on Terror.* New York: New York Review of Books.

Darity, William A. Jr., and Patrick L. Mason. 2004. "Racial Discrimination in the Labor Market." In *Race, Liberalism and Economics.* Edited by David Colander, Robert E. Prasch and Falguni A. Sheth. Ann Arbor: University of Michigan Press, 2004.

Davis, F.J. 1991. *Who Is Black? One Nation's Definition.* University Park: Pennsylvania State University Press.

Davis, Mike. 2006. "A History of the Car Bomb (Part I)." In *Tom Dispatch.com.* Edited by Tom Engelhardt: Nation Institute, 2006.

Deloria, Philip Joseph. 1994. "Playing Indian: Otherness and Authenticity in the Assumption of American Indian Identity." Ph.D. Thesis, Yale University 1994.

Deloria, Philip Joseph, and Neal Salisbury. 2004. *A Companion to American Indian History, Blackwell Companions to American History; [4].* Malden, MA: Blackwell Pub.

Delves Broughton, Philip. 2004. "French Schools to Put Turbans and Crucifixes on Banned List." *Daily Telegraph,* January 24.

Denniston, Lyle. 2003. "High Court to Hear Detainees' Appeals Kin of Prisoners Challenge Us View They Have No Rights." *Boston Globe,* November 11.

Derrida, Jacques. 1976. *Of Grammatology.* Translated by Gayatri Chakravorty Spivak. Baltimore: Johns Hopkins University Press.

———. 1990. "Force of Law: The 'Mystical' Foundations of Authority." *Cardozo Law Review* 11, no. 5–6: 919–1045.

Dershowitz, Alan M. 2002. *Why Terrorism Works: Understanding the Threat, Responding to the Challenge.* New Haven: Yale University Press.

Dreyfus, Hubert. 2003. "Being and Power Revisited." In *Heidegger and Foucault: Critical Encounters.* Edited by Alan Milchman and Alan Rosenberg. Minnesota: University of Minneapolis, 2003.

duCille, Ann. 1996. *Skin Trade.* Cambridge: Harvard University Press.

Dumbauld, Edward. 1937. "Neutrality Laws of the United States." *American Journal of International Law* 31, no. 2: 258–270.

El Guindi, Fadwa. 1999. *Veil: Modesty, Privacy and Resistance.* New York: Berg (Oxford International Publishers), Reprint, 2000.

Elkins, Caroline. 2005. *Imperial Reckoning: The Untold Story of Britain's Gulag in Kenya.* 1st ed. New York: Henry Holt and Co.

Engle, Karen. 2004. "Constructing Good Aliens and Good Citizens: Legitimizing the War on Terrorism." *University of Colorado Law Review* 75: 79–115.

Euben, Roxanne L. 1999. *Enemy in the Mirror: Islamic Fundamentalism and the Limits of Modern Rationalism. A Work of Comparative Political Theory.* Princeton: Princeton University Press.

Eze, Emmanuel Chukwudi, ed. 1999. *Race and the Enlightenment: A Reader.* Malden, MA: Blackwell Publishing.

Fanon, Frantz. 1965. *A Dying Colonialism.* New York: Monthly Review Press.

Fichte, Johann Gottlieb. 1979. *Addresses to the German Nation.* Westport, CT: Greenwood Press.

Fiss, Owen. 1998. "The Immigrant as Pariah." *Boston Review Online* 23, no. 7, October/November. www.bostonreview.net/BR23.5/Fiss.html.

Flusser, Vilem. 2003. *The Freedom of the Migrant: Objections to Nationalism.* Urbana and Chicago: University of Illinois Press.

Ford, Richard T. 2004. *Racial Culture: A Critique.* Princeton: Princeton University Press.

Foucault, Michel. 1977. *Discipline and Punish.* Translated by Alan Sheridan. New York: Vintage Books.

———. 1978. "Governmentality." In *Power.* Edited by James D. Faubion. New York: New Press, 1978.

———. 1979. *Discipline and Punish.* Translated by Alan Sheridan. New York: Vintage Books.

————. 1989. *Madness and Civilization: A History of Insanity in the Age of Reason.* Translated by Richard Howard. London: Routledge.

————. 2003a. *Society Must Be Defended: Lectures at the College De France 1975–6.* Translated by David Macey. New York: Picador Press.

————. 2003b. *Abnormality: Lectures at the College De France 1974–1975.* Translated by Graham Burchell. New York: Picador Press.

————. 2006. *Psychiatric Power: Lectures at the College De France 1973–1974.* Translated by Graham Burchell: Palgrave MacMillan.

Franks, Myfanwy. 2000. "Crossing the Borders of Whiteness? White Muslim Women Who Wear the Hijab in Britain Today." *Ethnic and Racial Studies* 23, no. 5: 917–929.

Fraser, Nancy. 1989. *Unruly Practices: Power, Discourse, and Gender in Contemporary Social Theory.* Minneapolis: University of Minnesota Press.

————. 1997. *Justice Interruptus: Critical Reflections on The "Postsocialist" Condition.* New York: Routledge.

Fraser, Nancy, and Axel Honneth. 2003. *Redistribution or Recognition?: A Political-Philosophical Exchange.* London; New York: Verso.

Galston, William. 2002. *Liberal Pluralism: The Implications of Value Pluralism for Political Theory and Practice.* New York: Cambridge University Press.

Gandhi, Leela. 1998. *Postcolonial Theory: A Critical Introduction.* New York: Columbia Press.

Gerges, Fawaz A. 1999. *America and Political Islam.* Cambridge, England: Cambridge University Press.

Gilman, Sander L. 2003. *Jewish Frontiers: Essays on Bodies, Histories, and Identity.* New York: Palgrave MacMillan.

Girard, Rene. 1986. *The Scapegoat.* Baltimore: Johns Hopkins University Press.

Glasgow, Joshua. 2003. "On the New Biology of Race." *Journal of Philosophy* 100, no. 9: 456–474.

Goldberg, David Theo. 2004. "The Power of Tolerance." In *Philosemitism, Antisemitism and the Jews: Perspectives from Antiquity to the Twentieth Century,* edited by Nadia and Tony Kushner Valman. Burlington, VT: Ashgate Publishers, 2004.

———. 2002. *The Racial State.* New York: Blackwell.

Gossett, Thomas. 1997. *Race: The History of an Idea in America.* New York: Oxford University Press.

Goswami, Namita. 2006. "Shifting Grounds: Identity, Partition, and the Anglo-Indian Subject of History." *South Asian Review* 27, no. 1: 74–98.

Goswami, Namita and Paul Courtright. 2008. "Who Was Roop Kanwar? Sati, Law, Religion, and Post-Colonial Feminism." In *Religion and Personal Law in Secular India: A Call to Judgment* 200–225. Bloomington: Indiana University Press, 2008.

Gourevitch, Philip. 1998. *We Wish to Inform You That Tomorrow We Will Be Killed with Our Families: Stories from Rwanda.* 1st ed. New York: Farrar, Straus, and Giroux.

"Government Unveil 'Charter of Values'." 2007. *Ansa English Media Service*, April 26.

Gracia, Jorge. 2000. *Hispanic/Latino Identity: A Philosophical Perspective.* Oxford: Blackwell.

Gracia, Jorge and Pablo De Greiff, ed. 2000. *Hispanics/Latinos in the U.S.: Ethnicity, Race and Rights* New York: Routledge Press.

Gramsci, Antonio. 1971. *Prison Notebooks.* New York: International Publishers.

Greenhouse, Linda. 2003. "It's a Question of Federal Turf." *New York Times*, November 12.

Guglielmo, Jennifer and Salvatore Salerno, ed. 2003. *Are Italians White?* New York: Routledge.

Guha, Ranajit. 1988. "The Prose of Counter-Insurgency." in *Selected Subaltern Studies.* Edited by Edward Said, Ranajit Guha, and Gayatri Chakravorty Spivak. Oxford: Oxford University Press.

Gutmann, Amy. 1993. "The Challenge of Multiculturalism in Political Ethics." *Philosophy and Public Affairs* 22, no. 3: 171–206.

Hardimon, Michael. 2003. "The Ordinary Concept of Race." *Journal of Philosophy* 100, no. 9: 437–455.

Harvey, Miles. 2003. "The Bad Guy." *Mother Jones.* March/April. http://www.motherjones.com/commentary/notebook/2003/03/ma-293.01.html.

Hasan, Najeeb. 2007. "Feds May Move on Local Mosques: A New FBI Case against Terror Suspects Could Be Set to Rock the Bay Area" *Metroactive*, April 4–10. http://www.metroactive.com/metro/04.04.07/terror-probe-0714.html.

Hays, Tom. 2006. Last 9-11 Detainee Released from Lockup. In *Associated Press*, http://news.yahoo.com/s/ap/20060722/ap_on_re_us/last_detainee. (accessed July 24, 2006).

Heidegger, Martin. 1950. "Question Concerning Technology." In *Martin Heidegger: Basic Writings (1977)*. Edited by David Farrell Krell. New York: Harper & Row, 1950.

———. 1996. *Being and Time, Trans. Joan Stambaugh*. Albany: State University of New York Press.

"Hérouxville Drops Some Rules from Controversial Code." 2007. *CBC News (online edition)*, February 13.

Hess, Gary. 1969. "The 'Hindu' in America: Immigration and Naturalization Policies and India, 1917-1946." *Pacific Historical Revew* 38: 335–340.

Hirschmann, Nancy J. 1998. "Western Feminism, Eastern Veiling and the Question of Free Agency." *Constellations* 5, no. 3: 345–368.

Hochschild, Adam. 1998. *King Leopold's Ghost : A Story of Greed, Terror, and Heroism in Colonial Africa*. Boston: Houghton Mifflin.

Homola, Victor. 2004. "World Briefing| Europe: Germany: Ban Extended to Nuns' Habits." *New York Times*, October 12.

Honig, Bonnie. 2001. *Democracy and the Foreigner*. Princeton: Princeton University Press.

———. 2002/2003. "A Legacy of Xenophobia." *Boston Review Online* 27, no. 6. December/January, www.bostonreview.net/BR27.6/honig.html.

Hoodfar, Homa. 1997. "The Veil in Their Minds and on Our Heads: The Persistence of Colonial Images of Muslim Women." In *The Politics of Culture in the Shadow of Capital*. Edited by Lisa Lowe and David Lloyd. Durham, NC; London: Duke University Press, 1997.

Hosken, Fran. 1981. "Female Genital Mutilation and Human Rights." *Feminist Issues* 1, no. 3.

Huntington, Samuel. 1993. "The Clash of Civilizations." *Foreign Affairs* 72, no. 3: 1–12.

Ignatiev, Noel. 1995. *How the Irish Became White.* London: Routledge.

Jackson, Derrick Z. 2004. "Bible Lessons These Clergy Forgot." *Boston Globe,* February 11.

Jane Doe V. State of Louisiana, through the Department of Health and Human Resources, 1985. 479 So. 2d 369 (1985).

Jensen, Joan. 1988. *Passage from India: Asian Indian Immigrants in North America.* New Haven and London: Yale University Press.

Kashima, Tetsuden. 2003. *Judgment without Trial: Japanese Imprisonment During World War II.* Seattle and London: University of Washington Press.

Kassab, Elizabeth. 2005. "Integrating Modern Arab Thought in Postcolonial Philosophies of Culture." *American Philosophical Association Newsletter* 14, no. 1: 207.

Kateri-Hernandez, Tanya. 1998. "'Multiracial' Discourse: Racial Classifications in an Era of Color-Blind Jurisprudence." *Maryland Law Review* 57: 97–173.

Khalidi, Rashid. 2004. *Resurrecting Empire: Western Footprints and America's Perilous Path in the Middle East.* 1st ed. Boston: Beacon Press.

Kim, David. 2002. "Asian American Philosophers: Absence, Politics, and Identity." *American Philosophical Association Newsletter (on the Status of Asian/Asian American Philosophers and Philosophies)* 1.

———. 2003. "Orientalism and America Enlarged." *American Philosophical Association Newsletter (on the Status of Asian/American Philosophers and Philosophies)* 2.

———. 2004. "Empire's Entrails and Imperial Geography of 'Amerasia'." *City* 8, no. 1: 57–88.

———. 2007. "What Is Asian American Philosophy?" In *Philosophy in Multiple Voices,* edited by George Yancy. Lanham, MD: Rowman & Littlefield, 2007.

Kitcher, Philip. 1999. "Race, Ethnicity, Biology, Culture." In *Racism: Key Concepts in Critical Theory.* Edited by Leonard Harris. Amherst, NY: Humanities Books.

Kramer, Jane. 2004. "Taking the Veil; How France's Public Schools Became the Battleground in a Culture War." *New Yorker,* November 22.

Kymlicka, Will. 1989. *Liberalism, Community and Culture.* Oxford: Oxford University Press.

Laborde, Cecile. 2005. "Secular Philosophy and Muslim Headscarves in Schools." *Journal of Political Philosophy* 13, no. 3: 305–329.

Lalami, Leila. 2006. "The Missionary Position." *The Nation,* 19 June.

Lelyveld, Joseph. 2002. "In Guantánamo." *New York Review of Books,* November 7.

Leonard, Karen. 1992. *Making Ethnic Choices: California's Punjabi Mexican Americans.* Philadelphia: Temple University Press.

Lewis, Neil A. 2006. "Judge Sets Back Guantanamo Detainees." *New York Times,* December 14.

Locke, John. 1947. *Two Treatises of Government.* New York: Hafner Press.

Loomba, Ania. 2005. *Postcolonial Studies and Beyond.* Durham, NC: Duke University Press.

Lopez, Ian F. Haney. 1998. *White by Law: The Legal Construction of Race.* New York: New York University Press.

Mahmood, Saba. 2001. "Feminist Theory, Embodiment, and the Docile Agent: Some Reflections on the Egyptian Islamic Revival." *Cultural Anthropology* 16, no. 2: 202–235.

———. 2005. *The Politics of Piety: The Islamic Revival and the Feminist Subject.* Princeton: Princeton University Press.

Maldonado-Torres, Nelson. 2004. "The Topology of Being and the Geopolitics of Knowledge." *City* 8, no. 1: 29–56.

Mamdani, Mahmood. 2001. *When Victims Become Killers: Colonialism, Nativism and the Genocide in Rwanda.* Princeton: Princeton University Press.

———. 2004. *Good Muslim, Bad Muslim: America, the Cold War, and the Roots of Terror.* 1st ed. New York: Pantheon Books.

Margulies, Joseph. 2006. *Guantanamo and the Abuse of Presidential Power.* New York: Simon and Schuster.

Martin, David. 2003. "With a Whisper, Not a Bang Bush Signs Parts of Patriot Act II into Law—Stealthily." *San Antonio Current,* December 24.

Mathew, Biju. 2006. *Taxi!* New York: New Press.

Mayer, Jane. 2003. "Lost in the Jihad." *New Yorker*, March 10.

———. 2005. "Outsourcing Torture: The Secret History of America's 'Extraordinary Rendition' Program." *New Yorker*, February 14.

Mehta, Uday S. 1992. *The Anxiety of Freedom: Imagination and Individuality in Locke's Political Thought*. Princeton: Princeton University Press.

———. 1999. *Liberalism and Empire: A Study in Nineteenth-Century British Thought*. Chicago: University of Chicago Press.

Melendy, Brett. 1977. *Asians in America: Filipinos, Koreans, Indians*. New York: Hippocrene Books.

Mendieta, Eduardo. 1999. "Is There a Latin American Philosophy?" *Philosophy Today, SPEP Supplement* 43: 50–61.

———, ed. 2003. *Latin American Philosophy: Currents, Issues, Debates*. Bloomington, IN: Indiana University Press.

Metcalf, Thomas. 1995. *Ideologies of the Raj, The New Cambridge History of India*. Cambridge, UK: Cambridge University Press.

Milchman, Alan, and Alan Rosenberg, eds. 2003. *Heidegger and Foucault: Critical Encounters*. Minneapolis: University of Minnesota Press.

Mills, Charles. 1997. *The Racial Contract*. Ithaca: Cornell University Press.

———. 2003. "White Supremacy." In *A Companion to African-American Philosophy*. Edited by Tommy Lee Lott and John P. Pittman. New York: Blackwell, 2003.

———. 2006. "Modernity, Persons, and Subpersons." In *Race and the Foundations of Knowledge*. Edited by Joseph Young and Jana Evans Braziel. Urbana and Chicago: University of Illinois Press, 2006.

Mitchell, Melanthia. 2004. "Muslim Chaplain Will Receive Honorable Discharge." *Associated Press*, September 16.

Mohanty, Chandra Talpade. 1991. "Under Western Eyes: Feminist Scholarship and Colonial Discourses." In *Third World Women and the Politics of Feminism*. Edited by Chandra Talpade Mohanty, Ann Russo, and Lourdes Torres. Bloomington and Indianapolis: Indiana University Press, 1991.

Mouffe, Chantal. 1993. *The Return of the Political*. London, New York: Verso.

———. 1996. "Democracy, Power, and the Political." In *Democracy and Difference: Contesting the Boundaries of the Political.* Edited by Seyla Benhabib. Princeton: Princeton University Press, 1996.

Mullen, Bill V. 2003. "Du Bois, *Dark Princess*, and the Afro-Asian International." *Positions* 11, no. 1: 217–239.

Myre, Greg. 2006. "Israeli Visa Policy Traps Thousands of Palestinians in a Legal Quandary." *New York Times*, September 18.

Nancy, Jean-Luc. 1993. "Abandoned Being." In *The Birth to Presence.* Stanford, CA: Stanford University Press, 1993.

Narayan, Uma. 1997. *Dislocating Cultures: Identities, Traditions, and Third World Feminisms.* New York: Routledge.

———. 1998. "Essence of Culture and a Sense of History: A Feminist Critique of Cultural Essentialism. (Border Crossings: Multicultural and Postcolonial Feminist Challenges to Philosophy, Part 1)." *Hypatia* 13, no. 2:86–106.

Neri, Geoffrey. 2005. "Of Mongrels and Men: The Shared Ideology of Anti-Miscegenation Law, Chinese Exclusion, and Contemporary American Neo-Nativism." *bePress Legal Series* Paper 458.

Neuman, Gerald. 1996. *Strangers to the Constitution: Immigrants, Borders, and Fundamental Law.* Princeton: Princeton University Press.

Ngai, Mae. 2004. *Impossible Subjects: The Making of Illegal Aliens in America.* Princeton: Princeton University Press.

"Note to Would-Be Immigrants: You Can't Stone Women Here: Quebec Town Adopts List of Official 'Norms'." 2007. *Edmonton Journal (Alberta)*, January 28, 2.

Nozick, Robert. 1974. *Anarchy, State, and Utopia.* New York: Basic Books.

"Nun Identity Card Photo Sparks Veil Debate." 2004. *Catholic News*, July 9.

O'Flaherty, Brendan, and Jill S. Shapiro. 2004. "Apes, Essences, and Races: What Natural Scientists Believed About Human Variation, 1700–1900." In *Race, Liberalism, and Economics*, edited by David Colander, Robert E. Prasch and Falguni A. Sheth. Ann Arbor: University of Michigan Press, 2004.

Okin, Susan. 1997. "Is Multiculturalism Bad for Women?" *Boston Review Online.* Oct./Nov. www.bostonreview.net/BR22.5/okin.html.

———. 1999. "Is Multiculturalism Bad for Women?" In *Is Multiculturalism Bad for Women?* Edited by Susan Okin, Joshua

Cohen, Matthew Howard, and Martha C. Nussbaum. Princeton: Princeton University Press, 1999.

Ortega, Mariana. 2001. ""New Mestizas," "'World'-Travelers," And "'Dasein': Phenomenology and the Multi-Voiced, Multi-Cultural Self." *Hypatia* 16, no. 3: 1–29.

———. 2006. "Being Lovingly, Knowingly Ignorant: White Feminism and Women of Color." *Hypatia* 21, no. 3: 56–74.

Owens, Keith. 2001. "Niggers, Old & New." *Metro Times*, December 12.

Paris, Jeffrey. 2002. "After Rawls." *Social Theory and Practice* 28, no. 4:679–699.

Parker, Kunal. 2001. "State, Citizenship, and Territory: The Legal Construction of Immigrants in Antebellum Massachusetts." *Law and History Review* 19, no. 3.

Pascoe, Peggy. 1996. "Miscegenation Law, Court Cases and Ideologies Of "Race" In Twentieth Century America." *The Journal of American History* 83, no. 1:44–69.

Pateman, Carole. 1982. *The Sexual Contract*. Pennsylvania State University Press.

Pfaelzer, Jean. 2007. *Driven Out: The Forgotten War against Chinese Americans*. New York: Random House.

Pliny, The Elder. 2005/77 ACE. "On the Human Animal." In *Natural History*. Oxford: Clarendon Press, 2005/77 ACE.

Powell, Michael. 2001. "Pakistani Exodus to Canada Brings Waits, Crowding." *Washington Post*, February 1.

Rangaswamy, Padma. 2000a. *Namaste America: Indian Immigrants in an American Metropolis*. University Park: Pennsylvania State University.

———. 2000b. *Namaste America: Indian Immigrants Inan American Metropolis*. University Park: Pennsylvania State University.

Rawls, John. 1971. *A Theory of Justice*. Cambridge: Harvard University Press.

———. 1999. *Law of Peoples*. Cambridge: Harvard University Press.

Romero, Roberto Chao. 2003. "Dragon in Big Lusong: Chinese Immigration and Settlement in Mexico, 1882–1940." Ph.D. Dissertation, University of California, Los Angeles.

Rorty, Richard. 1992. "A Pragmatist View of Rationality and Cultural Difference." *Philosophy East and West*. 581–596.

Rousseau, Jean-Jacques. 1979a. *Emile.* New York: Basic Books.

———. 1979b. *Basic Political Writings.* Edited by Peter Gay. Indianapolis: Hackett Press.

"Rumsfeld Praises Army General Who Ridicules Islam as 'Satan'." 2003. *New York Times,* October 17, 7.

Said, Edward W. 1978. *Orientalism.* 1st ed. New York: Pantheon Books.

Saito, Natsu Taylor. 1997a. "Alien and Non-Alien Alike: Citizenship, "Foreignness," And Racial Hierarchy in American Law." *Oregon Law Review* 76. Summer: 261–345.

———. 1997b. "Model Minority, Yellow Peril: Functions Of "Foreignness" In the Construction of Asian American Legal Identity." *Asian Law Journal* 4, May: 71–95.

———. 2003. "The Enduring Effect of the Chinese Exclusion Cases: The "Plenary Power" Justification for on-Going Abuses of Human Rights." *Asian Law Journal* 10: 13–36.

———. 2007. *From Chinese Exclusion to Guantanamo Bay: Plenary Power and the Prerogative State.* Boulder: University Press of Colorado.

Sajida Alvi, Homa Hoodfar and Sheila McDonough, ed. 2003. *The Muslim Veil North America: Issues and Debates.* Toronto: Canadian Scholars' Press.

Salyer, Lucy E. 1995. *Laws Harsh as Tigers: Chinese Immigrants and the Shaping of Modern Immigration Law.* Chapel Hill: University of North Carolina Press.

San Juan, E. 2002. *Racism and Cultural Studies: Critiques of Multiculturalist Ideology and the Politics of Difference.* Durham: Duke University Press.

Sawicki, Jana. 2003. "Heidegger and Foucault: Escaping Technological Nihilism." In *Heidegger and Foucault: Critical Encounters,* edited by Alan Milchman and Alan Rosenberg. Minneapolis: University of Minnesota Press, 2003.

Scaperlanda, Michael. 1993. "Polishing the Tarnished Golden Door." *Wisconsin Law Review* 1993: 965–1032.

———. 1996. "Partial Membership, Aliens, and the Constitutional Community." *Iowa Law Review* 81: 707–773.

Schiavone-Camacho, Julia Maria. 2006. "Traversing Boundaries: Chinese, Mexicans, and Chinese Mexicans in the Formation of Gender,

Race, and Nation in the Twentieth Century U.S.-Mexico Borderlands." Ph.D. Dissertation, University of Texas, El Paso.

Schmitt, Carl. 1985. *Political Theology.* Translated by George Schwab. Chicago: University of Chicago Press.

———. 1996. *The Concept of the Political.* Chicago: University of Chicago Press.

Schneider, David 1965. "Kinship and Biology." In *Aspects of the Analysis of Family Structures,* edited by Ansley J. Coale, Lloyd A. Fallers, Marion J. Levy, Jr., David M. Schneider, and Silvan S. Tomkins. Princeton: Princeton University Press, 1965.

Schuck, Peter. 1984. "The Transformation of American Law." *Columbia Law Review* 84, 1: 1–90.

———. 1998. *Citizens, Strangers, and in-Betweens.* Boulder: Westview Press.

Schutte, Ofelia. 2000. "Negotiating Latina Identities." In *Hispanics/ Latinos in the United States: Ethnicity, Race, and Rights.* Edited by Jorge Gracia and P. De Greiff, 61–75. New York: Routledge, 2000.

———. 2001. "Latin America and Postmodernity: Ruptures and Continuities in the Concept of 'Our America.'" In *Latin America and Postmodernity: A Contemporary Reader.* Edited by P. Lange-Churión and E. Mendieta, 155–176. Amherst, NY: Humanity, 2001.

Sheth, Falguni. 2003. "Statelessness, Rightlessness and Black Americans." Unpublished Manuscript. Amherst, MA: Hampshire College, 2003.

———. 2005. "Border-Populations: Boundary, Memory, Conscience." *International Studies in Philosophy* 37, no. 2: 131–157.

———. 2007a. "Am I That Race? Am I That Other? Mexican-Hindus and Hybrid Subjectivity in Early Twentieth Century United States." 20: Hampshire College; on file with author, 2007.

———. 2007b. "Race, Violence, Law: Some Questions About Foucault's Account of Sovereign Power." Conference paper presented at the Foucault Circle Meetings, Loyola Marymount University, Los Angeles, CA.

———. 2008. "The Hijab and the Sari: The Strange and the Sexy Between Colonialism and Global Capitalism. *Contemporary Aesthetics.* Special Issue on Race and Aesthetics. Edited by Monique Roelofs. Forthcoming.

Shirazi, Faegheh. 2001. *The Veil Unveiled: The Hijab in Modern Culture.* Gainesville: University Press of Florida.

Simons, Marlise. 2006. "Somali-Born Politician Allowed to Stay a Dutch Citizen." *New York Times,* June 28.

Simpson, Glenn R. 2003. "Military Files Charges against Muslim Chaplain." *Wall Street Journal,* October 13.

Spivak, Gayatri. 1988. "Subaltern Studies: Deconstruction, Historiography" In *Other Worlds: Essays in Cultural Politics.* London: Routledge.

Spivak, Gayatri Chakravorty. 1985. "Can the Subaltern Speak?" *Wedge* 7/8: 118–130.

St. John, Warren. 2007. "Outcasts United: On a Small Town's Soccer Fields, Refugees Find Hostility and Hope." *New York Times,* January 21.

Stoler, Ann. 1995. *Race and the Education of Desire: Foucault's History of Sexuality and the Colonial Order of Things.* Durham and London: Duke University Press.

Stoler, Ann Laura. 2006. *Haunted by Empire: Geographies of Intimacy in North American History.* Durham: Duke University Press.

Takaki, Ronald T. 1993. *A Different Mirror: A History of Multicultural America.* 1st edition. Boston: Little Brown.

———. 1998. *Strangers from a Different Shore: A History of Asian Americans.* Updated and revised edition. Boston: Little Brown.

Taylor, Charles. 1994. "Multiculturalism: Examining the Politics of Recognition." In *Multiculturalism: Examining the Politics of Recognition.* Edited by Amy Gutmann. Princeton: Princeton University Press, 1994.

Temple-Raston, Dina. 2007. *The Jihad Next Door: The Lackawanna Six and Rough Justice in an Age of Terror.* 1st edition. New York: Public Affairs.

Thomas, Elaine R. 2006. "Keeping Identity at a Distance: Explaining France's New Legal Restrictions on the Islamic Headscarf." *Ethnic and Racial Studies* 29, no. 2: 237–259.

Trainor, Brian. 2006. "The State as the Mystical Foundation of Authority." *Philosophy and Social Criticism* 32, no. 6: 767–779.

Velazco y Trianosky, Gregory. 2006. "Immigration, Identity, and the Law." Paper presented at the American Philosophical Association Meetings, Washington, DC, December.

Waldman, Amy. 2006. "Prophetic Justice." *Atlantic Monthly*, October: 82–93.

Waldron, Jeremy. 1998. "Liberalism." In *Routledge Encyclopedia of Philosophy*. Edited by Edward Craig, 601. London: Routledge, 1998.

———. 2003. "Security and Liberty: The Image of Balance." *Journal of Political Philosophy* 11, no. 2: 191–210.

Walzer, Michael. 1983. *Spheres of Justice: A Defense of Pluralism and Equality*. New York: Basic Books.

Waters, Anne, ed. 2004. *American Indian Thought: Philosophical Essays*. Malden, MA: Blackwell.

White, Michael, Alan Travis and Duncan Campbell. 2005. "Blair: Uproot This Ideology of Evil." *Guardian*, July 14.

Williams, Brackette F. 1995. "Classification Systems Revisited: Kinship, Caste, Race, and Nationality as the Flow of Blood and the Spread of Rights." In *Naturalizing Power*. Edited by Sylvia and Carol Delaney. Yanagisako. New York: Routledge, 1995.

Winter, Greg. 2002. "The Supreme Court: The Demonstrators; Thousands of Students Gather Outside Court in Support of Admission Policies." *New York Times*, April 3.

Wong, K. Scott. 2005. *Americans First: Chinese Americans and the Second World War*. Cambridge: Harvard University Press.

Woodbury, Marsha. 2003. "A Difficult Decade: Continuing Freedom of Information Challenges for the United States and Its Universities." *E Law* 10, no. 4.

Wypijewski, Joanne. 2003. "Living in an Age of Fire." *Mother Jones*. http://www.motherjones.com/news/feature/2003/03/ma_275_01.html.

Yanagisako, Sylvia and Carol Delaney. ed. 1995. *Naturalizing Power*. New York: Routledge.

Zack, Naomi. 1993. *Race and Mixed Race*. Philadelphia: Temple University Press.

Zunes, Stephen. 2001. "U.S. Policy toward Political Islam." *Foreign Policy in Focus*, as reprinted in Sept. 12, 2001, issue of AlterNet.

INDEX

Abraham, Matthew, 73–74
Abu Ghraib prison, 176–77. *See also*
  Guantánamo Bay prison
Abu-Lughod, Lila, 97
Adorno, Theodor, 1
affirmative action, 7, 139, 225n53
African Americans, 129, 156; as
  Border-population, 11–12,
  136–45; dehumanization of, 54;
  legal recognition of, 157–60;
  Muslims and, 198n6; "passing"
  as White and, 194n13
Agamben, Giorgio, 54, 181n9; Derrida
  and, 45–46, 195n20, 201n19;
  on exceptions, 116–17, 189n17;
  on fear of abandonment, 38–39;
  Homo Sacer, 16, 18–19, 44–46,
  134, 191n39; on sacrifice, 55;
  on sovereign power, 44–45,
  133–34, 167–68, 210n16
Ahmed, Leila, 206n86
Akhay Kumar Mozumdar v. United States,
  224n
Alcoff, Linda Martin, 195n26
Alexander, Jacqui, 158, 161
Algeria, 104, 199, 203n38, 205n73
Ali, Ayaan Hirsi, 94, 201n17
Alien Act (1913), 152
Alien Land Acts, 59, 148, 152–53,
  155, 190n29, 222n17; *Oyama v.
  California* and, 192n45

Almaguer, Tomas, 179n4
Althusser, Louis, 134
Anarchy and Lynch Law, 151
Andreasen, Robin, 29
apartheid, 129, 216n15
Arabs. *See* Muslims
Arar, Mahar, 203n42, 214n58
Arendt, Hannah, 1–3; on aliens, 111,
  119, 126–27, 216n15; on human
  rights, 119–20; on pariahs, 6, 11,
  113, 132; on sovereign power, 16
Ashcroft, John, 2, 92, 129
Asia Barred Zone Act, 152
Asian Americans, 160
Asian Indian immigrants, 12, 60,
  144, 147–66; cosmopolitanism
  of, 162–63; deportations of, 152;
  "foreignness" of, 191n36; independence movement among, 150–53;
  invisibility of, 157–65; Japanese
  immigrants and, 149, 155; Mexican American wives of, 12, 149,
  153, 162; population of, 148,
  221n1; racialization of, 154–57;
  U.S. v. Bhagat Singh Thind on,
  33–34. *See also* Sikhs
Asiatic Exclusion League, 149, 155
assimilation, 72

Bah, Adamah, 96, 106–7
Baha'i, 169

249

nihilism, 12–13, 173
niqab. *See* hijab
"Nisei" subjectivity, 161
"noncomformity," 71
North American Free Trade Agreement (NAFTA), 2, 63

Okin, Susan M., 101–3
Olson, Theodore B., 199n10
one-drop rule, 4, 27–29, 184n36, 184n37; caste system and, 34–35; "passing" and, 194n13
onto-politics and onto-power, 170
outcasting, 113, 141–44, 171; Border-populations and, 129–30, 144; concealment of, 143–44
Owens, Keith, 220n51
Oyama v. California, 192n45

Padilla, José, 92–93, 199n10
Paige, Rod, 138
Palestinian-Israeli conflicts, 183n24
panopticon, 6, 48, 134
Papson, Stephen, 184n35
pariahs, 11, 136–41; Arendt on, 6, 11, 113, 132; as Border-guards, 132–35; definition of, 132
pariah-parvenu dynamic, 6, 11
Paris, Jeffrey, 195n32
Parker, Kunal, 119, 126, 211n28
"passing" as White, 194n13
Pateman, Carole, 209n7
Patriot Act. *See* USA PATRIOT Act
Perez v. Sharp, 223n33
Perlmutter, Amos, 200n16
Philippine Repatriation Act (1935), 222n16. *See also* Filipino immigrants
Phillips, Trevor, 204n53
Phipps, Susie Guillory, 185n37, 185n40
Pipes, Daniel, 200n16
plenary power doctrine, 121–22, 158
Plessy v. Ferguson, 33–34, 185n37
Pliny the Elder, 68

pluralism, 73, 83, 88, 105–6. *See also* multiculturalism
Political Othering (PO), 24–25, 36
polygamy, 95, 101–3, 106, 108, 201n17
Pontecorvo, Gillo, 205n73
postcolonial theory, 7, 14–15, 161, 163–64, 167
Powell, Colin, 138
Prevention of Terrorism Act (POTA), 187n65
prostitution, 101, 103
Protect America Act (2007), 203n44
Puerto Ricans, 90, 164
Punjabis. *See* Asian Indian immigrants
punk aesthetics, 106
purdah, 10, 96–99, 103–5, 169, 201n17. *See also* hijab

Qu'ran, 10, 98
Qutb, Sayyid al-, 200n16, 202n28

race, 4–9, 68, 167–78; binary of, 159, 163–64; as bio-power, 35; *eidos* of, 36; enframing of, 35–39; essence of, 21; ethnicity versus, 57–58, 80–81; gender and, 161–62, 171; idea of, 194n5; metaphysics of, 39; "purity" ideal and, 48; strangeness and, 68; as technology, 8, 22–24, 170–71; as tool of sovereign power, 29–35; in U.S. Constitution, 191n38
racialization, 51–56, 111–12, 168–78; of Asian Indian immigrants, 154–57; definition of, 51; of Rwanda, 56–59; "unruliness" and, 9, 22, 154–55
racial profiling, 48, 89, 139, 188n5, 199n12, 217n21
racism: Foucault on, 8–9, 30–33, 117, 134, 168, 169; "medical," 80–81; Mills on, 123, 188n3; "new," 31; state, 8–9, 30–33
rape, 103
Rawls, John, 15, 75–78, 84, 90, 100, 108, 180n22

Printed in Great Britain
by Amazon